KU-630-954

45633

New Strategies in Social Research

NEW STRATEGIES IN SOCIAL RESEARCH

An Introduction and Guide

Derek Layder

Polity Press

Copyright © Derek Layder 1993

The right of Derek Layder to be identified as author of this work has been asserted
in accordance with the Copyright, Designs and Patents Act 1988.

First published in 1993 by Polity Press in association with Blackwell Publishers
Reprinted 1995

Editorial office:
Polity Press
65 Bridge Street
Cambridge CB2 1UR, UK

Marketing production:
Blackwell Publishers, the publishing imprint of Basil Blackwell Ltd
108 Cowley Road
Oxford OX4 1JF, UK

Basil Blackwell Inc.
238 Main Street
Cambridge, MA 02142, USA

All rights reserved. Except for the quotation of short passages for the purposes of criticism
and review, no part of this publication may be reproduced, stored in a retrieval system, or
transmitted, in any form or by any means, electronic, mechanical, photocopying, recording
or otherwise, without the prior permission of the publisher.

Except in the United States of America, this book is sold subject to the condition that it shall
not, by way of trade or otherwise, be lent, re-sold, hired out, or otherwise circulated without
the publisher's prior consent in any form of binding or cover other than that in which it is
published and without a similar condition including this condition being imposed on the
subsequent purchaser.

ISBN 0 7456 0880 9
ISBN 0 7456 0881 7 (pbk)

British Library Cataloguing-in-Publication Data
A CIP catalogue record for this book is available from the British Library.

Library of Congress Cataloging-in-Publication Data
Layder, Derek.
    New strategies in social research : an introduction and guide /
  Derek Layder.
      p.   cm.
    Includes bibliographical references and index.
    ISBN 0–7456–0880–9 (U.S.). — ISBN 0–7456–0881–7 (U.S. : pbk.)
    1. Social sciences—Research—Methodology.   I. Title.
  H62.L34   1993
  300'.72—dc20   92–30551
                                                                                  CIP

Typeset in 10 on 12pt Times by Graphicraft Typesetters Ltd, Hong Kong
Printed in Great Britain by TJ Press (Padstow) Ltd., Padstow, Cornwall.

This book is printed on acid-free paper.

Contents

Figures

Preface

This book is designed as a resource which is intended to be of use to those who are about to embark on, or need to know something about social research. However, it is not meant to be a general account of research methods. Neither is it a specialized text dealing with the narrower band of fieldwork methods, upon which this book tends to concentrate. Rather, it outlines a set of research strategies which may be employed in conjunction with more established methods and strategies. These strategies are particularly suited to research which not only concentrates on the discovery of new findings or data about a particular aspect of society, but which is also aimed at constructing theory from the material unearthed by the research.

Therefore, these strategies are most applicable to research of two broad (but not mutually exclusive) types. First, research which is exploratory in nature, that is, in an area which has had little or no research done on it previously. In this case, the absence of an established body of knowledge about the area in question means that the researcher is required to develop theoretical ideas about the research area or topic as well as gather empirical information on it. Secondly, where the research is pursued in an area which has already had a fair amount of attention paid to it, these strategies may be of use to researchers who wish to develop new lines of approach. In this case the researcher may be concerned not only to unearth new empirical information which may add to the existing stock, but may also wish to develop original theoretical ideas which either complement established ideas, or represent new ways of thinking about the topic.

Given this set of interests, the book should be of use to several different audiences. First, it will be helpful to undergraduates who need to know something about strategies of research, or are required to evaluate or understand particular pieces of published research as part of their coursework. Also, undergraduates who are required to undertake small research projects as part of their assessed coursework may find the book helpful as a way of 'getting started' or to guide the later development of the project. Secondly, postgraduate, academic and professional researchers may find the book useful either as an adjunct to the strategies employed in research projects that are already under way, or as a resource to be used in planning specific research projects. Thus, the book is relevant not only to first-time researchers, but also to those who are more experienced.

However, I hope that colleagues and students who are generally more concerned with theoretical issues and the philosophy of social science will find something of interest in this book as well. This is because it attempts to bring general theoretical issues together with the more practical concerns of research. In this regard the book has something to say about the relationships between theory, research and empirical evidence. Moreover, the book engages in a dialogue between what have hitherto been regarded as separate domains of sociological interest underlined by a division between 'theorists' on the one hand and 'applied researchers' on the other. Generally, my aim has been to close the gap between the practicalities, uncertainties and general 'messyness' of the research process, and the more formal, patterned, and sometimes rather insular world of social theory.

The idea of this book first occurred to me while I was engaged in writing another, *The Realist Image in Social Science*. In fact it 'followed on' from this book in such a way that it could be regarded as something of a companion volume. Having said this I must stress that in level and style the two are very different. *The Realist Image in Social Science* deals with some quite technical philosophical and theoretical issues about the nature of social science, and as such employs some rather abstract and involved arguments that require a fair bit of prior knowledge. In this sense, students beginning sociology would find *The Realist Image* somewhat difficult to follow. In contrast the present book deals with more 'down-to-earth' practical issues and does not presume too much prior knowledge on behalf of its audience. Nevertheless, there is a certain continuity between the two books in that the present volume endeavours to spell out some of the implications of the previous work for the concrete problems encountered while doing research.

As I say, I began sketching in the provisional contours of this book before I had finished the other and since I was, at the time, an Academic Visitor in the Department of Sociology, University of New England, Australia, I would like to register my gratitude to this institution. My thanks also go to Stewart Clegg, then at UNE (now at the University of St Andrews), who originally invited me over and made sure I had the space and time to write. I would also like to thank Margo Huxley for 'insisting' that I give a talk to a group of her students who were about to engage in small research projects as part of their coursework. This initially prompted me to think about the specific strategies that they could use. This experience contributed greatly to the thinking behind this book and specifically its attempt to provide a 'resource' for research.

As these initial 'seeds' grew into the developed form of the book various other people became important to its development. First, I would like to thank the editorial board of Polity Press who offered sound and invaluable advice on its content and form when it appeared before them as a proposal. When I had written a complete draft of the manuscript, John Scott went through it in detail and made many comments and suggestions for improvement, most of which I have tried to incorporate in the final text. I would like to thank John for his time and effort in this regard, particularly since he had to wade through a rather rough version of the manuscript. Next, I would like to express my appreciation for the advice, encouragement and helpful comments that Tony Giddens has offered throughout the writing of the book. In particular, Tony read through the penultimate draft and pointed out areas that needed improvement, amendment and expansion. Again, I found these comments to be invaluable. I would also like to thank Robert Burgess of Warwick University for reading through the complete manuscript and providing perceptive comments and useful advice on the overall text. Ann Bone copy-edited the book and suggested a number of improvements in style and content. While I am most grateful to all these people for their very constructive help in this project, this does not mean that they are in any way responsible for any shortcomings that the book may possess. These, of course, are entirely my own.

Finally, I would like to express my appreciation for the support, interest and influence of a number of people over the years, who have been rather more indirectly involved in the writing of this book. Elim Papadakis of the University of New England and Jack Barbalet of the Australian National University provided important collegial support during my stay in Australia. I would like to thank Robin Barrow and Jaap Tuinman of Simon Fraser University for taking an interest in my work, and for providing facilities and support during my stay in Vancouver in May 1991. During my time there I greatly appreciated the friendship and help of Lynne, Alex and Natasha Barrow, Geoff Madoc-Jones, Patrick Keeney, Kathleen Thomson, Jane Preston, Stuart Richmond, Brigitte Kappel, and Al Mackinnon. I would also like to express my gratitude to Leicester University Research Board for financial assistance during my study leave.

Conversations with friends and colleagues have undoubtedly affected my thinking in various ways. In this respect, I would like to thank David Ashton, Dave Field, Martyn Denscombe and Sharon Higson for their 'persistent' and welcome influence for some time now. A more diffuse debt of gratitude must go to Mick Gardiner, Drew Clode, Mike Harper, Fergus Whitty, Sue Massey and Steve Boyer, all of whom have contributed greatly to my sense of 'ontological security' over the years.

Derek Layder

1

Research Strategy and Theory Generation

The purpose of this book

How do you start a piece of social research? Where do the ideas come from? Once the research is begun how do the observations made and the data gathered during the course of the research help the researcher develop ideas which can explain or give shape to this empirical information? These questions are related to others which are often expressed in rather more formal terms: how does theory emerge from research? What is the relationship between theory and empirical evidence? In relation to this book an important question is, what strategies can the researcher use in order to get the best and most relevant information?

It is essentially to these sorts of questions that this book addresses itself. It does so in three main ways. First, by discussing two influential approaches to social research and the development of theory from research. In chapters 2, 3 and 4 I compare and evaluate these two approaches in terms of their usefulness as 'guides' both to first-time researchers as well as those who are more experienced. The second way in which this book deals with these questions is by providing a *research resource map* (figures 1.1 and 5.1). This is a 'map' of key features of society and social life which represent particular levels and dimensions of analysis which have already proved useful in social research. That is, each element or dimension is derived from, or can be found in, existing pieces of research, although typically all the elements will not be present in any one piece of research. However, it is the way I have arranged the elements into an overall framework that provides the distinctive feature of this map. As such, the map represents potential areas or sites of research.

By describing and discussing the characteristics of each of these elements as well as stressing their interconnections, the map is intended as a resource that can help in the formulation of research strategies. This it does in several ways. First, by acting as a 'prompt' or sounding board it can aid the development of initial ideas about research on specific topics (such as the nature of interaction in various kinds of settings like factories, coffee bars or hospitals). In this sense, the resource map can help a researcher (either first-time or experienced) to 'get started' by indicating fruitful lines of approach or general starting points. Similarly, it may be of use in research projects which are already under way by providing a fund of 'alternative angles' on research topics. In this sense, the researcher may be able to develop the research more fruitfully along different lines, or simply widen the scope of the research.

The third way in which the book deals with the questions posed at the beginning is by outlining a number of ideas about research strategy. Strategy refers to the manner in which particular methods and techniques are harnessed to the research so as to produce the most efficient means of collecting information (empirical data). Thus, chapters 6 to 9 suggest a number of strategies to this end. The strategies flow from, and are thus closely related to, the resource map and its elements. In this sense, they are primarily geared to helping the researcher with problems re-lating to theory construction during research. However, the strategies also branch out on their own. Chapter 6 develops a version of multi-strategy research as a highly efficient means of data collection. Chapter 7 suggests research strategies which directly aid the development of theory from research, while chapter 8 outlines strategies for investigating power, commitment and constraint in social life. Chapter 9 is devoted to the issue of historical analysis as a useful additional strategy for fieldwork with a contemporary focus. Chapter 10 provides some reflec-tions on the main themes of the book and a summary of the strategies discussed in Chapters 5 to 9.

Points of departure

In this section I shall say something about the issues that form the background to this book. Let me start by declaring that the central focus of this book is on the relation between social theory and research. Without suggesting that all research fits neatly into these categories, there seems to be, as Rose (1982) has pointed out, two dominant ten-dencies in the existing sociological literature. First, there is research carried out primarily to *test* theories, which uses structured techniques of data collection such as content analysis or a social survey with a standard questionnaire. Such research requires that details of sampling and data collection are tightly planned in advance and that the data are quantified and presented in a research report in the form of tables or other statistical means.

The second type of research concentrates on *theory construction* (or theory building), and more often uses participant observation and less structured interview techniques. In this case the whole research process will be much more flexible and, more often than not, certain aspects of research design and sampling will be decided during the course of the research. The data in this kind of research is usually qualitative and thus the evidence presented in the research report tends to be extracts from interviews or statements based on the researcher's observations.

As Rose points out, these types are polar extremes and many studies fall between them. For example, studies occasionally combine the theory-testing mode with the use of qualitative data, while some studies have attempted to construct theories from quantitative data. Similarly, not all pieces of research are clearly of either the theory-testing type or the theory-building type. For example, they may simply be investigating a social problem or describing some sociologically interesting area. In this sense, the research may be undertaken in the context of a theoretical framework, but is not strictly in the business of 'testing' theory (Rose 1982: 11). However, while noting these exceptions, the distinction is useful as a general indication of the form and content of much social research. In fact, Rose's book is an excellent example of the way in which this distinction can help to convey and illuminate the nature of methods and strategies of research as well as give some indication of how students and/or researchers can begin to 'decipher' research reports.

The gap between theory-testing and theory-building research

In the present book I find the distinction useful in coming to terms with the broader questions concerning the relation of theory and research. In chapters 2, 3 and 4, I examine the work of sociologists who may be said to represent both these types of research. Robert Merton's ideas about the development of 'middle-range' theory from research (chapter 2) is representative of the theory-testing type with its dominant emphasis on structured techniques and quantitative data. Merton's ideas have been very influential in social research (particularly of the theory-testing kind), although his wider concerns about the general nature of the relation between theory and research are often neglected or 'skipped over' in discussions of research method and strategy. On the other hand, the pathbreaking work of Barney Glaser and Anshelm Strauss (1967) on 'grounded' theory and field research conforms very much to the theory-building type with its overriding emphasis on qualitative data and the flexible or emergent use of sampling and research design. Again, however, Glaser and Strauss's more general ideas concerning the connection between theory and research tend to be overlooked in methods texts.

These two important approaches to the theory–research relation represent the background concerns of this book. I evaluate and compare the ideas of Merton and Glaser and Strauss with a view to developing an alternative approach which builds on the stronger features of each of these and excludes their less useful ones. As a convenient and shorthand way of describing this alternative I call this a 'realist' approach. However, this is not simply a convenient label, it also draws attention to the connection between my approach to research strategy and the recently emergent realist philosophy of social science (see comments below, and Layder 1990, for a detailed examination).

Now although this alternative attempts to incorporate the many strengths of both types of research, it falls somewhere between the theory-testing and theory-building types that Rose describes. This is for a number of reasons. First, it is not always easy to distinguish qualitative and quantitative data and the relevance of this will become apparent as the general arguments of the book unfold. Second, while acknowledging that quantitative forms of data and analysis have been used most frequently in conjunction with theory-testing research (and are perhaps more generally suited to this type, see Smith 1975), this book presses the case that quantitative analysis has a significant role to play in theory-building research. In this respect, I endorse the view that quantitative and qualitative data can be used in a complementary fashion.

Third, although the dominant focus of this book is on theory-building field research, I also emphasize that this necessarily includes elements of theory-testing (although perhaps not always of the conventional type) and that therefore the two cannot be thought of as completely separate. Finally, throughout the book I argue that aspects of general theory can (and should) play an important role in this kind of research. In this sense, theory has an informative role to play in the research (and vice versa), but is not directly involved in a process of 'testing' theoretical assumptions.

Differences in approach

The differences outlined above are not the only important ones to be considered. Merton's 'middle-range' approach and Glaser and Strauss's 'grounded' theory' approach differ from each other also in terms of their emphasis on the importance of meaning in social life, particularly the meaningful world of the people who are the subjects of research. Merton's framework is more 'scientific', in the sense of adopting an external, 'objective' and impersonal standpoint than is Glaser and Strauss's (although it is not true to say that it is any more systematic or 'valid'). In this sense, Merton's approach more closely approximates the methods used by physical scientists in order to study atoms, particles and molecules and so on.

In contrast, the grounded theory approach strongly underlines the human dimension of society, and the importance of meaning in people's lives, and thus concentrates more attention on the 'subjective' aspects of social life. One way of characterizing the difference is to say that the theory-testing view, represented by Merton, adopts a more distanced or remote stance towards the individuals who make up society, while the theory-building approach, represented by Glaser and Strauss, takes a more 'involved' and close-up viewpoint on these individuals.

Not only is there a difference of emphasis in relation to the question of analytic standpoint, but there is also a difference regarding the basic units of analysis. The middle-range theory approach tends to emphasize the importance of the collective and institutional aspects of society and their impact on the lives of individuals. On the other hand, the grounded theory approach tends to emphasize the importance of processes of interaction and the way in which individuals play a part in 'constructing' their social environment. In rather more formal sociological terms this is a difference in the emphasis placed on 'macro' (large-scale, institutional or collective) aspects of society, as against the 'micro' aspects of social life (small-scale, face-to-face situations). This is reflected in the division between one group of researchers who favour qualitative fieldwork in order to study the micro world of social interaction and everyday life (Becker 1970, Lofland 1971, Strauss 1987) while another group, favouring quantitative survey methods, tends to concentrate on the macro phenomena of social structure and institutions (Blau and Duncan 1967, Goldthorpe 1980, Wright 1980). Thus, the ideas of Merton and Glaser and Strauss about the nature of social research are representative of this more general division within sociological analysis.

The missing links in method: power, history and general theory

To be sure, as with the theory-testing and theory-building distinction not all research falls neatly into one or the other of the macro or micro categories but, nonetheless, they do indicate general tendencies. Now while methods texts are often very good at describing the methods and techniques that are associated with theory-testing and theory-building types of research, they tend to be less good at describing or encouraging the links between them. This is because very often methods texts treat them as rather separate areas of interest. In this sense, they are seen as methods, techniques and strategies that are to be applied in relation to different topics or types of research problem.

One of the main aims of this book is to attempt to bridge some of the gaps between quantitative and qualitative methods, theory-building and theory-testing research, macro and micro levels of analysis, and so on, by endeavouring to trace points of contact between them and thus helping to create a wider view of the relation between theory and research. In this respect, the literature on methods and strategies of research tends to underplay, or neglect completely, the role of three elements which, in my view, should be essential components of research. These are power, history and general social theory.

An examination of the issues surrounding the analysis of power is often missing from books on research method because it is assumed that power is part of the subject matter of social research rather than an initial methodological consideration. Of course, it is true that the various empirical forms of power do constitute an important part of the subject matter of social research. However, it is the very fact of its empirical omnipresence that makes it necessary to incorporate the analysis of power in the actual strategies that we employ in social research. This is a continuing theme of this book and, in particular, chapter 8 examines in detail the investigation of power and research strategy. Much the same is true of history. More often than not, the role and nature of historical research is left out of methods texts as if it were an entirely separate matter. Since the topic of history traces the changing forms of social behaviour and institutions over time, it is essential to incorporate such concerns in the strategies we use to conduct social research. This again is a dominant theme of the book and receives particular attention in chapter 9.

Another important element that is usually missing from methods texts is a concern with the contribution that general social theory can make to the research effort. Researchers are often dismissive of this kind of theory on the grounds that it is speculative and too far removed from the down-to-earth issues of empirical research. I take the view that this attitude actually hinders the general development of sociological understanding by preventing the harnessing of the insights of general theory to the requirements and procedures of social research. Furthermore, such a situation simply reinforces the gap that already exists between researchers and social theorists by stifling potential dialogue and erecting, rather than removing, barriers to cooperation.

This gap between research and theory is nowhere more evident than in the division between macro and micro forms of sociology. In this respect, social theorists have suggested that the macro–micro problem is *the* major problem in sociology. Unfortunately, however, these discussions tend to be of an exclusively theoretical nature (Knorr-Cetina and Cicourel 1981, Alexander et al. 1987), and thus the link with social research has been neglected. The approach outlined in this book, especially in the form of the research map, attempts to bridge this gap somewhat. The whole thrust of the book suggests that researchers (and thus the research methods and strategies that they use) must forego the idea that general theory bears no useful relation to the empirical world or to the practical issues of social research. Conversely, social theorists, particularly those working on the macro–micro problem, must realize that it cannot be resolved entirely in theoretical terms. (Even though it could be argued, as in Giddens 1990, that theory is partly autonomous from social research.) The approach to research strategy presented in this book attempts to encourage dialogue between these overlapping aspects of theory and research.

Bridging the gap: a realist approach

The approach to research outlined in this book is meant to convey the 'textured' or interwoven nature of different levels and dimensions of social reality. These levels and dimensions are, in fact, the elements which form the basis of the research map described more fully in chapter 5 and sketched in figure 1.1. They are: the self, situated activity, setting, context and history (as a dimension applicable to them all). In this respect I would claim that this approach reflects a greater appreciation of the multifaceted nature of the empirical world than do middle-range theory and grounded theory (MRT and GT from now on), which tend to restrict themselves to one or two of these levels or dimensions.

This closely relates to the problem of bringing macro and micro analyses closer together. Recent social theory has demonstrated that despite differences in proposed solutions to this problem, there is agreement on the complexity of the theoretical issues involved (Giddens 1984, Layder 1981, 1989). As compared with MRT and GT, the realist approach attempts to address this complexity by offering a layered or 'stratified' model of society which includes macro (structural,

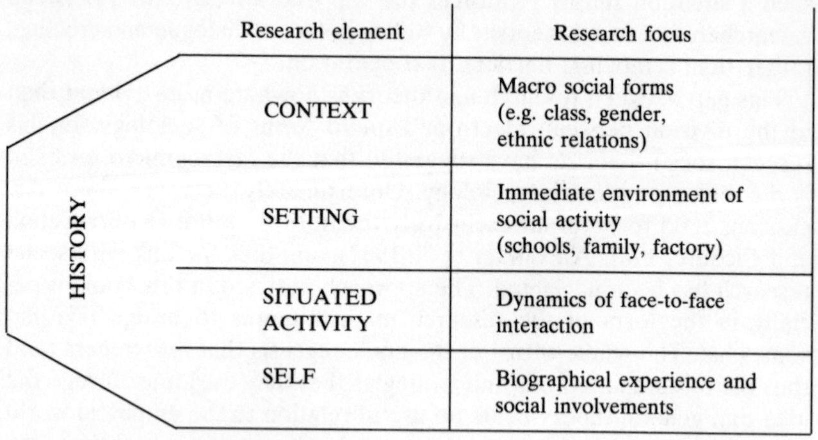

Research element	Research focus
CONTEXT	Macro social forms (e.g. class, gender, ethnic relations)
SETTING	Immediate environment of social activity (schools, family, factory)
SITUATED ACTIVITY	Dynamics of face-to-face interaction
SELF	Biographical experience and social involvements

(The left side of the table is labelled vertically: HISTORY)

Figure 1.1 Research map: an outline.

institutional) phenomena as well as the more micro phenomena of interaction and behaviour. This more comprehensive outlook has two important consequences.

First, it enables social research to address the problem of the division between macro and micro levels of analysis in sociology by concentrating attention on the organic links between them. (Thus, the research and theory it produces have a textured or interwoven quality.) Such an approach directly opposes those which assume either that one level can be reduced to, and explained by, the other more 'favoured' level, or that the less favoured level can be simply tacked on to the more 'important' focus of analysis. Strauss (1987) provides an example of this latter by suggesting that macro or structural aspects can be brought in to complement the analysis of micro phenomena as a matter of convenience or emphasis. Secondly, viewing society or social reality as a series of interdependent layers each with its own distinctive characteristics enables the researcher to be sensitive to the different units and time-scales that are involved in social processes and social change. Again, these are factors which are characteristically overlooked in the MRT and GT approaches.

The research map, social activity and social processes

The research map (comprising the elements self, situated activity, setting, context and history) describes levels of social organization which are also potential areas of research for those who wish to engage in exploratory fieldwork. In this sense, the map suggests a number of questions that the field researcher may ask either prior to or during data gathering which may prompt theoretical reflection, and thus, help in the understanding and analysis of a specific research problem. As a 'prompt' the map can be incorporated either as an aspect of initial research design, or it can be used as a means through which the researcher can relate his or her findings to more general theoretical issues in sociology. In this manner, the map can be used to generate practical and theoretical questions that are pertinent to many sorts, styles and problems of research. However, the map should not be regarded as a substitute or replacement for carefully developed and empirically grounded research itself, and the kinds of questions and forms of explanation that naturally grow from it. To the contrary, the map has to be understood as a resource that can be drawn on to complement, or 'add to', such research.

I shall not go into detail about the elements of the research map and their distinctive properties at this juncture since this will be the subject of chapter 5. However, in order to understand how they are empirically related to social activity I shall provide a thumbnail sketch of each of the elements and then go on to say something about how they are related to each other. The research focus indicated by the term 'self' refers primarily to the individual's relation to her or his social environment and is characterized by the intersection of biographical experience and social involvements. In 'situated activity' the research focus shifts away from the individual towards the emergent dynamics of social interaction. 'Setting' denotes a research focus on the intermediate forms of social organization (such as schools, hospitals, factories) that provide the immediate arena for social activity. 'Context' refers to the wider macro social forms that provide the more remote environment of social activity (such as gender or class relations).

As can be appreciated from these sketches all the elements overlap and interweave with each other. There are no clear empirical boundaries between them, although as I shall argue more fully in chapter 5, each element or area has its own distinctive characteristics which must be carefully registered in order to understand how they all combine to influence behaviour and social activity in general. The same goes for 'history' and 'power'. These two major features of social life enter into the operation of all the elements of the map, although they do so in ways that differ importantly. However, for the moment let us concentrate on how the research map can throw light on the analysis of social activity. In this respect, we have to understand the different elements as operating in two important dimensions; vertical (as a series of layers) and horizontal (as layers stretched out over time). In reality these dimensions operate simultaneously; however, in the map (figures 1.1 and 5.1) it is really only possible to depict the elements in a one-dimensional sense, as layers 'frozen' in time.

Generally social activity has to be understood in terms of social processes stretched out over time and space. Nonetheless, viewing the elements as a series of interwoven layers is useful since it helps us to understand how social activity is influenced by different aspects of society at specific points in time (or, at least, during very short periods of time). That is, if we were able to stop the action, so to speak, at a particular moment in time we would be able to see that social activity itself is made up of the various influences of different elements such as the self, the situation, the setting and so on.

For example, in order to understand what is involved in a particular instance of sexual harassment at work we have to be aware of how different macro and micro aspects combine to produce the specific instance. Thus, we have to be aware of how macro elements like gender divisions operate in terms of patriarchal power and occupational placement. In turn, we have to be aware of the way in which these influence the nature and prevalence of sexism at the workplace, as well as the way in which particular kinds of situations are more easily manipulated by sexist males. Similarly, one would need to bear in mind the kinds of identities, personalities and unique social experiences that each person brings with them to such situations and which render them more or less sensitive or vulnerable. That is, the micro processes of everyday life as reflected in the situations and identities of the persons involved can only be understood properly when seen in conjunction with more macro features.

However, if we examine social activity only in this way – as a relatively fixed moment in time – we end up with a somewhat artificial picture of social activity. Since social activity is a continuous process we have to understand the way in which it unfolds over time, and to do this we have to view the operation of the elements horizontally. In order to do this let us imagine the situation from the point of view of the experience of a particular person. If we limit the time-scale to a typical daily round of activity, we can appreciate that the person will move in and out of the influence of particular contexts and settings such as work, family and leisure and engage in numerous pursuits in the process, many of which involve face-to-face interaction with others.

If we extend the time interval (depending on the particular focus of our interest) we will see that like the person's daily movement between the influence of different settings and situations and so forth, over a period of months or even years in a person's life there will be similar movement. For instance, if we look at a person's life history we will see that they are influenced by a number of contexts, settings and situations as represented, for example, by changes in job, getting married, having children, getting divorced, becoming ill and being hospitalized, emigrating, retiring and so on. So, as the person continues through the course of their lives, he or she is influenced by a succession of contexts, settings, situations and identity shifts.

Depending on our interests as sociologists we would focus on a particular time-scale in order to understand a specific aspect of the social life of a person or a group of people. For example, we may be interested in everyday life in a particular setting, say a group of factory workers, or even the kinds of customer–proprietor interaction in a coffee bar or restaurant. Alternatively, we may be interested in longer-term involvements such as occupational or work careers. Another focus may be on the way in which two settings intersect and influence each other (such as career and family involvements, or the effects of drug addiction on family life) over fairly lengthy stretches of time. The kind of time-scale we choose will depend on our interests as sociologists and the kind of problem we want to investigate.

Time-scales and units of analysis in research

So far I have spoken of the way in which social activity itself unfolds over time from the viewpoint of a particular individual in relation to the elements of the research map. In this section I want to shift the viewpoint slightly and concentrate on the elements themselves. By adopting this viewpoint we shall be aware of two things. First, that social research is usually focused through one or more of these elements as its basic unit (or units) of analysis. Second, each element or unit of analysis is related to a slightly different time-scale. This is where the notion of history comes in as a time dimension which involves all the elements. Before spelling these things out in rather more detail, I must point out that more often than not such issues are overlooked both in specific pieces of social research and in texts which discuss research methods.

Very often, specific pieces of research are carried out in the context of a commitment to the idea that society or social reality is 'in process', although it is not always apparent that this notion can mean different things to different researchers. Clearly, to talk about changes in class structure and composition during the industrial revolution is quite a different proposition from talking about attitudinal changes in a group of parents in relation to their children over a period of three years. Similarly, Becker (1953) suggests that his analysis of marihuana use is an analysis of use over time, in effect an instance of social process. However, the time-scale involved and the unit of analysis (in this case the individual's conceptions and perceptions of the drug and its effects) are obviously quite unlike the time-scale and unit of analysis involved in, for example, Parsons's (1966) analysis of social evolution. Clearly, some empirical studies focus on a much narrower time band than others and combine this with a focus on micro changes and processes rather than macro (structural) change. Viewing reality as inherently processual does little to distinguish between research methods and empirical analyses which focus on quite different time-scales and units of analysis.

This leads us directly to the question of the role of historical analysis in social research methods. It is a curious feature of methods textbooks that they considerably neglect this extremely important feature of social analysis. On the other hand, while some sociologists attempt to develop models of social evolution and long-term processes of change based on historical data, they have little or nothing to say about methods of social analysis as applied to historical data. Thus, as a result of the lack of dialogue between academic subspecialisms, sociohistorical analyses have been largely displaced and insulated from basic questions of research method.

Having pointed out these gaps in the research methods literature, let me now say something about the way in which the research map is intended to make some inroads towards rectifying this situation. As I said, the dimension of history is pertinent to all the elements of the map (self, situated activity, setting and context). However, the notion of 'history' has to be unpacked in order to understand its variable relation to each of the elements. We have already touched on this in the previous discussion of social activity. There I pointed out that the social researcher could produce a rather different perspective on the analysis of an individual's activities by choosing different time frames and units of analysis. Thus, if we took the daily round of activity as our basic unit and time frame we would produce a rather different analysis than if we examined the individual's whole life history.

In fact, this marks out the distinction between self and situated activity in terms of the elapsing of time. From the researcher's point of view the time-scale involved is very different. The time frame involved in the researching of situated activity is much shorter, involving sequences or episodes of face-to-face interaction taken from the routine day-to-day round of activity. The time frame involved in a research focus on the self would refer primarily to the lifespan of the individual, although it is clear that self and situated activity constantly interweave with each other. The point, therefore, of the distinction is to draw attention to differences of analytic emphasis in research. However, this not only a distinction which relates to the researcher's point of view. Both day-to-day activities and the individual's biographical lifespan are 'experienced' differently by the people involved.

What I have said so far accords fairly well with Giddens's (1984, 1987) discussion. Giddens, however, makes a threefold distinction of forms of temporality: the durée of day-to-day life, the durée of the lifespan of the individual, and the 'longue durée' of institutions. What he says about the durée of institutions in a general sense also applies to both the settings and contexts of activity in my terms. That is, settings and contexts refer to aspects of society that may 'endure beyond the lives of those individuals whose activities constitute them at any given moment' (Giddens 1987: 145). It is important to understand that these institutional features interweave with the activities of day-to-day life and thus each gives continuity to the other.

As I say, these considerations apply to settings and contexts since they both represent institutional features of social life. However, the distinction between setting and context is meant to highlight the difference between the social forms that constitute the immediate environment of activity (such as workplace or family), and the wider, more general institutional forms (such as the power structures of gender and class). Of course, they influence each other and are bound together with the other elements through the social activities of people. However, the more widespread and pervasive nature of the contextual aspects makes them generally less responsive to localized pressure for change than immediate settings. Thus, settings and contexts typically differ in terms of their continuity and durability. In other words, they tend to operate on different time scales.

In so far as self, situated activity, setting and context all relate to time in slightly different though interrelated ways, they could be said to have their own 'histories'. This sense of history is obviously different from the conventional idea of a narrative of significant events over time, or the teasing out of long-term processes of change based on the analysis of historical data. In a sense, the 'individual' histories unfold 'inside' this larger historical sweep of social evolution since they are all affected by it. This raises the interesting question of exactly what is the relationship between this 'larger' sense of history and the others.

The approach adopted in this book encourages the researcher to be sensitive to these different time-scales and units of analysis where they are of relevance to the research problem at hand and where it is feasible as a research strategy. In chapter 9 I engage in a more detailed discussion of some aspects of these issues in relation to research strategy. I focus on the relationship between historical analysis in the wider sense and the other elements of the research map. In particular, I concentrate on the research problems associated with analysing middle-range institutional change, as opposed to the larger 'societal' sweep of much historical analysis. Important problems in this respect arise from the attempt to generate sociological concepts, descriptions and explanations from qualitative historical data. Also, I raise the question of whether it is necessary to have a historical understanding of the evolution of such social institutions before we can produce an adequate contemporary analysis.

A note on the use of the term theory

Throughout I shall be using the term theory in a much wider sense than is the case in conventional methods texts (and in even more general discussions of theory in sociology). In the standard methods text there is usually quite a bit of talk about 'theory' and the relationship between this and 'empirical evidence', or the relationship between theoretical concepts and their empirical indicators. However, theory in this sense has a very specific meaning. It refers to the narrow province of 'variables' through which the empirical problem is focused, and in terms of which the data or evidence are ultimately explained. Used in this way, theory is connected to a specific substantive area or problem, for example, drug use or suicide.

Now, although it is the case that researchers do not always begin with a clearly defined hypothesis (although many do), most methods texts do not concern themselves with the seemingly haphazard process whereby researchers arrive at an initial hypothesis. The standard methods text usually begins by focusing on an already formulated research hypothesis and then moves on to describe the way in which it is reformulated in the light of the data produced through the application of a specific research method or technique. This also usually includes some discussion of the way in which the concepts denoting the research variables are given operational meaning in the research itself. In other words, how the concepts of a theory come to have specific indicators in the empirical data uncovered by the research.

Although this is undoubtedly an important sense of the term theory, I wish to draw attention to some of its wider meanings, meanings which

I shall employ throughout the book. The first is contained in the idea that theories should be regarded as 'networks' or 'integrated clusterings' of concepts, propositions and 'world-views' (Pawson 1989, Layder 1990). In this sense they are rather more than simple specifications of the way in which two or more variables relate to each other in the empirical world. Understanding theory in this sense helps to direct our attention to the fact that theory construction in social research is always undertaken against a background of more general underlying assumptions.

Also, my own usage draws into the discussion of methods and practice in social research notions of theory and theorizing which are usually thought to possess a quite separate existence and domain of application. I have already drawn attention to the fact that there is a very significant lack of dialogue between those who call themselves 'theorists', on the one hand, and those who deal with primary data collection (empirical researchers), on the other. This situation persists despite the fact that theorists constantly assert that the ultimate justification of any theoretical enterprise is to render the world more understandable. Similarly, the hiatus endures despite empirical researchers' continual lip-service to the idea of the importance of theory. Of course, this latter may be a reflection of the fact that empirical researchers often define theory in the narrower terms favoured by methods texts. However, whatever the reasons for the insularity caused by this radical academic division of labour, my own view is that we should attempt to overcome these barriers and to encourage genuine dialogue. In this book I attempt, in a modest way, to develop some elements of such a dialogue.

I do this, first, by taking seriously the idea that theoretical ideas often act as background assumptions to empirical research and that where these are implicit they should be made explicit and the relevant connections detailed. Second, in a more positive sense, I argue that in any research project there *should be* room for more qualitative, open-ended forms of theory (rather than ones that narrowly specify the relations between precisely measurable variables). These forms of theory could serve to both contextualize the research project itself and to influence its outcome in some way. That is, where a research project is based almost exclusively on the narrow sense of theory mentioned above, then *ipso facto* there will be room for the complementary influence of this other kind of theory. Third, I think dialogue can be achieved by actually trying to specify the nature of the links between the seemingly more remote and abstract forms of theorizing (as found in the writings of Talcott Parsons, Louis Althusser and Anthony Giddens), and the actual practice of research and the formulation of research projects.

Another 'theoretical' theme which is infrequently treated (if at all) in conventional discussions of research methods has to do with philosophical questions about the bases of knowledge which underlie different methods and strategies. Very often such discussions are left to 'specialists' who deal with philosophical and methodological issues in social science but who rarely engage in research of a primary data-gathering kind. Conversely, 'deeper' aspects of methodology are all too often left to one side in methods texts (perhaps because of a claimed lack of competence, see, for example, Rose 1982). Often, however, such things are overlooked completely because they are assumed to be irrelevant to the preeminently practical problems of research. This is a blinkered attitude which must be countered at every opportunity. Indeed, if, as I have said, such questions are at the centre of basic issues of research practice then it behoves anyone about to employ or explicate specific methods to confront such issues head-on.

Philosophical questions concerning the nature, validity and scope of our knowledge bear on questions of method and strategy. In chapters 2, 3 and 4, this theme plays an important role in my discussion of MRT and GT. I argue that both these approaches are inherently limited by the theory of knowledge which underlies them and that their explanatory power and scope can be usefully enhanced by modifying and extending their terms of reference.

Finally, philosophical issues are related to the question of the image or model of social science which underlies discussions of research methods and strategy. This is where the discussion connects back to the term 'realism'. The realist model of social science has been developed as an alternative to the conventional positivist notion (Harré and Secord 1972, Keat and Urry 1975, Bhaskar 1979, Layder 1990). Put very simply, a central feature of realism is its attempt to preserve a 'scientific' attitude towards social analysis at the same time as recognizing the importance of actors' meanings and in some way incorporating them in research.

As such, a key aspect of the realist project is a concern with causality and the identification of causal mechanisms in social phenomena in a manner quite unlike the traditional positivist search for causal generalizations. In this book I shall not be going into the technicalities of the issues and debates that surround the realist project in social science (on this, see Layder 1990). However, it is true to say that one of the underlying general themes of this book concerns the question of how a realist view of social science affects the practice of social research and the formulation of strategy and method. In this respect I feel that many aspects of the approach adopted here (for example, the stratified model of social life implicit in the research map) are consistent with the basic principles of realism.

How to use this book

Having given some indication of the contents and the progression of the argument, let me now say something about the best ways to use the book. The book is designed as an integrated whole, and thus I would encourage the first-time reader to read through it completely in order to get a feel of the overall argument. A complete read through is also necessary to appreciate the context from which I draw my arguments and establish my objectives. In this respect, chapters 2, 3 and 4 are essential to a rounded understanding of the research map in chapter 5 and the research strategies outlined in chapters 6 to 9. However, the book is also designed to be used as a 'reference' text. In this sense, it may be used periodically, in a selective manner, to help tackle particular kinds of research problem when they arise. Therefore, after a sense of the overall discussion has been acquired, the book may then be used as a reference work or resource which may be 'dipped into' on a recurrent basis.

For those who continue to use the book in this manner it is worth pointing out that there are several ways in which the organization of the text has been designed to facilitate its use as a resource or reference book. In this regard, the organization of chapter 5 is rather different from the rest. This chapter outlines the research map, mentioned previously, and proceeds by giving a description of each element of the map in turn. These elements (self, situated activity, setting, context and history) can be thought of as general ways of focusing specific research projects. This may involve one, or perhaps several, of the elements. The researcher who is begining a project on a sociological topic may ask him self or herself which of these elements, or which group of them, is most pertinent to the project and then go to the appropriate sections of the text. I have tried to aid this kind of selective rereading by including at the end of each section a list of some of the most important research questions that are raised by a focus on the particular element in question.

Chapters 2 to 4 and 6 to 9 differ in their format in this respect. In these I have included either a checklist, a summary or 'guidelines for research' at the *end* of the chapters. Chapter 2 ends with some guidelines for field researchers who wish to utilize aspects of theory-testing research in conjunction with a theory-building approach. Chapter 3 ends with a description of the variety of qualitative approaches to research other than the theory-building type. This provides a checklist of alternative objectives and strategies which may be drawn on by researchers who have theory generation as their central aim. Chapter 4 concludes with some 'new methodological rules' for grounded theory. This provides a summary of the main changes that I feel are necessary in order for the grounded theory approach to extend its terms of reference and increase its explanatory power. Chapter 6, which deals with the whole array of sociological research methods and how they interrelate with qualitative fieldwork, ends with a list of the key issues associated with a multistrategy approach. Similarly, chapter 7, dealing with the question of using research strategies to develop theory, and chapter 8, which discusses the analysis of power, commitment and constraint in fieldwork, both conclude with some guidelines for field research. Chapter 9, dealing with the historical dimension, ends with a summary of the main issues.

Both the chapters themselves and the concluding sections may be reread independently, in relation to the specific problems, topics or issues encountered by the researcher. The concluding chapter 10 consists of two distinct emphases. The first two sections discuss some general issues arising from the approach I develop, while the final section is in the form of a practical guide to the new strategies set out in this book. In particular, this deals with the issues discussed in chapters 5 to 9. It is hoped that such a list of 'main points' makes it easier to know which part of the book needs to be 'raided' in order to deal with a specific problem or issue.

2

Middle-Range Theory and Research

So far I have suggested that middle-range theory (MRT) is associated more with theory-testing research while grounded theory (GT) is generally linked with theory-building research. In this chapter I provide some more details about the nature of MRT. I shall give a detailed account of GT in the next chapter but it is worthwhile perhaps to summarize some of the main differences between these two approaches to research so that they may be borne in mind while reading this chapter. In essence, MRT encourages research which is led by a clear theoretical idea formulated prior to the research. For example, consider the proposition 'where people are surrounded by close supportive relationships (such as in a marriage or the family, or in certain kinds of religious community) they are less likely to commit suicide.'

In the context of this proposition research can proceed to test out its truth by gathering evidence relating to suicide in particular types of setting. This requires that the basic terms of the proposition to be investigated can be adequately measured in an empirical sense. For the purposes of the research a representative sample is decided upon (for example, a religious group, or a group of unmarried males) and various methods and techniques employed to collect data. This results in a set of findings which feed back into the initial propositions, either as confirmation of them, or as a requirement that they be rejected or modified in some way.

In contrast, the GT approach encourages the initiation of research without any preconceived theoretical ideas about the topic being researched (such as patient care in hospitals, or the careers of scientists) or the findings that may result from such research. The aim is to develop theory and concepts from the data as the research unfolds. Obviously, researchers cannot rid themselves of all preconceived notions, but the point of grounded theory is to encourage the researcher to be as flexible as possible when interpreting the findings of the research. In this respect, the researcher should adopt theoretical ideas which fit the data collected during the research rather than collecting data that fit a preconceived hypothesis or theoretical idea.

Sampling in this form of research cannot be decided dogmatically in advance. The size of the sample (how many people interviewed or observed) will depend on how well confirmed the emerging theory is, or becomes, during the research. Similarly, the nature of the sample and the choice of comparison groups (what kinds of people will be studied) will be decided as the theory emerges from the data. For example, in a project on patient care the initial focus may be on people with a specific kind of illness, but the data collected may begin to suggest that these may be usefully compared with patients with other types of illness. In this sense, theory about patient care (and the same would apply to research on scientists' careers) will emerge from, and be firmly grounded in, empirical data.

Thus, in the GT approach the data dictates the form of the theory, rather than the theory dictating the collection of certain kinds of data, as in MRT. These, then, are some of the important distinguishing features of MRT and GT. In what follows I shall be unpacking more of the detail of MRT with a view to identifying its advantages and limitations, especially in comparison with GT.

The nature of middle-range theory and research

Robert Merton's ideas on social research are firmly rooted in the idea that the social sciences should, as far as possible, attempt to follow the model of the natural sciences (physics, chemistry and so on) in terms of methods and procedures. Such an approach adopts a rigorously objective stance towards its subject matter. In this respect, understanding the social behaviour that may be the subject of a research project becomes a matter of establishing the objective social causes of that behaviour. In short, it is a matter of establishing how particular social variables influence other variables. For example, how rates of suicide vary with the closeness and supportive character of the community setting, or how forms of parental control over children vary with social class position. MRT attempts to describe just these sorts of relationships between empirically measurable variables.

Merton's views on MRT are a systematic attempt to describe the close relationship between theory and social research. Thus, as Merton puts it, MRT falls between the 'minor working hypotheses' that are typical of the earlier phases of research (and are not really much more elaborate than the hunches or insights that are ordinarily employed in everyday life) and the all-inclusive 'grand' theories which aim to explain a wide span of social phenomena. By 'grand' theories Merton had in mind such examples as Marxist theories of social development which give an account of the historical development of modern societies over a huge span of time and geographical space. Also Parsons's (1951) theory of the 'social system', an elaborate conceptual framework which attempted to account for a great many features of modern western societies, was regarded as a prime example of grand theorizing. While in most respects the theories elaborated by Parsons and Marx are very different from each other, with regard to their generality, scope and inclusiveness they are quite similar. The large-scale nature of such theories makes them very difficult to test in terms of empirical observations and research methods.

In contrast, middle-range theories describe the relations between empirically measurable variables (of the kind mentioned previously), which can therefore be 'tested' against empirically observable evidence. Clearly, MRT is directed at middle-range phenomena as well. That is, it concerns itself with the recurrent aspects of social life, rather than those that are unique and fleeting since these are not general enough to count as properly social characteristics. (This is very much in line with Durkheim's views expressed in *The Rules of Sociological Method* of 1895, see Durkheim 1982.) Conversely, problems of long-term social development fall outside the scope of MRT proper because they are too encompassing and thus difficult to test. Such theories, as in the case of Marxism, have had to be broken down into smaller, more manageable and more specific areas and problems of investigation.

Developing middle-range theory

In a paper called 'The bearing of sociological theory on research' (in 1967b) Merton uses the example of Durkheim's analysis of suicide (Durkheim 1952) as the model upon which we should base our MRTs. Durkheim began his analysis with the observation that in a number of different populations Catholics have a lower suicide rate than Protestants. As such, this represents a regularity which can be expressed as an empirical generalization. Such generalizations should not be mistaken for theory proper. Moreover, they could only become theoretically significant if they could be related to, and derived from, a set of other propositions or assumptions. In order to show how this is, in fact, a feature of Durkheim's analysis, Merton offers us a statement of the assumptions which Durkheim used as the basis from which he derived specific hypotheses about suicide and which he later confirmed by empirical investigation.

In this respect, the assumptions which allowed Durkheim to deduce the relationship between suicide rates and religious affiliations were the following (Merton 1967b: 151):

1 Social cohesion provides psychic support to group members subjected to acute stresses and anxieties.
2 Suicide rates are functions of unrelieved anxieties and stresses to which persons are subjected.
3 Catholics have greater social cohesion than Protestants.
4 Therefore, lower suicide rates should be anticipated among Catholics than among Protestants.

These assumptions highlight the fact that empirical descriptions only become theoretically relevant when they are related to more abstract assumptions: for example, relating rates of suicide to the extent of social cohesion (supportive relationships). Once this is done, then the original empirical finding becomes increased in scope. In this case, the connection between religious affiliation and suicidal behaviour is restated as a more general relation between social cohesion and behaviour. Thus, other connections can be made between suicidal behaviour in different kinds of settings such as marriage and the family. Also, it means that the theoretical assumptions can be applied to areas of inquiry other than suicidal behaviour. For example, says Merton, other kinds of 'maladaptive' behaviour have been found to be related to the lack of social cohesion in various settings.

Establishing the theoretical significance of an empirical regularity allows further research on differences in suicide rates to add confirmation to (or disconfirm) the initial set of assumptions. This makes for the cumulative and systematic development of theory since it is given a firmer grounding by continually testing it against empirical evidence. Also, the framework of assumptions means that the analyst does not have to rely solely on observed trends in order to make predictions. For example, one can predict from the theory that where there is a decrease in social cohesion, there will be a tendency towards increased rates of suicide.

Finally, although Merton admits this is not altogether true of Durkheim's formulation, a theory must be *precise* and *determinate* in its formulation and in the predictions it yields. Such precision reduces the likelihood that alternative hypotheses could be responsible for the same predictions. Precision in the form of an MRT and in the empirical consequences it predicts is an essential aspect of its 'testability'. In this respect, Merton endorses the trend towards the use of statistical data in sociology because it allows precision in the control and testing of theory. While Merton is definitely not against the use of qualitative data in sociology, he does regard it as less systematic than MRT (and thus not as scientific). Certainly, the kind of theorizing encouraged in the grounded theory approach would not be regarded as properly scientific since it is, in Merton's eyes, too flexible, imprecise and open-ended.

Role research and the theory-testing approach

Although Merton uses Durkheim's analysis of suicide as an illustration, the approach is applicable to a large number of areas including theories of role-sets, role conflict, reference groups, social mobility, development of social norms and so on. I shall use the topic of role research to highlight some of the features of Merton's approach that have had a significant impact on theory-testing social research in general. Basically, roles are defined in terms of the social 'expectations' that surround a social position (parent, worker, manager, school teacher, policeperson and so on). A parent is expected to care for his or her children and not to abuse them in any way, a policeperson is expected to uphold the law, a manager is expected to have leadership qualities, and so on. Some roles are more clearly defined than others, some have more officially defined and detailed expectations attaching to them. Compare, for example, the rather loosely defined role of 'friend' with that of 'senior sales manager in company X'.

However, one of the assumptions associated with earlier work on the topic was that for every role there must be broad agreement or consensus about the relevant expectations between all those affected by the behaviour of the role player. This generated a number of research projects to investigate this phenomenon. Merton himself (1957) suggested that research should concentrate on those people who are responsible for defining the role in question and not just on the role itself. This 'role-set' could then be investigated to examine such questions as; the level of agreement or disagreement about expectations among those concerned; whether some people had more power than others to impose their definitions and expectations; the extent of conflict generated by disagreement over expectations.

The study by Gross et al. (1958) of the 'school superintendent' role in Massachussets explored the amount of agreement or consensus there was among the superintendents themselves and between the superintendents and school board members (prominent members of their role-set). The interviews were standardized and the interviewees were asked to consider how far they felt obliged to do, or not to do, certain things (such as accepting full responsibility for subordinates' decisions, or keeping an eye on the private life of subordinates and so on). Interviewees were asked to consider 30–40 such items and their answers were precoded in terms of the degree to which they felt bound by the expectations (strongly obliged, moderately or mildly obligated). Gross et al. found that there was more agreement among the superintendents themselves than there was between them and their school boards and that dissensions with the latter led to a certain amount of conflict over particular issues.

Similar work has been done in relation to the role of 'police officer' by Preiss and Ehrlich (1966) in the USA, and by Cain (1973) in the UK. Preiss and Ehrlich examined in detail the different dimensions of expectations associated with the role (scope, pervasiveness, formal, informal and so on). They also traced the way in which police officers' perceptions of their roles changed as they advanced in their careers. Cain looked at the police officer's role in both rural and city environments with a view to testing the proposition that the greater power of some role definers (colleagues or local community) was due to the effects of working within these different social contexts.

These projects are good examples of theory-testing research based on the propositions of role-set and role conflict theory. The approach demands that theoretical concepts are provided with empirical indicators which can be measured precisely. For example, 'degree of consensus on role expectations' was translated into a measurable empirical indicator through survey questions on 'felt obligation to do certain things' in Gross et al.'s study. In Cain's study 'perceived interdependence with role definers' was indicated by such things as the measured extent of cooperativeness or support received by police officers in certain work environments. In each case, data was collected (mainly through survey questionnaires), and the results tabulated and presented in statistical form. The information thus obtained was then interpreted in relation to its implications for the original hypothesis or set of propositions.

Varieties of approach

The distinction made above between 'the original hypothesis' and/or a 'set of propositions' raises an important issue. Merton's original ideas on MRT seem to stress the importance of the testing of a clearly formulated hypothesis (an anticipated relation between two variables such as 'status' and 'power' or, 'rate of suicide' and 'amount of social cohesion') for the development of research-based theory. While it is the case that some research attempts to test a clearly formulated hypothesis, these few examples discussed above show that this is not always so, and that other kinds of 'testing' form an integral part of this sort of research.

For example, as the work of Gross et al. demonstrates, such research may also involve a general 'exploration' of the empirical implications of a particular concept, or set of related concepts, or the assessment of their empirical applicability (such as the amount and nature of consensus on role expectations). Similarly, this kind of research may involve unpacking particular empirical dimensions of a concept (such as Preiss and Ehrlich's 'instrumental' and 'expressive' aspects of role expectations, or the variations between interpositional and intrapositional consensus in Gross et al.). Sometimes the research as a whole may include a combination of these related sorts of aims and objectives without testing any specific hypothesis as such. Alternatively, the testing of a specific hypothesis (Cain's study) may be undertaken in conjunction with one or more of these broader sorts of tasks. The common thread in these broader activities is the fact that they are undertaken in the context of a wider, more comprehensive set of ideas (such as role theory) on a particular topic.

An important point is that research that begins from an accredited body of theory and empirical evidence does not necessarily preclude elements of theory construction. For example, Gross develops a theory of 'role conflict resolution' on the basis of the research into school superintendents. A central aim of Preiss and Erhlich's study was to 'reformulate' role theory in the light of their findings. In both cases there was a clear intention to develop 'new' theory while 'testing out' or assessing the viability of existing theories. In this sense, the existing theories play a major part in the formulation of the new theory (which may, in fact, simply turn out to be a minor modification of current ideas, or an extension and elaboration of these ideas). What gives this kind of theory construction its identity is the fact that it is an outgrowth from an existing body of theory and evidence.

It is clear that in practice social research is not always structured around the testing of a hypothesis as is stressed in MRT. Rather more vaguely formulated ideas and more diffuse and 'exploratory' aims are often built into this kind of research. None the less, it is true to say that much of the spirit of MRT remains as an important ingredient of this kind of approach. Let me summarize what this entails:

1 The research has to be general enough to be considered important, and 'manageable' enough to pose no problems associated with empirical testing and observation. The theory itself will be halfway between, on the one hand, provisional hunches and intuitions, and on the other, grand, speculative and total systems of theory.

2 Theory is connected to research primarily through a deductive procedure. That is, a testable hypothesis or proposition is logically deduced from an existing set of assumptions. The empirical data that is then collected either confirms or disconfirms the original hypothesis or proposition.

3 All the initial theoretical assumptions and elements have to be given corresponding empirical 'indicators' in order that they may be empirically observed and 'tested'.

   (a) These indicators may be carefully defined empirical 'variables' which can be measured with precision. In this case, empirical data collected on the variables will give the researcher an idea of the relations between them (for example, authoritarian control of children is more typical of working-class parents than middle-class parents).

   (b) If the research is not designed primarily to test an hypothesis as such, then nevertheless, any concepts, propositions or assumptions that are abstract in nature must be given empirical indicators which are potentially measurable, observable, and thus testable, in the light of the evidence unearthed by the research.

4 The requirement of testability through empirical observation is further buttressed by the need for precise measurement techniques of the sort provided by statistical and mathematical models. This means that quantitative data and data-gathering techniques are a precondition for this kind of research. This does not imply that qualitative data and methods are ruled out, but it does imply that they are regarded as somewhat less systematic and precise and thus less 'scientific'. In this sense 'softer' qualitative data and methods can be used as a supplement to the more solid and 'scientific' quantitative forms.

5 The results or findings of such research are intimately related to the initial assumptions in two main ways;

   (a) If a hypothesis was subjected to empirical testing then the results of the research would either confirm or disconfirm it. If it was disconfirmed this might be because the form of the test (that is, the methods of measurement and techniques of data collection) were faulty. This, in turn, would lead to a retest through further empirical research. If it could be confidently asserted that the form of the test was adequate in the first place then this would more likely lead to a reformulation rather than a complete discarding of the original hypothesis. In either of these cases there is a reluctance to jettison entirely the original hypothesis because it follows from assumptions and empirical evidence derived from previously accredited research.

(b)   If the research was more loosely formulated (say, the investigation of a particular concept or set of concepts, or had more exploratory objectives), the findings or results have to be evaluated in terms of the assumptions that form the initial context of the research. Thus the empirical usefulness of the research has to be assessed in relation to the wider context of assumptions and evidence in which it is embedded.

The scope and testability of MRT: the role of history

Merton maintains that MRT is both limited (to specific assumptions and hypotheses) and general, in the sense of extending beyond particular cultures or historical epochs. This seems to imply that MRTs are universally applicable regardless of any differences between societies in terms of economic and political institutions. But it is precisely these sorts of differences that are important in accounting for the development of particular societies and cultures and differences in social behaviour. Such differences figure prominently in the work of many historical sociologists, particularly the classical sociologists such as Karl Marx, Emile Durkheim and Max Weber.

However, as we have seen, Merton explicitly rejects speculative theories of history and social development such as Marx's, on the basis that they are too difficult to test. As Giddens (1987: 42) has pointed out there is no need to suppose that 'the testable can be identified with what is limited in scope'. Thus, there is no reason to assume that 'grand' or general questions of social development are inherently speculative and unconnected with the details of empirical research. In this respect, the large-scale and long-term processes of social change must be viewed as legitimate aspects of social analysis and research, and cannot be written off in the way that Merton's conception of MRT implies.

This point is an important one with regard to my later discussion of research strategies. In particular I stress the importance of the social, political and economic institutions and the historical processes that influence the shape and substance of social activity. These concerns are conspicuously absent from the MRT and GT approaches, and thus have to be brought into the research process in some way. I would therefore support Giddens's call to bring back the larger questions of social development if this means a more sophisticated appreciation of their role in social research which may not be primarily concerned with them. My point is that although one does not want the focus of research into social activity to be 'lost' to the more pressing demands of larger research questions, none the less, the information which they yield can become a resource which may enrich such research. Hence, social research must be freed from the limiting effects of MRT which insists on disconnecting 'testable' empirical research from larger concerns.

Testability, research and other approaches to theory

Merton's description of MRT tends to reinforce a separation between it and more general theories. First, Merton insists that although MRT goes beyond descriptive generalizations about empirical evidence, it must not stray beyond specifying 'determinate relationships between particular variables' (1967b: 148). In this sense, theory is empirically defined by the variables it is concerned with, and thus it must not be confused with 'general sociological orientations' or the general process of clarifying concepts. As we have also seen, MRT has nothing to do with total or unique systems of theory (as in Marx and Parsons).

In this manner, MRT tends to be defined in terms of the substantive areas (or topics) that are its focus of interest, such as suicide, role behaviour, organizational structure, forms of deviance and so on. Moreover, despite Merton's suggestion that MRTs have a certain compatibility about them, and that potentially they could be joined together to form cumulative general theories, it is clear that what Merton means by this is very different from the more abstract 'general social theory' which is the province of sociological specialists. By drawing a clear demarcation between MRT and general theory, Merton reinforces the separation between them.

Also, Merton's idea that we should break up larger theories into narrower, more researchable, testable or observable portions may lead to an inadequate empirical application of the theory. For example, in trying to apply Marx's ideas on class inequalities in society, it is no use simply focusing on measurable indicators of inequality such as level of income, education and consumption, as if they in themselves, could determine the validity or usefulness of the theory. Marx's theory of class is set in a more encompassing framework of ideas and concepts such as the nature of capitalist exploitation and domination, the influence of economic power on social relationships and so on, and this must be registered in some way in the definition of the problem that is to be the focus of the research.

To take another example, in order to utilize Giddens's notion of 'the dialectic of control' in the study of empirical forms of power, it has to be recognized that it can only be understood properly in the wider context of the 'theory of structuration' from which it derives. To completely isolate it from this wider context in order to 'test' its empirical usefulness would be quite inappropriate and would fail to produce a valid or efficient test (see discussion of the 'dialectic of control' in chapter 8). Researchers can, and must, draw on more general theories (or aspects of them) and employ them in empirical research. However, the researcher must be careful not to wrench particular ideas or concepts out of their wider theoretical context when formulating an empirically researchable problem or topic.

The usefulness of MRT and other theory-testing approaches

As a form of theory-testing research in which variables can be measured and observed with ease (and where they are not subject to a great deal of contention or controversy) MRTs can provide useful information. For example, such an approach would be useful in testing hypotheses about the relation between measurable variables such as 'income level' and 'rates of participation in community activities'. Nevertheless, it would be beneficial to widen the scope of such research in order to seek to understand *why* particular relations between the two variables exist. This would demand some understanding of the broader structures of power and domination, the nature of local labour markets and so on, as well as the meanings that these things have for the individuals involved.

The reason for this is that, very often, structural features of society are not best thought of simply as measurable variables. For instance, some kinds of power relations cannot be reduced to these terms. Often, power relations in factories and industrial organizations are hidden behind the scenes of the daily round of activity, and are seemingly unaccompanied by overt conflict (see chapter 8 for a general discussion of power). Certainly, power relations are definitely associated with various styles of management and forms of worker behaviour (in that they influence, and are influenced by, such behaviour). However, in themselves, they have to be understood as social forms which stand apart from, and underlie, these more overt activities. In this sense, they are best thought of as mechanisms which underlie and generate routine activities. MRT, then, must be seen as one resource among others which may be drawn on to supplement the research attack on particular substantive problems. That is, it can be seen as one element in a multistrategy approach (see in particular, chapter 6).

Much the same may be said of other theory-testing approaches. Interestingly, Hammersley (1985) has argued for a theory-testing approach in the context of ethnographic research. The ethnographic approach tends to use qualitative methods and forms of data to describe and analyse particular settings, groups or organizations, and is sometimes associated with a theory-building approach. In this context, however, Hammersley's call for theory-testing ethnographic research provides an interesting adjunct to Merton's ideas on MRT. Hammersley points out that the ethnographic tradition has produced a large amount of empirical research but that it has remained primarily descriptive. He suggests that it should concern itself much more with the cumulation of theoretical knowledge. Using a number of ethnographic studies of schools in the UK Hammersley offers a model for theory-testing ethnography.

Reviewing the work of Lacey (1966 and 1976), Hargreaves (1967) and Ball (1981), Hammersley concludes that they provide the basis for a theory which accounts for the polarization of pupils in certain kinds of school setting. The theory claims that if pupils are allotted to different classes according to their general intellectual abilities, or abilities in particular subjects, their attitudes towards these rankings will become polarized. Those given the highest rankings will accept them and the values they embody, while, more significantly, those given the lowest rankings will reject them and as a consequence this will lead to various kinds of 'disruptive' behaviour. A research programme could be developed to test this theory and its various ramifications. Such a programme would concentrate on the selection of case studies which are crucial for the theory. For example, initially one might choose a school where one would expect the theory to be endorsed. One might then choose another case which could be expected to provide weaker support for the theory, or even suggest alternative explanations. In this way, theory would be developed in a cumulative fashion, building on the work of previous ethnographic studies of schools.

Hammersley's model differs from Merton's in certain crucial respects. First, it utilizes data from ethnographic studies which are primarily qualitative in nature, such as extracts from interviews or field notes (although as Hammersley points out, the studies that he cites use some quantitative measures as well). Here, Hammersley reinforces the important point that although ethnographic studies produce much good empirical data, they should also use quantitative indicators whenever possible, and pay careful attention to the representativeness of their samples. Secondly, the theory that is to be tested makes reference to 'variables' that cannot necessarily be expressed in quantitative terms. In this respect, Hammersley claims that he is just as concerned with the social factors that underlie and give shape to the observable events.

However, in certain other respects Hammersley's approach is strikingly similar to Merton's. The centrality of a tightly specified theory and the testing of specific hypotheses derived from it are also features of MRT. Also similar is the idea that the cumulative development of theory from successive research projects through a theory-testing approach requires a *narrow* research focus. As Hammersley says 'If the development and testing of theory is to be pursued effectively, the research focus has to be narrow. Attempts to provide a rounded and detailed description of the institution or behaviour under study or to integrate macro and micro levels of analysis are, it seems to me, counterproductive as far as theorising is concerned' (1985: 251).

In the same manner as MRT, Hammersley's approach can be regarded as one among a number of possible approaches to research which would provide useful information and contribute to the cumulative development of theory. However, this cumulative development has to be understood in rather wider terms than is presently implied in Hammersley's model. If theory and research are to develop in a truly cumulative way, then theory-constructing approaches such as Glaser and Strauss's 'grounded theory', as well as more general forms of theory, must have a central place alongside theory-testing approaches. It is not enough to insist that research pay more attention to theoretical aims and then to define theory in a very limited way. It needs to be recognized that theorizing may take a number of forms, and may be related to the empirical world of research in a number of ways. A truly cumulative approach to theory would seek to integrate these seemingly diverse efforts.

It seems entirely negative of Hammersley to dismiss attempts to integrate micro and macro levels of analysis in social research on the grounds that they inhibit the establishment of tightly formulated theories with a narrow empirical focus. One of the central theoretical problems in sociology concerns understanding the relationship between macro and micro aspects of social life, and much scholarly effort has gone into coming to grips with it. It would be a wasted opportunity if theoretical and empirical research endeavours were not coordinated in some way. In this respect, theory-testing and theory-constructing approaches (as well as those that fall somewhere in between) should not be seen necessarily as competing with each other, but as serving specific research needs in relation to specific kinds of empirical problem.

MRT and theory construction

In describing MRT Merton focuses primarily on the question of theory testing and thus he says little about how theoretical ideas emerge through the process of research itself. However, elsewhere, he discusses the way in which research can lead to the initiation and development of theory. Merton claims that research is not restricted to the verification or testing of theory and that, in fact, it plays a more active role. This is because 'an explicitly formulated theory does not inevitably precede empirical inquiry . . . as a matter of plain fact, the theorist is not inevitably the lamp lighting the way to new observations' (1967a: 47). By way of illustration, Merton indicates four ways in which empirical research helps in the formulation of theory.

1   What Merton calls the 'serendipity pattern'. This refers to the situation in which an unanticipated research finding which is not consistent with prevailing theory or with other established facts stimulates the development of a new theory or the extension of an existing one. For example, a researcher concentrating on a particular problem, say role behaviour, unearths hitherto undiscovered empirical information which casts considerable doubt on the established body of role theory. This leads either to the development of a completely new theory, or to the substantial reformulation of existing theory.
2   The repeated observation of previously neglected facts or data creates pressure to elaborate on an existing theory or concept or framework. In this sense, research on various aspects of role behaviour led to extensions and modifications of the theory. For example, repeated observations of the operation of 'informal expectations', as opposed to officially defined ones in police behaviour, added a new dimension to established theory (Preiss and Ehrlich 1966).
3   The invention of new research methods and procedures can lead to a shifting of the focus of interest in theory. Merton gives the example of the emergence of interest in the theory of propaganda which, he suggests, was partly stimulated by the development of such research methods as 'content analysis' and the 'panel technique'.
4   The research process forces the researcher to establish 'operational definitions' of concepts, that is, measurable aspects of the variables under consideration. This aids the clarification of concepts in the

theory or theoretical framework. Thus, for example the operational definition of 'consensus on role expectations' used by Gross et al. was the extent to which people felt obliged to do certain things. The findings that emerged from this then fed back into the initial assumptions and clarified the concept of consensus. It led to the conclusion that consensus (or complete agreement) about role expectations had to be thought of in a more loose and flexible manner.

If we examine these four it is clear that although they do describe ways in which social research may feed back into theoretical understanding, it is only the first and third of these that directly address the question of how new theory is generated. The second and fourth are really only concerned with the elaboration or clarification of existing theory. While the invention of new mehods and procedures of research may well have the effect of establishing new areas of theoretic interest, such breakthroughs are few and far between. They certainly do not form part of the routine activities of social research. This leaves us with the serendipity pattern, where the chance discovery of anomalous findings stimulates fresh theorizing. In this case new theory is developed only in response to chance empirical discoveries which require novel explanations. Accordingly, the generation of new concepts and theories is not something that the researcher intends to do, or can predict in any way. This is because the researcher's exposure to anomalous empirical findings is entirely accidental.

All in all, there appears to be nothing in Merton's approach which concentrates on the issue of theory generation as a routine or strategic feature of research. As it stands, routine theorizing in the MRT approach tends to be in the service of confirming or disconfirming preconceived theory. This means, first, that theory does not have an organic relationship with the emerging data of research such that it responds to, and is to some extent shaped by, newly uncovered data. In this sense, theory only adapts to the dictates of empirical evidence, after the event of the research, and without the benefit of the closeness of the data. Modifications or reformulations of the theory in the light of research evidence have to be achieved in a relatively 'blind' way, somewhat removed from the immediate circumstances and emergent processes of the research. Moreover, such modifications and reformulations will retain the shape and content of formalized hypotheses about the relations between variables.

Secondly, such an approach does not make the most efficient use of empirical data. A more intensive concentration on empirical evidence as a resource which is continuously suggestive of theory (at least potentially) would result in a more efficient use of the data uncovered by research. This, of course, would require that we adopt a wider notion of theory and theorizing than that implicit in theory-testing approaches generally. In fact, it is to theory-constructing approaches applied mainly in the context of qualitative research (like that of Glaser and Strauss) that we have to turn in order to develop this idea more fully.

Guidelines for fieldwork

Clearly, we must conclude that if MRT (or any similar theory-testing approach) is taken as the sole guiding principle for research, then it will tend to limit the theory-generating potential of the research. However, for the researcher who is about to embark on a fieldwork project in which the primary aim is to construct theory it is important not to overlook these approaches as resources which can be drawn on to help in the formulation of theoretical ideas and concepts. Of course, it is also possible that the field researcher will decide that the aims of the research are more descriptive than theoretical, such as providing information on a social process (for example, professional–client counselling, or training to be a nurse) or on a group (such as homosexuals, or students, or footballers) about which little work has been done, or where there are gaps in knowledge. It is also true, as we have seen in this chapter, that some research is rather more loosely associated with the theory-testing approach. In this sense, while it shares the objective, 'scientific' methods of theory-testing, it is often concerned with things other than the strict testing of a tightly formulated hypothesis (for example, it might be concerned with providing 'basic' information for future research and theorizing).

Thus, for the fieldworker who has already decided on a topic or area (such as patient care, or a particular occupational group like musicians or lawyers), and who has theory construction in mind, the following questions may provide useful starting points for thinking in theoretical terms. The basic question is: What elements of the theory-testing approach could be useful to me in my research? This can be subdivided into: Can I draw on some of the findings of theory-testing research and use them for my own purposes? What elements of the general approach of theory testing could be of use to me in attempting to develop new theory?

1 Using a hypothesis as a resource

In this case the field researcher must ask: Can I draw on the hypotheses of theory-testing research in order to structure my own research? In this sense well-established relationships between specific variables such as different forms of parental control and social class, or illness behaviour and social class, may provide valuable starting points for further exploratory research. For example, Cain's study of the police in the UK established that in a city setting the police 'role' was more likely to be defined by colleagues rather than the local community, and that in a rural setting the reverse was the case. This was because in the rural setting the police worked in relative isolation from colleagues and depended very much on the cooperation of the local community in the clearing up of crime and general policing duties. In the city setting, police work was more team-based and thus individual officers depended more on colleagues for back-up and the sharing of information.

Such hypotheses about the power of role definers may become the basis for a more detailed, exploratory study within the area of police work. For example, one might want to know exactly how city police cooperate with and depend on each other, or whether in fact such dependence leads to strain or conflict in an officer's relations with colleagues (of the same rank or of different ranks). This might lead to the development of theoretical ideas which move away from a concentration on the power of role definers as such. Nonetheless, initially thinking in these terms starts the flow of new ideas or stimulates an interest in new dimensions of police behaviour or a different area of police work.

The focus of research interest need not be limited to the police. For example, the hypothesis about the power of role definers in different settings could be extended to other occupational roles (doctors, nurses, factory workers, artists, chiropractors). In these cases the original hypothesis would apply in a rather looser sense, since the particular circumstances of the work will be somewhat different. However, simply trying to apply it to these other settings may stimulate new lines of thought about role behaviour or other aspects of activity in these settings. The research focus could be even further removed from the world of work and occupations and applied to more informal contexts such as family or friendship situations. Again, thinking initially in terms of an established relationship between two (or more) variables could provide a valuable starting point for new theoretical ideas and concepts.

2   Using particular aspects of theory-testing research

Another type of question for the fieldworker to ask is: Can I draw on any of the component elements of theory-testing research and use them independently as a means of developing new lines of thought? Such elements may take the form of a concept, or conceptual distinction, which forms part of a more comprehensive framework, or an empirical fact or description which is taken from the context of the original research. For example, the conceptual distinction between 'instrumental' and 'expressive' (Preiss and Erhlich 1966) role expectations may be extracted from its role theory framework and used in a more general sense as a means of exploring different aspects of behaviour. A particular concept such as 'an elaborated code' in relation to language use (taken from Bernstein's theory of class-based speech codes, in Bernstein 1971, 1973) might become the starting point for thinking about the way language is used in situations in which class has a less important influence.

Similarly, extracting other more empirical or descriptive aspects of research conducted in the context of a theory-testing approach may serve the same function. Thus, for example, Hammersley's ideas about the polarization of school pupils in situations where they are ranked academically may stimulate ideas about whether, or in what sense, attitudes and behaviour formed in the school spill over into non-school areas such as family and friendship. Or it could initiate thinking about whether types of ranking in other areas of social life (such as in some sporting activities) leads to a rejection of the values embodied in the ranking system by those who occupy the lowest ranks. Again, these simply provide ways in which theoretical thinking may be stimulated, in this sense, the original theory-testing context is drawn on as a resource for theory building; there is no necessary commitment to the whole framework of the original research.

3 Using quantitative data as a resource

The researcher must ask the question: Can quantitative data be useful in formulating theory and concepts? As we have seen, theory-testing approaches have traditionally used quantitative measures and statistical techniques in order to lend precision to their findings. Quantitative data should not be thought of as the exclusive property of theory-testing approaches. In theory-constructing fieldwork, quantitative data can be useful for checking theoretical 'hunches' or intuitions that may arise as the researcher becomes more acquainted with a particular topic. In the light of quantitative checks it may be found that such hunches may have concealed misleading or over-enthusiastic interpretations of the data (see discussion of Silverman's work in chapter 6). Also, quantitative data may be an important stimulus to theoretical ideas in fieldwork which is primarily qualitative (see discussion of my research on the acting profession also in chapter 6).

4 Using general theory as a resource for fieldwork

Here the researcher must ask: How can the work of writers like Parsons, Foucault, Giddens and Habermas, among others, help to illuminate the empirical area of my research? How can it help me develop further theoretical ideas? General theory can be used in both theory-testing and theory-building types of research. However, here 'theory testing' has to be understood in a rather different sense to that used in the more conventional approaches. Thus it does not refer to research which either confirms or disconfirms a purported relationship between two or more variables. Rather, empirical research provides a 'test' of general theory if it illustrates the usefulness of general theory to the understanding of empirical data.

In this sense, the research may be pertinent to large segments of a general theory or simply to one aspect of it. For example, Bloor and McIntosh (1990) employ Foucault's notions of power, resistance and surveillance in their study of therapeutic communities and health visiting in the UK. (See also my discussion of Giddens' notion of 'the dialectic of control' in relation to occupational careers in chapter 8.) While it is clear that the empirical data of research can illustrate the usefulness of concepts and ideas taken from general theories, it is also the case that such theory can stimulate theoretical ideas in fieldwork which has a theory-building aim.

3

Grounded Theory and Field Research

The context: ethnography and qualitative methods

Compared with MRT, grounded theory and the fieldwork associated with it is anchored in a quite different methodological tradition and vision of sociology. It stems from the symbolic interactionist perspective which is founded principally on the work of G. H. Mead (1967). Mead's work subsequently gave rise two major variants of symbolic interactionism which were originally based at two American universities, Chicago and Iowa. The Iowa school, as it became known, preferred to utilize the positivist framework which emphasized strict control over variables, rigorous testing of hypotheses and propositions, and the quantification of results. In constrast, the Chicago school has taken a quite different tack with regard to sociological method.

Instead of stressing the role of an objectively 'detached' observer whose task is to describe social behaviour in terms of causal forces external to the individuals concerned, the Chicago school emphasized the more 'involved' role of the social researcher. In this 'humanistic' vision of social science, a *verstehen* approach was required whereby the researcher should seek an empathetic understanding of the behaviour of those people being studied. This goal could only be accomplished if the analyst paid considerable attention to the way in which social meanings emerged in situations and thereby affected the behaviour of those involved. In short, as Blumer (1966: 542) has pointed out, the researcher must attempt to describe how the actors themselves act towards the world on the basis of how they see it, and not on the basis of how that world appears to the outside observer. This humanist strand of symbolic interactionism favours research methods and strategies such as participant observation, in-depth or semi-structured interviews, and documentary evidence, which seek to tap the subjective understandings of the people who are the subjects of the research.

This perspective has been a major influence on field research in sociology, although as others have noted (Burgess 1984, Hammersley 1990) there is a rather larger context to qualitative research in general. Cultural anthropology, in particular, has always employed an 'ethnographic' method (the direct observation of behaviour) in order to gather data on particular societies that seem alien from the standpoint of modern industrial societies. However, as Burgess has pointed out, some British sociologists, especially those studying schools and classrooms, have used the term 'ethnography' to describe their work. Much work in anthropology, sociology and social psychology that relies on an observational approach and a relationship between the researcher and those being studied has been described in various ways as 'fieldwork', 'ethnography', 'case study', 'qualitative research' among others (Burgess 1984).

Hammersley (1990) notes that in the past 30 years ethnography and other forms of qualitative method have become much more central in social science especially in particular areas such as education and medicine. Apart from a concern with observing activity and describing actor's meanings, Hammersley claims that the underlying justification for ethnography is based on 'a critique of quantitative, notably survey and experimental, research' (1990: 597). Such research tends to impose the researcher's assumptions and therefore reduces the chances of discovering evidence which would question the basis of these assumptions. Also, studying people in settings that have been specially set up by the researcher is not a good basis for making claims about what goes on in 'natural' everyday settings. Moreover, says Hammersley, such research neglects processes of development and change and the creative role of individuals and groups. Thus, the main assumption underlying qualitative method is that the 'social world must be *discovered*' and 'that this can only be achieved by first-hand observations and participation in 'natural' settings, guided by an exploratory orientation' (Hammersley 1990: 598).

Hammersley goes on to argue that while much ethnography places great emphasis on the 'description' (of societies, small communities and organizations) as a central goal of research, there are other strands that emphasize a form of 'theoretical description'. I shall consider these variations in more detail further on, but it must be noted here that while Glaser and Strauss's notion of grounded theory is related to this wider context of qualitative analysis and method, there are also significant differences of emphasis. Specifically, grounded theory shares the assumption that the social world must be *discovered* using qualitative methods and employing an *exploratory* orientation. However, grounded *theory* (as the very term implies) is concerned neither with description pure and simple, nor with what Hammersley refers to as 'theoretical description'. In this sense Glaser and Strauss's approach is highly distinctive and quite unlike other forms of qualitative approach.

Methods and strategies of fieldwork

The method of 'participant observation' allows the closest approximation to a state of affairs wherein the sociologist enters into the everyday world of those being studied so that he or she may describe and analyse this world as accurately as possible. Participant observation represents the ideal form of research strategy because this method requires that the sociologist for all intents and purposes 'becomes' a member of the group being studied. Although there may be no deliberate attempt to disguise the natural curiosity of the sociologist, nevertheless, being a participant enables the professional identity of the sociologist to be submerged so that the group can be studied from the point of view of a typical member.

There have been a number of classic participant observation studies in America. For instance Becker (1963) used this method in his study of jazz musicians and drug takers; Polsky (1967) used his experience as a pool-room player in order to study pool hustlers; Humphreys (1970) acted as a 'watch queen' to study homosexual behaviour in public rest rooms. As Burgess (1984) has pointed out, these studies constituted the major site for the discovery of American ethnography by British sociologists. This influenced a number of British studies, notably in the fields of deviance (Young 1971), the sociology of labour and industry (Benyon 1973, Pollert 1981, Cavendish 1982) and the sociology of schools and classrooms (Willis 1977, Hargreaves 1972, Delamont 1976, Burgess 1982).

By playing down, or even disguising, a professional sociological interest, the participant observer has unique access to the otherwise somewhat 'closed world' of a social group. By gaining the trust of the people in the group the participant observer is initiated into the values, routines and social meanings that the group holds dear. Thus the sociologist is able to observe firsthand the typical experiences and attitudes of group members, and is able to describe their world in terms of the same language and expressions.

Of course, the complete ideal of participant observation is not always possible or even desirable, especially since the deception involved in disguising one's real motives raises quite serious ethical issues. Alternatively, 'close' observation of a group requiring something less than complete participation is often chosen as a research strategy. In fact Gold

(1958) has identified three other fieldwork roles that a researcher may adopt instead of that of the complete participant. These are the 'participant as observer', the 'observer as participant' and the 'complete observer', and they represent degrees of closeness to the group achieved by the researcher during the fieldwork.

The most common strategies involve some combination of the middle two roles since they require the researcher to adopt a level of involvement in the everyday routines of the group, as well as a degree of detachment implied and necessitated by their observer status. Very often these methods and strategies are combined with, or supplemented by, unstructured or semi-structured interviews with 'key' informants. Completely unstructured interviews are something akin to naturally occurring conversations with group members in which important information about the workings of the group is imparted to the researcher.

In semi-structured interviews the interviewer has a list of topics or questions that he or she wants to cover, although this list will be flexibly adhered to according to the emergent demands of the interview situation. Semi-structured interviews are designed to let interviewees respond in an open-ended way. This differs from the kind of formal structured interview in which a fixed-choice questionnaire is administered and which forces the respondents to reply in terms of precoded categories (such as 'strong agreement', 'mild agreement' or 'disagreement' with a particular statement). By contrast, the semi-structured interview is geared to allowing people the freedom to respond in any way they choose. In this manner, the individual's own interpretations and meanings are allowed to surface in the interview data. As with participant observation (and its variants), these methods are designed to elicit qualitative data which reflects and records the meanings and understandings (the 'subjective worlds') of the people being studied (rather than a quantitative expression of the relations between 'variables').

Grounded theory: a qualified formalism

Arguing against Merton and others who favour positivistic methods, Glaser and Strauss (1967) have championed the use of qualitative methods and data, arguing that they can be used systematically and that they can give rise to reliable, precise and valid social research. In fact, they argue that qualitative methods are the only methods suited to the emergent nature of field research. Echoing Blumer's (1969) arguments against the static and artificial nature of many sociological research variables, Glaser and Strauss stress that qualitative methods and data uniquely capture the unfolding nature of the meanings, interpretations and processes that the sociologist is studying. However, apart from participant observation, they view more 'remote' forms of observation, semi-strutured interviews and documentary materials as having equivalent weight as research instruments, depending of course on the exact circumstances of the research.

Glaser and Strauss's ideas were developed as a result of firsthand involvement in research into the hospital care of dying patients (1965), and also through an acute dissatisfaction with the state of sociological theory. According to these authors, theory generation had been stultified by an over-emphasis on the verification of extant theories exemplified in the work of Merton (MRT), Parsons ('grand' social systems theory) and Blau (exchange theory). Such theories are generally 'speculative' in nature because they have not grown directly out of research, and thus remain ungrounded. As a consequence, these theories very often lack validity because they do not 'fit' the real world and thereby remain irrelevant to the people concerned. Glaser and Strauss point out that these ungrounded formal theories dictate, 'before empirical examination, presumed relevancies in problems, concepts and hypotheses, and the kind of indicators that "should" apply . . . to the neglect of emergent relevancies of concepts, properties and indicators' (1971: 177).

Substantive and formal theory

In order to overcome such inadequacies the authors suggest that all formal theory must first proceed through, and emerge from, a substantive grounding in data. Thus they distinguish between *substantive* theory and *formal* theory. Substantive theory is theory 'developed for a substantive area such as patient care, race relations, professional education, geriatric lifestyles, delinquency or financial organizations'. By contrast, formal theory is theory 'developed for a formal or conceptual area of sociological inquiry such as status passage, stigma, deviant behaviour, socialization, status congruency, authority and power, reward systems, organizations or organizational careers' (Glaser and Strauss 1971: 177–8).

Substantive and formal theories differ in terms of their degrees of generality, but both are generated by some form of comparative analysis. If the researcher's focus is on the generation of substantive theory, comparative analysis is made between or among groups within the same substantive area. Glaser's own work (1964) on scientists' careers can be used to illustrate a substantive focus. Thus a focus on the substantive area of scientists careers (as opposed to the formal area of organizational careers) meant that comparisons were made between different career stages such as junior investigator, senior investigator and supervisor, and also in this particular case across two promotional systems within the organization.

However, if the focus is on generating formal theory, for example a formal theory of organizational careers (rather than a substantive theory of a particular organizational career), then the comparative analysis is made between different cases and substantive theories falling within the same formal area, without relating the resulting theory to any one particular substantive area. Glaser has attempted to do this in relation to the formal area of 'organizational careers' by providing a 'sourcebook' containing a diversity of empirical materials on many different types of organizational career (Glaser 1968).

From this it is clear that it is possible to construct formal theories on the basis of particular substantive theories grounded in data (primarily qualitative data, although the use of quantitative data is not ruled out by Glaser and Strauss). Formal theories cannot be developed in some prior or independent way which short-cuts an initial substantive grounding. The comparative method which involves comparing groups of both maximum and minimum similarity is the most powerful means of generating substantive and formal theory because of its coverage of many diverse properties of the groups studied. Such exercises in comparison force or encourage the researcher to develop categories, properties and hypotheses as they emerge from the collection and analysis of the data.

There is, however, another way of generating formal theory from grounded substantive theory and this involves what Glaser and Strauss call a 'rewriting technique'; this involves writing about substantive material in a more formal sociological manner. One variant of this is simply to omit substantive words, phrases or adjectives. The authors demonstrate this technique by reference to their substantive analysis of dying patients in hospital (1965), which they attempt to relate to the formal area of 'status passage' theory. This latter involves the study of career-like movements through beginning, transitional and end statuses and embraces occupational careers as well as other types of career such as that of deviance, or marriage, or illness. Thus, with the example of the 'careers' of dying patients they point out that 'instead of writing "temporal aspect of *dying* as a non-scheduled status passage" one could write "temporal aspects of non-scheduled status passage"' (1971: 179).

Whether formal theory is produced through a process of rewriting or through the generation of new concepts and analytic devices, both techniques depend on the comparative method and the existence of a bedrock of substantive material. Producing formal theory from substantive material by comparative analysis ensures that the concepts and categories so produced will be appropriate and relevant. Also, it means that one's analysis as a whole will be grounded in empirical reality. This feature strongly distinguishes this kind of theory from other types (particularly 'grand theory') which Glaser and Strauss claim are generated from assumptions and speculations about what 'ought' to be the case, rather than what 'is' the case in empirical, factual terms.

Linking grounded theories

As part of the wider design of the grounded theory approach, Glaser and Strauss stress that the generation of particular theories should be seen in the context of an attempt to develop a more cumulative body of theory. In this respect, grounded theories should be extended and linked to other grounded theories. The authors' own linkage of their grounded theory of 'status passage' (1971) with what they call 'awareness theory' (the degree of awareness of people in different contexts about 'what is going on' in particular episodes of interaction) is an example of the extension they mean.

It is only by making these kinds of connections that sociologists can build a cumulative body of theory. Otherwise, grounded theories will be relegated to the status of 'respected little islands' of (mainly substantive) knowledge separated from others. Glaser and Strauss suggest that the cumulative progress of theory is enhanced by the encouragement of multiple substantive and formal theories, and thus their stance is in contrast to 'the directly monopolistic implication of logico-deductive theories, whose formulators talk as if there is only one theory for a formal area or perhaps only one formal theory for all areas' (1971: 182).

Ethnographic studies (which concentrate on providing detailed descriptions of observed behaviour) may contribute to the later development of grounded theories. However, Glaser and Strauss clearly regard the role of the practitioner of grounded theory as being very different from that of the ethnographer. The researcher interested in developing grounded theory is 'an active sampler of theoretically relevant data', rather than 'an ethnographer trying to get the fullest data on a group' (1971: 183). That is to say that in the service of generating theory the researcher must select comparison groups according to their theoretical relevance in furthering the development of emerging categories, properties, hypotheses and the integration of the theory. The constant selection and control over comparison groups is part of the dynamic and emergent design of the research process and encourages the development of properly grounded theory.

According to Glaser and Strauss, although grounded theory can be expressed in a propositional, codified and axiomatic form, they prefer to use it as a running theoretical discussion to emphasize 'theory as process'. This discussional form of theory stresses the idea of theory as an ever-developing entity which can be extended and modified, as against the idea that theories are perfected products whose purpose is served merely by being confirmed or negated. Rather, theory should be viewed as a constant and flexible accompaniment to the incremental collection of data and the unfolding nature of the research.

These, then, represent the main features of grounded theory. Glaser and Strauss generally present it as a counter to the established conceptions of theory and research as found in the works of Merton, Parsons and Blau. However, in one respect grounded theory is similar to Merton's conception of systematic theory. Thus, grounded theory is 'middle range' in scope, falling between the minor working hypotheses of everyday life and all-inclusive 'grand' theories, just as Merton insists is the case with MRT proper. However, it must be emphasized that this is where the similarity ends since Merton favours a deductive procedure in the formulation of hypotheses. This tends to promote the search for evidence which confirms or disconfirms the preformed hypothesis, rather than a concentration on what the freshly gathered data can yield in terms of emergent concepts and theoretical ideas. As I pointed out in the previous chapter, Glaser and Strauss view Merton's conception of research as one which encourages the researcher to find data to fit the theory rather than to generate theory that fits the data, as is the case with grounded theory.

Other qualitative approaches to research

As I pointed out at the beginning of this chapter, the grounded theory approach is one among a number of qualitative approaches. In order to further highlight its distinctive character, let me consider some of these other kinds of approach in more detail. In chapter 2 I made it clear that the distinction between theory-testing and theory- constructing research was not always clear-cut. At the end of that chapter I reinforced this by giving several examples of research that fell somewhere between the two extremes. The same principle applies here with qualitative and ethnographic research. Clearly, as Hammersley says, all these approaches are characterized by a concern with discovery and exploration through firsthand observation. However, they are not all concerned to the same extent, or even at all, with the construction or generation of theory.

1   The descriptive or anti-formal approach

A number of writers who share the same general symbolic interactionist framework as Glaser and Strauss have tended to adopt an approach which minimizes the importance of theory and scientific method. According to this view, theorizing simply moves the researcher away from the empirical world and into an alien abstract world. Instead, the sociologist must faithfully describe and reconstruct the world of those she or he is studying from their subjects' point of view without the encumbrance of theory or methodological techniques (see Becker, quoted in Rock 1979: 190). The data of social research will be based on direct personal experience through participant observation. Moreover, the findings will be expressed in language which reflects the commonsense worlds of those being studied (Rock 1979: 95). Any training or grounding of the researcher in social theory of any kind is irrelevant, and possibly disadvantageous, since it does not defer to the authority of the empirical world (ibid.: 214).

This kind of stance has led to a form of qualitative research which aims to 'investigate and describe the social world as it really is beyond all presumptions and prejudices' (Hammersley 1990: 606). Becker's own work on marijuana users and the occupational culture of jazz musicians (1963) and a study of student culture in medical school (Becker et al. 1961) are good examples of this type of research. As Hammersley has observed, the coherence of such accounts 'often lies primarily in their focus on the particular community, group or situation that they study; rather than in any substantive or theoretical issue' (1990: 606). He goes on to point out that this is reflected in the titles of some ethnographic studies which refer solely to the phenomenon described. For example, Street Corner Society (Whyte 1943); Hightown Grammar (Lacey 1970); The Mountain People (Turnbull 1973); The Nude Beach (Douglas et al. 1977).

In my view, these studies often provide valuable empirical information, albeit restricted to a primarily 'descriptive' rather than 'theoretical' or 'explanatory' form. However, if such studies are coupled with a proscriptive attitude towards theorizing of any kind on the grounds that it is somehow wrong or misplaced, then their value is rather more limited.

There is no need to limit social research by eschewing the value of theory and scientific method. Descriptive ethnography of this type may coexist with qualitative analyses which seek to develop theory and to employ systematic methods of study. There is no reason for the two to be seen as *competing* approaches.

2 Information-gathering approaches

This refers to research which employs qualitative methods with a view to filling in gaps in knowledge about social processes, or to confirming or verifying previous findings, or to investigating a social problem. (Or even some combination of the three aims.) In that such research may employ a descriptive format, it is similar to the previous type. However, it is unlike the previous category in that it does not strive to give a detailed account of the 'closed' or bounded social world of a group or community. Rather it focuses on segments of society or social processes (which may in fact overlap) about which there is a lack of information. Secondly, such research is not consciously anti-theoretical, or hostile to theory. Its focus is primarily substantive and problem-oriented and may be motivated by a question of social policy.

Good examples of this kind of research can be found in the overlapping areas of medical sociology and deviance. For instance, McKeganey's (1990) study of the level of drug abuse in an area in Glasgow attempts to assess the nature and extent of needle sharing among injecting drug users and the meaning of such activities to the users. The study arose out of a 'social problems perspective' (p. 114), that is, the growing recognition that injecting drug use represents one of the main risk activities for contracting and spreading HIV (AIDS) infection. The research therefore attempted to gain an understanding of current levels of risk among a sample of injecting drug users. Such research has clear policy implications about intervention strategies aimed at reducing levels of sharing among injecting drug users. Also, McKeganey et al. (1990) have conducted an ethnographic study comparing female street-working prostitutes and male rent boys in Glasgow in terms of risks of HIV infection and the practice of safer sex. This study was aimed at plugging gaps in knowledge by providing locally based information on the nature of risk practices between male and female prostitutes and their clients.

These types of study, oriented to a social problem and primarily intended to gather information, can also take the form of replications of previous studies of a similar type. In this case, they would be concerned with either confirming findings over time or assessing how generally they can be applied (for instance by assessing their relevance to other geographical and social contexts). Such research seeks to verify or disconfirm previous findings and, in this sense, it resembles theory-testing research but without reference to a tightly formulated hypothesis. At the same time, it is clear that while not primarily concerned with theoretical issues, such studies may feed into more theoretical work in the longer term by providing a body of knowledge on, for example, 'risk-taking behaviour'.

3   Clarifying concepts and assessing their usefulness

A variation on the information-gathering approach is the idea of focusing on an important concept which has been associated with a particular area with a view to illustrating its usefulness or its limitations for research. In this respect, qualitative analysis can yield information which can clarify or redefine such concepts by exploring their empirical dimensions. For example, Backett's (1990) study of families in the UK explored the empirical components of the concept of 'family health culture'. On the basis of the evidence gathered, Backett questions some of the assumptions built into the concept of family health culture as it has been used in previous studies. For example, she found data at variance with the assumptions that health-related beliefs and behaviours of men and women, and adults and children, are similar in the same family group.

4   Applying theory and concepts from general frameworks

Sometimes, ethnographic studies and qualitative analyses are guided by general theoretical frameworks or particular concepts taken from these frameworks. In this respect, such studies are not simply limited to a commitment to a wider framework of symbolic interactionism. As we have said, ethnographic data have been used in the context of the discipline of anthropology and have also been associated with other theoretical frameworks such as Marxism or feminism or ethnomethodology. In this sense, particular studies demonstrate the utility or otherwise of such frameworks as a whole, or of particular concepts (like 'alienation' or 'patriarchy'), for the organization and analysis of qualitative data. Willis's (1977) study of working-class school-children in the UK illustrates how some Marxist concepts can make sense of ethnographic data. Willis demonstrates how the rebellious and disruptive attitudes of the boys and their general concern with 'having a laff' as opposed to studying for educational qualifications subsequently seals their fate as low-level manual workers. During his analysis Willis draws on Marxist concepts (like Louis Althusser's notion of 'ideological state apparatuses') to show how 'the lads' participate in reproducing the very class system in which they are entrapped.

Burawoy's (1979) analysis of factory workers' 'games' in the USA is similarly influenced by a Marxist perspective, as is Cockburn's (1983) study of deskilling in the UK printing industry. Equally, studies such as Charles and Kerr (1986) have demonstrated the usefulness of a feminist perspective in understanding women's 'normal' relationship to food. The authors claim that on a day-to-day basis almost all women have a problematic relationship to food and that this can lead to eating disorders such as anorexia nervosa and compulsive eating.

The primary emphasis in such studies is the investigation of a social phenomenon, with the employment of more general theoretical frameworks (or parts thereof) in order to organize and give sense to the findings. In the main, these studies are concerned with illustrating the usefulness of an existing framework, rather than developing new concepts or theoretical ideas. Of course, however, the same approach could be used to develop theory by using the existing framework simply as a starting point for theoretical reflection. Furthermore, the concepts or theory that provide the 'organizing framework', as it were, for an ethnographic study do not necessarily have to be drawn from an extensive, interrelated body of general theory, such as Marxism, feminism and so on. As in the previous type of approach (in relation to the concept of 'family health culture'), a particular concept which has general currency in a particular area may be used as an organizing device. For example, concepts such as 'primary' and 'secondary deviance' or 'residual rule-breaking' (Scheff 1966) may be used to organize data on petty crime or milder forms of mental illness.

5 Sensitizing concepts and theoretical description

A type of approach which provides an intermediate position between the above four and Glaser and Strauss's out-and-out theory-constructing type is the exploratory kind of fieldwork which aims to develop concepts and descriptions which are theoretically insightful and thus provide useful starting points for further research. In this sense, once developed, they act as 'sensitizing devices' which help subsequent researchers to formulate theoretical ideas or to organize their data. Goffman's concept of a 'total institution', developed from his study of a mental hospital (1968), is a good example of such a transition, as is Hughes's (1937) notion of 'career' as a two-sided (objective and subjective) concept. (See the discussion in chapter 7.)

Conclusion

Although these different approaches to ethnography and qualitative analysis can be thought of as separate 'approaches' in so far as one can point to fairly clear examples of them all, it is also clear that they can be used in conjunction with each other. In this light, the grounded theory approach can be thought of in a dual sense. First, it is distinctive in so far as it stresses the role of systematic theory-building (both substantive and formal) as an integral element of research. It is also distinctive in that it stresses the importance of sampling as part of the emergent nature of the research and the theory. In another sense, grounded theory could be seen as an 'end product' of research which draws on all or some of the elements contained in the other approaches described above. In this way, the central aim of the research is to develop 'new' theory, but in so doing it may draw on other approaches ('information-gathering', 'theory-applying' or 'concept-clarifying' research) in order to reach this goal. Essentially, this is the kind of research I want to stress in the rest of this book. The next chapter therefore attempts to amend and extend the GT approach with a view to endorsing a more open approach to theory generation in fieldwork.

4

Grounded Theory on a Broader Canvas

So far I have suggested that the grounded theory approach makes extremely efficient use of research data as a means of constructing theory. Also, compared with both theory-testing approaches and more 'exploratory', qualitative approaches it gives systematic attention to theory building, thus allowing a cumulative development of empirical and theoretical findings. However, at various junctures I have indicated that in order for GT to deploy its stronger features to maximum effect, it needs to incorporate other elements. Most notably, it must draw on other approaches to research as well as forms of general theory so that it may secure more sophisticated and comprehensive grounded theories. In this chapter I shall examine in more detail the question of amending and extending GT as a fieldwork strategy. First I shall introduce the main theme, the importance of theoretical 'discovery' or 'innovation' in GT and how this can be augmented by thinking of research paradigms in general in a more open sense. This theme will then be applied to other issues including: the importance of structural analysis and power; the relation between institutions and activity; the need for a redefinition of GT; the importance of historical analysis. I conclude with a brief discussion of the macro–micro issue since it runs through all the others.

The importance of discovery and openness

Sometimes students or even professional field researchers have been schooled in a particular sociological perspective or framework such as Marxism, feminism, developmentalism or ethnomethodology. In other cases, researchers have come to embrace or favour such a perspective after independent thought has led them to the conclusion that it explains more, or more adequately accounts for, a wide range of empirical facts.

In such cases it is very tempting for researchers to gather empirical data on a particular phenomenon (say intergang violence or hooliganism, women's eating habits, or client–professional relationships) and then apply only their favoured theoretical framework to this data as a means of explaining, understanding and organizing the empirical evidence. So, for example, gang violence or adolescent deviance is explained in terms of a Marxist perspective wherein disaffected working-class youths are attempting to recover some meaning and control over their lives by resisting conventional lifestyles and work routines. Or data on women's eating habits and conceptions of food are analysed from a feminist perspective in terms of women's subjugation to men, in the form of domestic labour, or under patriarchal power.

In some instances such applications of general theoretical frameworks are illuminating and provide useful insights. However, if all fieldwork data is interpreted in terms of a prior framework favoured by the researcher then it will lead to a blinkered outlook. In this kind of situation knowledge cannot progress since the data of research is always interpreted as reinforcing or verifying the existing perspective of the researcher. Thus it is very difficult for genuinely new theory or forms of explanation to emerge if the research data is simply labelled or conceptualized in terms of the favoured framework. In this sense, if theory does 'develop' in the light of the empirical findings of research, then it will tend to be an outgrowth of the master framework. As we saw in chapter 2, if taken to an extreme, the theory-testing approach will produce the same effect. That is, researchers are encouraged to replicate studies or confirm previous findings under different conditions and so on, with a view to establishing the credibility or otherwise of particular 'established' theories or hypotheses or bodies of knowledge.

Both these strategies conform in some measure with what Kuhn (1970) has described as the progress of 'normal science' in relation to the natural sciences. In normal science, scientific activity is concerned with 'routine' problem-solving within an accepted or established 'paradigm', or framework of ideas, concepts and theories. These paradigms first come into being as revolutionary displacements of previous paradigms (for example, Einstein's relativity theories displaced Newton's theories of motion which had held sway for two centuries) but, once established, they become the context in which most scientific research is undertaken. Thus 'normal', as opposed to 'revolutionary', science becomes the investigation of small empirical problems which represent minor parts of the paradigm which have not yet been filled in or 'resolved' in some way.

However, in the social sciences it must be remembered that we are not dealing with one dominant paradigm but a number of competing (or complementary) frameworks of ideas, including GT itself. In this situation, much of the innovatory potential of knowledge and research will derive from the cross-fertilization of ideas from different frameworks. Thus it is important that lines of communication between them are kept open and that opportunities for dialogue are maximized. Research which begins from an accredited explanatory framework such as Marxism, functionalism, developmentalism or another, and then proceeds to 'explain' empirical evidence in its terms, simply works to reinforce the boundaries between frameworks.

The GT approach promises much in the way of escape from this situation. First, it moves the researcher away from the idea that 'producing' theory is something of a sacrosanct activity reserved only for those who have been initiated into the mysteries of some 'master' framework or perspective. Secondly, GT holds out the promise of a healthy theoretical 'anarchy' wherein communication between frameworks is encouraged, and as a result innovative and synthetic forms of theory and research strategies are produced. So far, these promises have been largely unfulfilled.

Towards a more open GT

Although in one sense GT encourages researchers to think creatively in theoretical terms, in another way it runs into the same difficulties as the all-embracing perspectives mentioned above. This is because there are elements in GT which push it towards being yet another framework, or total perspective, which has rather closed boundaries. In the previous chapter I suggested that GT should draw on other research perspectives as resources for theory construction. To the extent that this has not been a conspicuous part of its approach so far, this very fact tends to cocoon GT from other, potentially helpful influences. There are a number of other elements that push in this direction and I shall be dealing with them in some detail in the rest of this chapter. Here I simply want to point to the manner in which GT is excluded from wider debates and issues in the philosophy of social science by distinguishing itself rather inflexibly from other positions. Apart from the intrinsically isolating effects of this, it has direct consequences for the skills that researchers require for fieldwork and the strategies available to them.

In this respect, Glaser and Strauss distinguish their position from the rigidly deductive procedures entailed in middle-range theorizing, as well as its tendency to encourage theory which 'chases the data', so to speak, rather than emerging out of the data. By making this conclusive break with MRT Glaser and Strauss undervalue the usefulness of the objective methods and procedures that underpin this tradition. This is reinforced by the extreme emphasis on grasping the emergent nature of meaning in the milieu that is being researched, and the insistence that grounded theory should 'fit' and be relevant to the people to whom it refers. Such an emphasis underlines the unsuitability of objective, scientific concepts as an important means of capturing everyday experience in sociological terms.

All in all, Glaser and Strauss's position insulates itself from the possibility of a convergence of aims and interests between humanist and more objective or scientific forms of research and theory. This is just the sort of convergence that is envisaged by some versions of 'realism' (Keat and Urry 1975, Bhaskar 1979, Outhwaite 1988, Layder 1990). Realism attempts to rescue some of the useful aspects of an objective scientific approach to social phenomena while rejecting those aspects that have proved to be inadequate or troublesome. It is a matter for debate as to how far realism has successfully combined the strengths of humanism and a scientific attitude. However, the important point is that realism has recognized that with their respective concerns with causality and meaning, both have something to offer in the understanding of social reality. As a consequence, both may contribute to our knowledge of the aims of social research as well as to its execution.

Glaser and Strauss's conception of grounded theory needs to be prised open to accommodate this kind of dialogue between positions. This is necessary since the idea of an approach to theoretical discovery becomes nonsensical if certain forms of 'discovery' are excluded because they fall beyond the legitimate boundaries of GT. This is by no means to advocate an unprincipled eclecticism which licenses the joining together of sundry approaches regardless of compatibility or usefulness. On the contrary, my arguments to open up grounded theory to important developments in philosophy and social theory are based on the assumption that only certain forms of synthesis and integration of approaches are possible, but that where they are, they should be vigorously pursued.

Research skills and strategies

The issue of widening the outlook of GT is not just an abstract one. It links directly with the question of the sorts of skills that are required in field research. The realist position encourages the researcher to seek out aspects of society which are not immediately apparent or 'obvious' in the normal course of observation, interviewing or the examination of documentary evidence. For example, some aspects of the operation of social institutions or relations of power are not clearly visible or detectable if the researcher focuses on the observable behaviour and activities of people in particular settings. The GT approach tends to encourage the researcher to focus on the 'close-up' features of social interaction and, in this sense, neglects the seemingly more remote aspects of the setting and context. These 'structural' or 'macro' aspects of society must play a more central role in fieldwork analysis.

The fieldworker must be aware of the existence and operation of structural phenomena in order to be sensitive to their implications for emerging theoretical ideas and concepts. For example, in my research on the acting profession I observed a group of actors, (men and women) and a director rehearsing a play at a provincial theatre in the UK (Layder 1981: ch. 6). There were several aspects of their behaviour which were immediately striking. For instance, there was a liberal use of 'camp' language: that is, the use of terms of address like 'love', 'dear' or 'darling' regardless of the sex of the speaker or listener. One actor described these verbal interchanges as 'little cuddles without touching'. Also, there were many instances of physical comforting when the 'insecurities' of actors became apparent or critical. Themes of personal vulnerability and self-exposure emerged as the director attempted to bring out the best performances of the actors. These and many other facets of behaviour could be easily observed and described fairly accurately in a straightforward manner.

However, it is important to realize that these forms of behaviour cannot be understood simply in terms of the mixture of personalities involved, or the dynamics of the rehearsal situation. The wider work setting and the economic context of the acting profession play key roles here. In this sense, institutional or structural features of society are intimately interwoven with behaviour and activity. First, it has to be appreciated that there is chronic unemployment in the acting profession. Second, when they do work, actors are usually employed on a short-term basis (for the run of the show, or the making of a film or a TV programme, or even a season in a permanent ensemble). This means that, at the best of times, work is intermittent, and that when it is available actors will move between employers and employing organizations.

This creates a highly discontinuous work and career situation, and has the effect of producing uncertainty and insecurity in actors and their work relationships. The importance of being able to 'trust' other people in the profession and to make this trust 'visible' becomes extremely important in the occupation generally, as well as in specific work situation. One of the ways actors deal with this is through the use of camp language and other expressions which communicate 'little cuddles without touching'. In this sense, the interpersonal behaviour and skills that are on overt display in rehearsal are directly related to the more remote, and less visible, economic and social context of the occupation. In other words, the way in which the occupation is socially organized 'behind the scenes', so to speak, is an important influence on the 'up-front' activities and behaviour of the actors.

The importance of structural analysis

Understanding the way in which social structure interweaves with activity is an absolutely essential aspect of fieldwork and demands that the researcher inquires beyond overt aspects of interaction to investigate its structural components. However, the grounded theory approach often has the opposite effect, by encouraging the researcher to attend to those features of behaviour that are immediately apparent and observable. This is for several related reasons. First, there is a general distrust of structural concepts and forms of analysis both in the GT approach and the interactionist tradition more widely. Secondly, where advocates such as Glaser and Strauss do employ a notion of 'structure', they use it in a rather restricted sense. That is, their usage refers rather more to the *immediate* environment of behaviour than to the manner in which the wider (and to some extent impersonal) context of action is socially organized.

In Strauss's later work there is some recognition that structural aspects do exist at different levels. However, he reasserts the priority accorded to the immediate features of interaction by arguing that grounded theorists do not 'assume that given structural conditions . . . must necessarily be relevant to the interactional/processual phenomena under study' (Strauss 1987: 80). These prohibitions on the use of structural concepts need to be amended. In particular, it needs to be asssumed that structural features are inextricably interlocked with social activities and that we cannot understand the one without the other. As the previous research example makes clear, if we do not assume this (or if we assume that structural analysis is of limited importance), the researcher will 'miss' important connections between data and theory. Let us deal in a little more detail with the GT view of structure.

One reason why GT (and similar approaches) tends to restrict the notion of structure to features which are 'close in' to the action is a fear of reification. For example, at one point in *The Discovery of Grounded Theory* Glaser and Strauss write, 'why not take the data and develop from them a theory that fits and works instead of wasting time and good men in an attempt to fit a theory based on "reified" ideas of culture and social structure' (1967: 262). This echoes Blumer's (1969) idea that the central phenomena of interest to sociologists are 'acting units' (individuals and groups) rather than the 'structures' and 'systems' which are found in orthodox sociological approaches.

In both these critical comments there is a tendency to reject concepts (like that of structure) which seem to imply that there is a social realm which is independent of people. According to the critics of this view such reified modes of thinking imply that social phenomena are endowed with thing-like properties which somehow control the destinies of individuals. Contrary to this, humanists stress that it is important to view human beings as the creators of the social world and as being capable of transforming this world whenever necessary. Now, I do not wish to suggest that this problem of reification is simply a figment of the imagination. Indeed there have been, and will continue to be, social analysts who tend to employ reified usages of concepts like structure and system and so on.

However, often there is a confusion involved here, to the effect that the very use of terms like 'structure' *automatically* involves a reified mode of analysis. This is not the case, as I think the example from the acting profession makes clear. To suggest that there is a structural (or institutional) realm with characteristics distinct from those associated with face-to-face encounters does not, in itself, imply reification. This is because although institutions and face-to-face encounters are partly independent of each other, they are also intimately connected through social activity.

The interdependence of institutions and activity

The fact that institutions and social activity are deeply intertwined does not mean that they are somehow 'dissolved' into each other and that the differences in their properties can be disregarded. Exactly how these two dimensions of social life are related is a very complex issue, but essentially they are mutually dependent on each other. Institutions (structures) have an external dimension and are rather impersonal in nature. On the other hand, face-to-face activity is tied to specific situations and to the specific people involved. However, institutions are not just an 'external' resource for people to draw on in formulating their behaviour, they also directly enter into activity in the form of actors' reasons and motivations. Conversely, by enacting their reasons and motivations, people not only secure their practical intentions and objectives but, as a side-effect, they also reproduce the external form of institutions.

The ethnographic study by Nijsmans (1991) of a counselling and training institute in London provides some good examples of these themes. Nijsmans's study attempted to explore the 'organizational rules' involved in such a therapeutic setting and how they were used by its members. Nijsmans emphasizes the importance of professional values and conceptions of adequate counselling work and how they were embedded in the working practices of the institute. In this respect, the therapeutic aspect of the counselling setting required that it should provide a safe, stable environment free from external interruptions and influences. Only in such an environment could the patient feel free to enter into emotional states that were necessary for his or her eventual recovery, but which might also be felt as confusing or disorienting. In practical terms this meant that in the counselling setting there should be clear boundaries between time, space and the discussion of fees.

Although there were no written rules, there were a number of rules and procedures that were common practice. With regard to the time frame in which counselling sessions were conducted there was a house rule to the effect that they should conform to '50 minutes, once a week, same time each week'. Although this provided the guiding baseline, as it were, for professional practice, individual counsellors interpreted the rule with a certain degree of latitude according to its appropriateness to specific situations or to their style of counselling. As Nijmans points out, 'some would end the session right on time, even in the middle of a client's talk with a rather abrupt "Time is up. I will see you next week." Others held a more "human" view and allowed for extra minutes to "wrap things up" or to make a more appropriate ending' (p. 4). The same discretionary element applied to the 'once a week' rule depending on whether the counsellor believed the client needed more or less 'holding' or 'weaning' from the counselling relationship. A similar rule concerning the 'reliability of space' to provide a securely bounded area for the client was translated into 'same time, same space' house rule.

The house rules represent professional values that are embodied in the working practices of the counsellors. In this sense, such rules are 'external' resources that counsellors draw on in order to make practical decisions about when, and in what manner, to terminate sessions with clients and so on. In drawing on the rules, of course, the counsellors invest them with their own judgements about what is best for their clients in particular situations. In this conjunction of house rule and the professional's interpretation of the rule, professional values and standardized organizational practice become directly drawn into the counsellors' reasons and motivations for dealing with clients in certain ways. At the same time, the fact that the counsellor treats his or her client in these ways reaffirms the importance of the house rules in the first place. In other words, such practices reproduce the institutional or organizational features of the setting.

Unless it is constantly borne in mind that institutions and face-to-face activities are interdependent while, at the same time, possessing rather different characteristics, then it is all too easy to lose sight of the importance of one or the other in field research. In this sense, the grounded theorists' reluctance to take structural analysis seriously (either through a distrust of such concepts, or by assuming that the analysis of behaviour or interaction has priority) risks overlooking the importance of the structural dimension.

Structural analysis and power

Associated with the notion of structure is that of power. Power is not a subject which is greatly discussed in the context of grounded theory and needs to be brought to the forefront of issues concerning field research strategy. Writers working within a GT approach often deal with the subject in a rather implicit way. However, once pinned down, so to speak, it is clear that the notion of power is used to refer to a situation involving a relationship between two or more people in which control is exercised. The focus on the situated and action-centred character of power has the effect of overlooking its structural dimensions. This is related to the close-in notion of structure which focuses on the here and now of everyday encounters. Thus power is treated as a question of the capability of a person or group to make another person or group do what they want despite any resistance offered. This notion of power is exemplified in the situation in which an armed robber makes a bank clerk surrender money under threat of death (Luckenbill 1979).

Without doubt, this view of power is particularly useful when the focus of interest is on the observable aspects of the relationships between people or groups. However, such a focus ignores other dimensions of power relations. In particular, the situated focus deflects attention away from questions concerning how collective power resources (money, information, property, armed force, the force of law and so on) are possessed and distributed unequally and 'stored', as it were, in institutional and organizational containers. Such conditions of power are embodied in business and industry, in systems of stratification of all kinds, in labour markets and in gender and ethnic relations in modern societies. To narrow one's focus to the manner in which particular power holders exercise power over others in particular situations ignores the nature of the social conditions which underpin, and secure, control over collective power resources. It also overlooks the way in which relations of power between groups based on the ownership or possession of various resources are reproduced over time and establish the conditions which enable particular individuals to exercise power.

The need for a wider definition of grounded theory

Although Glaser and Strauss recognize the need for 'formal' theory, they define it in such a way as to exclude types of formal theory which are not grounded in data in the same way as their own version of grounded theory. For field research which uses the grounded theory approach it is necessary to widen our understanding of formal theory in order to maximize the potential for theory generation. I argue further on that it is necessary to include in our definition of grounded theory both theory that is *limited* by empirical data as well as that which is *guided* by empirical data. Similarly, there is a need to incorporate strands of general theory or so-called 'metatheory' into fieldwork in order to strengthen the basis of the GT approach.

On Glaser and Strauss's definition, formal theory allows us to go beyond particular empirical areas and thus enables a cumulation of theoretical knowledge by linking separate islands of research and expertise. This is because formal theory is related to a formal or conceptual area of inquiry such as stigma, status passage or socialization, as compared with a substantive or empirical area such as patient care, professional education or industrial relations. As such, formal theory represents a shift in generality which allows the connections between areas of theory to be more easily identified. Unfortunately, grounded formal theory does this only partially. Certainly, it provides a means through which dialogue between similar formal theories can occur. However, the strict distinction between 'proper' theory (that is, grounded theory) and other, 'speculative' kinds means that there can be no dialogue with other kinds of formal theory. It also implies that Glaser and Strauss's definition of grounded theory is the *only* way of expressing a sense of connectedness between theory and the empirical world.

Empirical data and theory

The distinction between grounded theory and speculative theory does not take account of the difference between theory that is *limited* by empirical data and theory which is simply *guided* by empirical data. Grounded theory fashions its link with the empirical world by limiting itself to what can be observed or recorded in some way, about the behaviour and interactions of those people who are being studied. Thus GT is limited to recording the exact features of the world as they present themselves to an observer, rather like a photograph presents us with a direct representation of the scene framed by the camera lens.

However, because the focus of the camera picks out a limited visual field that excludes the wider context, this may lead to a distorted idea of what the photograph depicts. For example, a close-up of a group of people who are smiling and waving to the camera may veil the fact that their surrounding circumstances may be grim indeed! We cannot tell whether the scene is taking place in the context of an urban centre, rural isolation, ravaging war or peacetime routine domesticity. Similarly, the camera's technology does not allow it to penetrate below the visual surface, and thus we cannot tell whether the smiling faces mask a high degree of tension and conflict within the group.

In an analogous way, grounded theory is limited in its focus on, and penetration of the social world by insisting that its concepts exclusively emerge out of the observed data of research and that they should directly represent the perspectives and behaviour of the people being studied. Such a focus cannot tell us about the mechanisms which may exist below the observable, sensorily detectable surface and which contribute to the formation of the observable features. Similarly, the narrowness of focus prevents us from having a real appreciation of the wider context in which people are pursuing their activities. In this sense, the whole thrust and meaning of theory is irresistibly driven by the empirical world as it *appears* to our senses. In this manner, theory is hedged in by our sensory limitations instead of being concerned with the actual processes and mechanisms of the empirical world as they really exist and reach beyond these limitations.

Types of grounded theory

Why should research and theory be so limited? We need a conception of grounded theory which accommodates a wider variety of research strategies which could be directed at the goal of theory generation.

Such a conception must include and absorb strands of theory whose content and meaning are not rigidly determined by empirical evidence or data, but are merely guided by them. As a result, the adequacy, validity and relevance of theory cannot always be understood as a simple appropriation of, or correspondence with, the empirical world.

For example, many theories which refer to structural or macro features of society are of this type, such as theories of occupational organization, formal organization, gender and ethnic segregation, class and power formations and so on. Such theories tend to be based on 'models' which help us understand the processes and mechanisms of the empirical world. However, they are not restricted to recording the observable features of interaction or the social meanings that inform and influence people's daily activities. These models represent the way in which the wider settings and contexts of activity are socially organized. In this sense, they represent the social conditions under which focused, or face-to-face encounters occur.

As I say, there are many theories of this type such as labour market segmentation theory (Krekel 1980), or theories of occupational autonomy and labour market shelters (Freidson 1982), or Etzioni's (1961) typology of compliance in formal organizations (such as hospitals, factories, businesses, schools, universities and so forth). The adequacy of these theories cannot be judged in terms of whether they directly mirror what people say or do in specific situations. Rather, they have to be judged in terms of whether they describe wider empirical conditions, patterns and processes in a powerful and accurate way that is superior to other theories.

There are two main reasons which account for the difference between such theories and grounded theories. The first concerns the fact that such theories have characteristics which are partly (but definitely not completely) independent of empirical evidence or data. That is, these theories have to be understood as clusterings (or networks) of related concepts. In this respect, the meanings of particular concepts cannot be properly grasped unless they are understood in the context of the wider network. The implication of this is that the theory itself cannot be judged simply in terms of its correspondence with empirical observations. Secondly, as we have seen, such theories concern themselves to a much greater extent with macro structural (or institutional) features, which are not as easily observed as face-to-face behaviour and activity.

We have to be reconciled to the fact that although behaviour and meaning is amenable to direct empirical study through observation or conversation with subjects, the same is not true for structural phenomena. This means that unlike the concepts specifically designed to describe and explain behavioural phenomena, those used to depict structural phenomena will not necessarily have directly observable counterparts in empirical data. Of course, these empirically guided theories are not exclusively about structural phenomena. As I said in the section on structural analysis, institutions and activity are inseparable and inter-dependent aspects of social life. Thus these theories often operate with a mixture of types or levels of theory. This is particularly the case with the analysis of empirical areas like occupational organization which tend to highlight the intersection of behavioural and structural phenomena. As we have seen, this is true of the studies of the acting profession, and the counselling and training institute discussed in previous sections.

The importance of general theory

Clearly, theory which is guided rather than limited by empirical evidence is not 'speculative' in so far as it attempts adequately to represent empirical forms. There is no question of attempting to force data into conceptual clothes that do not fit. The issue is about widening the manner in which grounded theory conceptualizes the empirical world and how we theoretically characterize it. The same applies to what has been termed 'metatheory'. This term implies that such theory is too abstract to be of importance to the down-to-earth social researcher who can continue to work quite efficiently without its 'dubious' benefits. Issues and debates such as the agency–structure problem, or the macro–micro problem, and the question of the philosophical basis of social science are all examples of this kind of theory. The term metatheory has also been applied to the work of general theorists like Parsons, Habermas Giddens, Foucault and so on.

Such forms of theory are anathema to grounded theorists on the basis that they are purely speculative and seemingly require no recourse to empirical research in order to substantiate their claims (see comments by Becker in Rock 1979). This is also a rather common attitude among overly pragmatic social researchers who assert that any theory which strays beyond a certain level of generality or abstraction is vacuous and of no possible use to social research. Such proscriptions are misplaced and have the effect of impoverishing social research. Social research, and GT in particular, needs to expand its resource base by incorporating the insights of other types of theory which bear different relations to the empirical world.

In the chapters that follow I attempt to do this with a number of empirical issues and several strands of general theory in relation to research strategies. In particular, I do this with several aspects of Giddens's structuration theory. However, let me conclude this section by highlighting a fieldwork study which draws on some of the concepts and theoretical ideas of Michel Foucault. This study vividly demonstrates the advantages to be gained by drawing on aspects of more general theory, not only for research itself, but also for stimulating new theoretical ideas and insights. Bloor and McIntosh (1990) gathered fieldwork data (using semi-structured interviews and participant observation) on health visiting and therapeutic communities in the UK with a focus on the client–professional relationship involved.

Although the researchers did not set out with Foucault's work on power, surveillance and resistance in mind, they found after completing the research that they had data pertinent to these issues. Thus the research was written up in such a manner as to highlight various aspects of these issues as they bear on the professional–client relationships in health visiting and therapeutic communities. The authors took Foucault's theme that power is not a commodity that is possessed by an individual or group ('sovereign' power), but rather a body of practical techniques and knowledge which are exercised in social relationships ('disciplinary' power). The notions of surveillance and resistance are intimately connected with this view of power. In health visiting and therapeutic communities surveillance is essential to the work of the professionals in the sense that they have to monitor various aspects of the behaviour of their clients. Resistance, on the other hand, refers to the way in which the exercise of power by such professionals is resisted by the clients themselves.

I shall not dwell too much on providing illustrative details from this study since my purpose is a more general one. It suffices to mention that the main point of the analysis was to provide a typology of client resistance. In this respect, the researchers identified five types of client resistance: two types of ideological dissent, collective and individual, non-cooperation, escape or avoidance, and concealment (which was the most common form of resistance in both settings). In conclusion, the authors point out that because most analyses that have used Foucault's ideas have used documentary materials, theirs is one of the first studies 'of the contemporary exercise of power in professional–client relationships' which uses fieldwork materials.

This is an important step forward, and connects with my general call for GT (and fieldwork more generally) to draw on aspects of general theory. It is interesting also that this study demonstrates the viability of using strands of general theory 'after the event' of the research, as a way of organizing and analysing the data. Clearly, general theory can be employed both as an initial part of the research design (loosely conceived, of course) as well as a post-research strategy. Both forms have the effect of stimulating innovative forms of theory either by using ideas or concepts as initial 'sounding boards', or as a retrospective means of establishing an explanatory pattern on the data.

Commonsense 'fit' and relevance

Glaser and Strauss propose that grounded theory should 'fit' the data and be 'relevant' to the lives of those who are the subjects of the study. That is, the theory must be 'accessible' to the people in the study in the sense that it describes some aspect of their everyday experience which they recognize and understand. For example, in their study of hospitalized dying patients, Glaser and Strauss identify what they call 'awareness contexts' which surround the patient. A grounded theory of 'awareness contexts' must fit and be relevant to the medical staff and family of the patient in the sense that they recognize when a 'closed awareness context' is operating (when the patient is excluded from knowledge of the terminal nature of his or her illness). Alternatively, 'mutual pretense' awareness (where people pretend not to know of the impending death of the patient) must 'make sense' to those involved (patient, staff and family) as part of their daily experience.

As this example makes clear, when we are dealing with the focused, situated aspects of behaviour and interaction, the notions of fit and relevance are undoubtedly pertinent. In particular, the notion of 'fit' is most apt when the theory in question attempts to describe, or represent in some way, the perceptions and experiences of people in particular settings. However, the more the researcher focuses on the description or analysis of the settings themselves (for example, hospital organization, the structure of the medical profession, the sociopolitical context of medical practice and so on), then the less relevant the notion of fit becomes. This is because descriptions of the context of activity involve structural features which stretch beyond the boundaries of people's commonsense meanings, experiences and perceptions.

Much the same applies to the criterion of 'relevance'. Of course, any grounded theory which hopes to shed light on behaviour and meaning in some setting or situation must, in some sense, be 'relevant' to the lives and experiences of those people. However, the more attention is focused on the setting, the more one attempts to trace the form of social relations as they extend away from face-to-face situations in time and space. Their analysis, therefore, requires an approach which is not dependent on the same notion of relevance. In the analysis of face-to-face encounters it is important to think of the 'relevance' of theory as related to the social skills and knowledge of the people involved. However, the more one moves towards the analysis of institutional phenomena, the 'relevance' of theory has more to do with its *general* empirical anchoring. In this context 'relevance' applies to the way in which the theory identifies social conditions and resources (and the inequalities which stem from them), which inform and empower activity.

In the analysis of institutional or structural phenomena, 'relevance' in the sense of implying people's knowledge of these aspects of the wider environment of their activity is not particularly appropriate. This is because such technical knowledge is unevenly distributed in society, and thus may not be 'known about' (or only vaguely discerned) by the people who are most subject to the influence of these wider structures. There is certainly no reason for researchers to *assume* that people know, or *should* know about (or could be expected to analyse) the institutional circumstances of their activities.

In this respect it is very important to distinguish this type of knowledge from the knowledge of the local social environment and social skills required in order for people to participate in a general way in social interaction. In this sense, people know a great deal about their experiential worlds of work, family, leisure and so on, and display complex social skills in the enactment of their day-to-day lives. For fieldworkers who are concerned with generating theory it is crucial to appreciate this distinction. Different criteria of fit and relevance are pertinent to institutional and interactional levels of analysis and to the different kinds of grounded theory that spring from them.

History and historical analysis

The humanist perspective tends to focus on the here and now of interaction in contemporary social life, particularly in urban locations. It has been claimed that this represents a concern with the episodic, transient and rather trivial aspects of society and social life to the exclusion of the more important and enduring aspects (Gouldner 1971). To a limited extent this characterization reflects a very real difference in the typical subject matter of interactionism as compared with more traditional, macro approaches. It is also true that this focus has a tendency to exclude important aspects of society.

However, to suggest, as Gouldner does, that interactionism is only concerned with minor, lightweight issues compared with the more im-

portant ones dealt with in macro approaches is something of a carica-
ture. This is because, while much of the subject matter of interactionism
does tend to dwell on episodic and transient aspects of social behaviour,
this does not mean that the approach is trivial and lightweight as compared with approaches which adopt a more macro focus. Much of social
behaviour is transient and fleeting, but this is its nature. It is not less
important because of this.

For example, Glaser and Strauss's study of dying patients in hospital
draws attention to the shifts in 'awareness' among those who are involved
with the patient, including doctors, nurses and family members. Such
shifts may be very swift and result from an accidental disclosure of
information to those who were previously unaware, or the 'awareness
context' may change over time as a consequence of the deliberate
'leakage' of information by doctors and nurses (Glaser and Strauss 1965).
Such detailed, and sometimes momentary, changes in behaviour and
interaction can indeed be seen as transient in relation to particular
instances, but in so far as they pick out typical and recurrent features
of interaction in and around terminal patients, they cannot be deemed
unimportant to a rounded understanding of the problems arising in
such situations.

They are important in another sense as well. As Giddens (1987) has
pointed out during a review of Erving Goffman's work, the phenomena
of everyday behaviour are implicated in macro phenomena as deeply as
macro or 'structural' or 'institutional' phenomena are implicated in the
micro world of everyday interaction. The micro world cannot, therefore,
be 'written off' as an irrelevant or residual subject matter. However,
and this is the more pertinent aspect of Gouldner's comments, what
seems to be missing from the interactionist's analytic scenario is a
parallel concern with the wider, structural or macro aspects of social
life, as they are implicated in the behavioural phenomena which are
their characteristic focus.

This, of course, relates back to the issues about structure and power.
However, in this context it is a key to understanding why the grounded
theory approach has tended to overlook the question of history. The
behavioural phenomena of the everyday world are an absorbing focus
in their own right, but this has been fuelled by another factor which has
acted as a 'protective seal' around the micro world of interaction. As I
have said, situated activity possesses its own partly independent properties, but it is a mistake to imagine that the micro world is self-contained
and self-sufficient. Everyday behaviour takes place against the backdrop
of wider social, economic and political circumstances which impress
themselves on this behaviour just as much as these circumstances may

be seen as the eventual product or outcome of this type of behaviour. The real problem is how to characterize the relation between the micro and macro worlds in general, and in terms of the analysis of particular empirical phenomena.

In this respect, the grounded theory approach must break away from its primary focus on micro phenomena. The very fixity of this concentration is a factor which prevents grounded theory from attending to historical matters of macro structure as a means of enriching contemporary or, as I shall call them, present-centred forms of research on micro phenomena. It should be possible to augment the processual and dynamic analyses of interactional phenomena by a parallel focus on the historically antecedent forms that provide their institutional backdrop.

This is not to insist that all micro analyses must be accompanied by a relevant, and substantial, macro analysis. What is needed is the analytic support for such supplementary macro analyses where these are deemed necessary or, at least, where they are regarded as potentially enriching. It must be remembered that although micro phenomena are most definitely not completely autonomous from their institutional contexts, they are partially so, in so far as they possess distinct and irreducible properties. This alerts us to the fact that it is possible to provide an adequate, sensible and more-or-less complete contemporary micro analysis without reference to its historical antecedents at the macro level.

The decision about whether or not to include a historical dimension in contemporary micro research will depend initially on the nature, scope and objectives of the research. After these have been settled, the discretion of the researcher will come into play in judging whether the research will be enhanced by the inclusion of a historical dimension. The possibility must not be precluded, for all intents and purposes, on the grounds that the research topic or area is inherently exhausted by a present-centred focus on micro-level data.

A comment on the macro–micro link

I have argued that current conceptions of grounded theory need to be extended and amended to incorporate aspects of social reality that are normally thought to fall outside of its legitimate parameters. In more general terms this means that grounded theory must attend to what in sociology are usually referred to as macro phenomena (institutions, power and authority, labour markets, formal organization), without in any way compromising its parallel concern with the micro world of face-to-face or situated interaction. This means that a major problem focus of an emended grounded theory approach would centre on the ligatures which bind macro and micro features together in the continuous flow of social life.

Such a concentration and focus is in direct opposition to both the thrust of grounded theory itself as presently constituted, and to some currently rather fashionable ideas which suggest that macro phenomena are simply agglomerations of micro events and can thus be reduced to statements about micro phenomena (Collins 1981, Knorr-Cetina 1981). I think I have made it plain that I am of the opinion that the attempt to deny the reality of macro phenomena is a naive and retrograde step which would simply halt the progress of any proposed rapprochement between these deeply entrenched approaches to social analysis. The recognition of the reality of macro phenomena and its registration in our social theories and research would be a promising first step along the road to the eventual integration of macro and micro analyses. This is because such a step would enable us to focus on the real problem which concerns the question of the exact nature of the ligatures that bind macro and micro phenomena together in ongoing human activity.

Conclusion: some new rules for GT

Let me finish by providing some rules of thumb for developing grounded theory under the wider terms set out in this chapter. As such, these rules both summarize the main points covered in the previous discussion and provide guidelines for field researchers.

1 Within limits, GT must be viewed flexibly, as an approach which is potentially open to the influence of other approaches to research and theory. In particular, GT must be sensitive to the advantages to be gained from combining important features of both humanism and scientific realism in social analysis. A number of practical rules of thumb follow from this initial 'rule'.

2 Field researchers must search for the influence of macro structural features on the behaviour and interaction they observe and/or record. Since institutions and activities are closely tied together, the researcher must *assume* the importance of structural features even if they are not immediately apparent. The examples of the acting profession and the counselling institute are good illustrations of this. The point is not to downplay the importance of the micro world of face-to-face interaction, but rather to avoid undervaluing the importance of structural analysis.

3   Associated with the above rule, researchers must also assume the importance of power 'behind the scenes' of activity. This is because macro structural phenomena are always influenced by power and power relations. As with the question of structure, researchers must investigate power beyond its situated and interpersonal aspects.

4   The definition of grounded theory must include theories which are guided by, rather than simply limited by empirical data. Such theories attempt to depict structural features of social life which may be difficult to observe in an immediate way. In this sense such theories cannot be expected to directly 'mirror' or describe behaviour and activity. Rather, these theories depict explanatory models of the settings and contexts in which activity takes place.

5   The same applies to 'general theory' and so-called 'metatheory'. Field researchers must not assume that such theories are simply 'speculative' and unconnected with the empirical world. Rather, they must be viewed as possessing a different relation to empirical evidence than that presupposed by GT. Some aspects of such theories (a concept, or several, or a segment of the whole theory) may be very useful in ordering fieldwork data, or in stimulating ideas or lines of thought about new concepts or theoretical insights. (The Bloor and McIntosh study is a good example of both.)

6   Field researchers must recognize that the 'fit' and 'relevance' of GT will mean rather different things when applied to the analysis of institutions as compared with the analysis of interaction.

7   While a historical dimension should not be thought of as mandatory for fieldwork, its relevance and potential for enriching an analysis should be seriously considered.

8   Finally, the above points imply that in order to be able to capitalize on the openness and breadth of scope of this amended GT approach, field researchers should possess particular kinds of skills. Specifically, researchers need perceptual skills that allow them to inquire beyond the surface happenings of social life in order to detect the influence of structural factors. Secondly, they need to be able to deal with analytic procedures which reflect this empirical depth. Thirdly, they need to be sensitive to the theoretical implications of underlying features of the empirical world.

5

A Resource Map for Research

The nature of the research map

In this chapter I outline in detail the elements of the research map provisionally discussed in chapter 1. I illustrate the main characteristics of each of the elements of the map in turn. These are: the self, situated activity, setting, context and the general dimension of history (see figure 5.1). It will be recalled that the elements refer to levels of social organization which are closely interrelated, but which for analytic and research purposes can be scrutinized separately. I shall begin with the elements at the micro end of the scale (the self) and work towards the more macro features (context). However, this is simply for convenience of exposition and does not imply that micro features are somehow more basic than macro features. The exposition could have begun equally well at the macro end because in the analysis of social life it is not useful to generalize about the relative importance of macro and micro factors. Such matters can only be decided by examining the particular facts of the matter. In general terms it is best to understand macro and micro features as intermingling with each other through the medium of social activity itself. I shall return to the implications of the map for the macro – micro problem and fieldwork at the end of this chapter. However, it is worth bearing this general problem in mind as the discussion unfolds.

In the previous chapter I restricted my discussion to research which had been influenced by interactionism and the GT approach in particular. However, in this chapter I draw on a range of research which displays a diversity of topics, styles and methods in order to illustrate each of the elements of the map. This is because specific examples of research are chosen primarily to highlight the characteristics of each of the levels of social organization in the map, and not because they conform to any particular theoretical or methodological framework. Thus, examples of

Research element	Research focus
CONTEXT	*Macro social organization* Values, traditions, forms of social and economic organization and power relations. For example, legally sanctioned forms of ownership, control and distribution; interlocking directorships, state intervention. As they are implicated in the sector below.
SETTING	*Intermediate social organization* Work: Industrial, military and state bureaucracies; labour markets; hospitals; social work agencies, domestic labour; penal and mental institutions. Non-work: Social organization of leisure activities, sports and social clubs; religious and spiritual organizations.
SITUATED ACTIVITY	*Social activity* Face-to-face activity involving symbolic communication by skilled, intentional participants implicated in the above contexts and settings. Focus on emergent meanings, understandings and definitions of the situation as these affect and are affected by contexts and settings (above) and subjective dispositions of individuals (below).
SELF	*Self-identity and individual's social experience* As these are influenced by the above sectors and as they interact with the unique psychobiography of the individual. Focus on the life-career.

(left margin, spanning all rows: HISTORY)

Figure 5.1   Research map.

research (mainly from the USA and the UK) are drawn from a number of theoretical perspectives and employ a range of methodological styles. In this section of the book the point is to concentrate attention on particular aspects of social life and social organization to see how they are reflected in research itself. This is to help the researcher think in terms of possible research starting points or types of question that can be asked in order to give further impetus and guidance to an ongoing project. In the later chapters (6 to 10) I adopt a more prescriptive tone, suggesting specific types of methods and strategies that may help to generate concepts and theoretical lines of thought in field research.

How to use the map

The map may be used in two main ways. First (although perhaps of less importance overall) the map can be used as a way of understanding the constituent aspects of pieces of published research. Since in most research reports the elements of the research map outlined in this chapter will co-mingle in various ways, the map itself provides a means of understanding, evaluating or 'deciphering' research reports (Rose 1982). I must emphasize, however, that since this is not intended to be its primary purpose, the map represents but *one way* of deciphering a research report. In this sense it must be thought of as complementary to more comprehensive frameworks for deciphering social research (the prime example being Rose 1982).

The more central purpose of the map is to help in the planning and ongoing formulation of field research which has theory generation as a primary aim. A major problem for both students and professional researchers is how to get started. This is reflected in the questions that confront potential researchers, such as: What shall I research? What are the sociological questions that I am going to address? In this respect the map can help a student or researcher to 'get started' on a specific project by providing initial ideas and questions that relate to the analytic framework of the project. This 'framework' can be used in a provisional manner simply in order to get the resesarch under way and may be subsequently dispensed with as the research develops its own theoretical momentum. Alternatively, the 'framework' may become more directly involved with emergent theory. In either case the map may be used as a resource for initial ideas on research.

Another way in which the map may be useful is as a resource for research which is already under way. In this sense the map may act as a 'prompt' or 'sounding board' for theoretical ideas or suggestions for lines of empirical enquiry as the research proceeds. This is particularly important in cases where, as the research has gone some way forward, the initial ideas or impetus for the research have proved unfruitful for further theoretical development. For all intents and purposes the research has come to something of a blind alley. In this sense the map may be used as a resource that may provide new 'lines of attack' or fresh angles on the problem, issue or topic at hand.

For both these purposes it is best to read through the whole chapter first. Particular attention should be paid to the questions or guidelines for research that appear at the end of each section. These questions and guidelines are specifically designed to stimulate ideas for the student or researcher engaged in fieldwork. After getting a feel of the map as a whole, the student or researcher should then identify which elements are of most interest or importance to their research topic and then reread the appropriate sections. It is more than likely that a specific project will involve a number of the elements in combination. This raises the issue of what I term 'selective focusing' whereby the researcher concentrates most attention on one or two areas while the others remain rather more in the background. I discuss this issue at several points in this chapter although I reserve a more thorough discussion of it for the next chapter.

1 THE SELF AND SITUATED ACTIVITY

Although I have already suggested that 'self' and 'situations' are separable elements of analysis in fieldwork I want to begin by introducing them together. This is because in practice selves cannot easily be separated from the social situations in which they are routinely embedded. As with all the elements in the resource map, when it comes to their application in social research it is a matter of *emphasis* as to which element has the main focus. There are no hard and fast cut-off points. Having said this, however, I would like to say that there is a definite point in distinguishing the notion of self from situated activity since it directs attention to the way individuals respond to, and are affected by, their social involvements as against a focus on the *nature* of the social involvements themselves. As I say, this is a matter of emphasis, and I shall be dealing with situated activity as an element in its own right presently.

The notion of self points to an individual's sense of identity, personality and perception of the social world as these things are influenced by her or his social experience. Some field research on deviant activity in urban settings has focused on these subjective aspects. For example, Becker's study of marijuana use (1953) attempted to show how regular users of the drug could not be understood as 'addictive' personalities or as people who were inherently predisposed towards deviant activity of this kind. Rather, they had to be understood as people who had had very specific types of social experiences, and who had, as a result, undergone subtle changes in their identities and perceptions. In short, there was a change from being a non-user of the drug to a habitual user.

This involved the establishment of a new aspect of identity and self-conception, the acquisition of a motivation to use the drug which did not exist beforehand, and a transformation in the meaning that the drug had for the person involved.

Becker's interviews with marijunana users led him to suggest that to become a habitual user a person must pass through a sequence of stages or experiences during which they learn to use marijuana for pleasure. This learning process takes place in relation to the person's participation in a community of regular users who are able to direct and define the newcomer's ambiguous and perhaps somewhat alarming initial experiences with the drug. Becker describes the three stages involved as (1) learning the correct technique of smoking the drug in order to produce real effects; (2) learning to recognize the effects or, in other words, learning to get high; and (3) learning to enjoy the sensations produced by the drug. By learning to associate certain experiences such as distortions of time and space with being 'high', and by learning to control and enjoy such effects the newcomer gradually aquires a 'taste' for the drug and begins to use it on a regular basis.

Becker's analysis concentrates on the changing meaning that the drug has for the person as they become more experienced with it, and how this altered meaning feeds into the way the person thinks about himself or herself. All this, of course, takes place in the context of involvement and interaction with a community of experienced users. It is only possible for the person to undergo these changes in self-conception and perception of the drug and its effects by actively communicating with others on a regular basis. In this respect Becker's analysis demonstrates the power that the social world has in producing certain kinds of behavioural predispositions in individuals.

This said, however, it is also true to say that Becker's interest is in how individuals respond to certain kinds of social experiences. In this respect he is interested in how the drug user's self-conceptions and motivations are developed along with the changing meaning that the drug has for them. Although he emphasizes that such things can only occur in a specific social setting, he is not primarily interested in the setting itself. For instance, he does not attempt to describe the typical kinds of social relationships that exist in the drug subculture, or the manner in which the community is organized. Similarly, Becker is concerned to point out that changing conceptions and perceptions of the drug and its effects are only acquired in specific situations of use. However, again, he is primarily concerned with the individual's response to these situations and encounters rather than dealing with the form and substance of the encounters themselves. As I have said this is all a matter of emphasis and focus since any 'individual' activity like habitual drug use always takes place in socially defined situations and against the background of a specific setting and context. Nonetheless, Becker's analysis does highlight the way in which the individual or subjective components of action may become a central focus of field research. In this respect something less than full attention is trained on situated interaction while analysis of the setting and context is kept very much in the background.

In a similar vein, many of Goffman's acute observations of social life are of this nature, with a primary focus on the strategies that individuals employ to deal with the social situations they encounter. For instance, his analysis of adult riders on fairground rides stresses the ways in which they express emotional and intellectual 'distance' from the role of rider. Goffman (1961) suggests that adults employ a number of behavioural techniques such as sitting stiffly and suppressing any outward signs of pleasure, in order to convey the impression that they are not 'seriously' involved with such pursuits and that their real interests are in protecting their children. Goffman's centre of attention here is on the fleeting aspects of social life and the way in which certain images of self are created or sustained by individuals in everyday encounters.

An example of an analysis which uses a slightly longer time frame is that by Lyn Lofland (1966) in her study of behaviour in public settings in which she observed and analysed the ways in which people 'entered' and 'waited' in public establishments. As the time frame used in the analysis becomes longer we can begin to understand how sequences of behaviour are connected over time and how certain stages or phases of the activity become distinguishable. The concept of 'career' has been used to analyse these linked series of phases and thus its use has been generalized from the area of occupations and work. However, it was Everett Hughes (1937), in his studies of work, who first pointed out the usefulness of the concept of career since it directed attention to both the objective and subjective components of social life.

The subjective career of the self

I shall return to the more objective components of careers and career processes further on, although it should be mentioned here that this aspect of career analysis has often been neglected by those engaged in fieldwork or those who have been in some way influenced by interactionist schools of thought (see, for instance, Collin and Young 1986). Despite this it has to be said that the subjective dimension of careers is extremely important for any social analysis. Stebbins (1970a) has drawn attention to the subjective side of careers (as opposed to the more objective elements such as career patterns or career lines) and its implications for the identities and self-concepts of those undergoing them. The subjective career, in this sense, refers to the more private meanings of such things as promotion blockage at work, or the experiencing of marital tension in the career of a marriage. The subjective career traces the implications these sorts of things have for the future 'progress' of the strands of social life in question.

The focus here is clearly on the biographical elements of social experience and represents another aspect of the link between individual identity and experience and the situations and settings that are the stuff of everyday social life. These aspects of analysis are very much a part of the general fieldwork and grounded theory traditions and can be seen to play a part in many pieces of research (Roth 1963, Davis 1963, Becker 1963, Goffman 1968). However, there is also a tendency in this kind of study to see the individual's personality and psychological traits and responses as more or less totally constructed by the social world.

The emphasis on the social construction of an individual's psychological responses is most useful when it is used to counter extreme psychological explanations which view the individual as a quite separate unit possessing a fixed inner core or essence. This view often overstates the influence of early childhood experiences on the later personality and identity characteristics of adults and, as a consequence, underplays the influence of the social environment. However, it would also be a mistake to rule out entirely the influence of such experiences and how they imprint themselves on the psyche of the individual and thus, in turn, feed into their behaviour (see, for example, Storr 1989).

An example of this sort of thing arose in my own research on the occupation of acting (Layder 1976, 1981, 1984). Many actors and actresses expressed the view that they thought that acting attracted people who were neurotic, unstable and insecure about their own identity. Acting out dramatic roles allowed them to mask their personality insecurities and engage in forms of wish fulfilment in an adult version of 'let's pretend.' That some people pursue a career in acting for these reasons is a plausible idea. However, it is also the case that the nature of the occupation and career is such that it produces an insecure and uncertain environment for all but the most successful and this in itself can lead to psychological vulnerability and seemingly neurotic forms of behaviour. (In a study of actors in the USA, McHugh (1969) suggests that this uncertainty is partially offset by the supportive community of colleagues.) Such evidence points to the fact that any fieldwork that purports to give a balanced view of the form and direction of social behaviour must at least acknowledge the possibility of the subtle interplay of psychological interior and social environment on an individual's behaviour. (See Hochschild 1983 for a discussion of emotion along these lines.)

Self, setting and context

I have already drawn attention to the fact that selves are directly implicated in social behaviour and thus it is often difficult to separate self-identity and situated activity. Let me now examine a study which highlights the interrelation between self-identity and the settings and contexts of social activity. This raises the question of 'selective focusing' which I alluded to at the begining of this chapter. The study demonstrates the way in which a focus on self-identity can also be linked to a secondary emphasis on setting or context. The research is an ethnographic study of routine police work in Northern Ireland (Brewer 1990). It focused on how the police dealt with, and responded to, the threat of danger from possible paramilitary attack in terms of their feelings and self-images. The area of Belfast where the research was carried out was not a high risk area, nonetheless, the police have to deal with the possibility in their day-to-day lives.

Brewer analysed the ways in which the police dealt with their feelings about danger in terms of three different vocabularies or forms of talk that they used as a means of 'normalizing' the dangers. The first of these, the 'skills vocabulary', emphasized the fact that as members of the Royal Ulster Constabulary they possessed the expertise, knowledge and commonsense to ensure their survival. Such feelings were reflected in talk about 'knowing who to trust', 'what places to stand in without being a target' and other expressions describing vigilant behaviour. The second form of talk employed a 'fatalistic vocabulary'. This emphasized the fact that even though precautions may be taken – 'if it's going to happen, you'll never prevent it,' or 'if your number comes, your number comes.' The final 'routinization vocabulary' emphasized the fact that risks are an ordinary part of the job. This gives rise to expressions like 'it's a way of life for us' or 'you don't think about it, you just take things as they come.'

Brewer goes on to analyse the different factors which give rise to, or help to sustain, the use of different vocabularies or mixtures of them. In this respect factors such as 'the location of the police station', 'previous involvement in dangerous situations' and 'the extent to which the family acts as a support and escape mechanism' all play a role in encouraging the use of various forms of talk about danger. These vocabularies enable the police to express their feelings about being targets in an occupational culture which otherwise inhibits emotion (Brewer 1990: 672). They also function to 'normalize' the threat of political violence and thereby render it a manageable feature of everyday life.

In terms of the elements of the research map, Brewer's research focuses primarily on the sorts of issues involved with self and situated activity. There is an emphasis on the way in which the police deal with occupational hazards by deploying forms of talk. These vocabularies enable them to express their feelings about danger, and to sustain certain images of themselves in order to deal with routine occupational demands. Clearly there is some obvious overlap with situated activity here in that the police employ these vocabularies in interaction with their colleagues. However, the predominant focus of interest is on the way in which individuals draw on specific vocabularies rather than on the dynamics of activity and interaction between the police as such. More important are various aspects of the setting and context of police work in Northern Ireland. Most important is the wider macro context of political division and violence. While Brewer does not make this a focal aspect of the study, it is clearly a major contextual feature, which gives sense to the whole notion of 'talk about danger' in the first place.

Brewer does point to some aspects of the settings of police work such as the influence of the family and the location of police stations, although generally there is no systematic analysis of the occupational setting itself. That is, questions about how police work is internally organized, how the status and power hierarchy impinges on the lower-status members and so on are not important features of the research. This is because Brewer has chosen to focus on the area of self and situated activity, while drawing on various aspects of setting and context in a selective manner to reinforce the points made about the main focus of the research (talk about danger).

Checklist for field research

To conclude this section let me summarize the sorts of research topics and questions that are raised by a focus on self and situated activity. In this sense they can be used as a checklist or as guidelines for field research.

1 The general topic or area of concern is with the way individuals respond to particular features of their social environment and the typical situations associated with this environment. Within this general

area we can indentify the following more specific questions.

2   What conceptions of self and identity are bound up with certain lines of activity over differing lengths of time? What specific mechanisms are involved? Examples of these kinds of activities are those involved in crime and deviance, marriage and the family, illness, work and careers.

3   What meanings and perceptions are bound up with these activities and how do they help shape and generally influence these activities? Do these meanings and perceptions change over time? If they do, what causes them to change?

4   What other subjective feelings, motivations and experiences are associated with particular 'careers' or lines of activity? This includes such things as feelings of entrapment, fulfilment and elation, level of ambition, attitudes towards authority and so on, at work, in private life (family marriage and partnerships), at school, college, in leisure activities such as sport and relaxation, and so forth. What is the interplay between social and psychological factors involved in the formation of these subjective feelings and experiences?

2   SITUATED ACTIVITY

I must continually stress that all the elements I identify in this map shade into and interweave with each other and this is no less the case with the notion of 'situated activity'. However, although this means that there are substantial areas of overlap between situated activity and the other elements in the map, nevertheless, this category does have some distinctive characteristics. Let me first indicate some of the distinctive emphases found in research which focuses primarily on situated activity, before describing its interrelation with other elements. As compared with the previous section which concentrated on the connections between self and social involvement, the area of situated activity shifts focus away from the individual's response to various kinds of social situations towards a concern with the *dynamics* of interaction itself.

This concern with the dynamics of interaction stresses the way in which gatherings of, or encounters between, several individuals tend to produce outcomes and properties that are a result of the interchange of communication between the whole group rather than the behaviour of the constituent individuals viewed singly. That is to say, interaction has emergent features as a result of the way in which the behaviours of the constituent individuals intermesh and coalesce. Empirical examples of situated activity point to the fact that they vary considerably along a number of dimensions such as the extent to which they endure in time and are spread out in space. Consider, for example, the differences in this regard between a one-off encounter between strangers brought together briefly during the daily round, and the recurrent and routine interactions between friends working in the same office or factory. As is already implied in the idea of the spatial spread of activity, the kind of setting in which it takes place is of considerable importance to the activity itself. In this respect activities vary according to the extent to which they tend to be limited to specific settings and specific individuals. Let me illustrate something of this variability by looking at three examples of situated activity.

The first is drawn from the work of Glaser and Strauss (1965) in their study of hospitalized dying patients. From this study Glaser and Strauss developed ideas about the nature and function of 'awareness contexts' in social interaction. After observing and analysing the forms of interaction around dying patients involving nurses, doctors and members of the patient's family, Glaser and Strauss were led to the view that the extent of people's awareness of the patient's forthcoming death was quite variable. Sometimes it was the patient who did not know that he or she was dying, while others did and attempted to keep the information secret. From this observed variation in the degree of 'awareness' of those involved, Glaser and Strauss constructed four types of 'awareness context'.

The first they called an 'open' awareness context and this indicated a situation in which everyone (including the patient) knew of the patient's death, and spoke about it freely and openly. A 'closed' awareness context is one in which the patient typically does not know that he or she is dying while the doctors and nurses do. 'Suspicion' awareness is where the patient suspects and realizes that others are trying to avoid disclosure. Finally, 'pretense' awareness depicts a situation in which both the patient and doctor (and, perhaps, nurses and family) are all aware that the patient is dying but pretend not to be, that is, they avoid openly admitting this to each other.

As can be appreciated, to the extent that a particular context obtains in any situation, then interaction will be significantly coloured by it. For example, where there is 'mutual suspicion' much of the interactants' behaviour will be geared to gaining as much information as possible about how much the other people know. Pretence awareness could lead to spurious forms of interaction in which crucial issues are clearly avoided and conversations are 'guided' on to safe topics. (See also Lemert 1962 for an example of this kind of thing in relation to interaction in and around individuals suffering from paranoia.) Such awareness contexts alter with circumstances and therefore allow us to trace through the ever-changing nature of interactive processes. Thus, for example, closed awareness may pass through subsequent phases of suspicion and open awareness depending on whether critical information is deliberately or accidentally disclosed.

Now, although the notion of awareness contexts is extremely pertinent to situations of dying, Glaser and Strauss suggest that it has more general applicability for the analysis of interaction. Situations of espionage have a clear relevance here, where the control of information about the true identity of the spy is of pivotal importance. However, it is equally clear that the notion of awareness contexts is pertinent to any small group situation in which information about key members is unevenly distributed. Coalitions among family members formed to deal with difficult or sensitive individuals are a common feature, as is the control and interchange of information between friends about other (mutual) friends. What can be said to whom and in what circumstances, are issues that are part of the fabric of everyday encounters, and the notion of awareness contexts can throw light on their dynamics. In this sense the model of awareness contexts is relevant to many situations other than the one for which it was originally intended. This is because it refers to recurrent patterns of social interaction, rather than to the specific aspects of situations (including the individuals who form them).

Let us now consider another empirical analysis of interaction in which there is a slight shifting of concern to the specific situation in which it occurs and the specific group of people involved. This is not to say that the analysis is not relevant to similar situations, or that there are no generally applicable features, but rather that there is more emphasis on capturing the unique interactional dynamics of a particular group of people. The fieldwork concerned is Donald Roy's (1973) study entitled 'Banana time:job satisfaction and informal interaction'. The study reports on a two-month period of participant observation of a small group of factory machine operatives in the USA working in a room relatively isolated from the rest of the factory. The workers were engaged in simple repetitive operations working extra-long days, six days a week. The problem that Roy focused on was how the workers dealt with the massive monotony and boredom that was engendered by the work task itself. His description and analysis of the informal interaction in the 'clicking' room generally concerned itself with how the men 'kept from going nuts' (or psychologically survived) in the face of such an unstimulating work environment.

At first, Roy did not notice that there was an underlying meaning to what he perceived to be 'flurries of childish horseplay'. However, growing familarity with the system of communication between his co-workers (there were three, George, Ike and Sammy, George being the lead man) enabled Roy to understand the sense that lay behind the apparent nonsense. In fact, the workday was broken up into a series of 'times' and 'themes' which occurred at hourly intervals throughout the day and were repeated daily. First, there was 'peach time' in which Sammy provided the peaches for a mid-morning snack. Ike invariably complained about the quality of the peaches and this 'fed the fires of continued banter' between them. Banana time followed peach time by about an hour. Each day, Sammy would bring a banana for lunchtime, but he never got to eat it because Ike would surreptitiously steal it from his lunchbox and eat it himself, accompanied by protestations from Sammy and George. Banana time was followed by window time, and then in the afternoon, pickup time, fish time and coke time. Each 'time' was a daily ritual and was accompanied by a series of verbal exchanges and thought processes which carried over until the next interruption.

Interwoven with these times were 'themes' that ran through the verbal interplay initiated by the times. Again, these were standardized in their repetition and centred on such things as 'kidding' or serious themes like 'the professor' theme. This latter derived from the fact that George's daughter had married the son of a local college professor. Whenever the subject came up, Sammy and Ike listened in awe, and Roy indicates that this, in fact, was the source of George's superior status. Roy goes on to suggest that these times and themes functioned to break up the monotony of the work by providing an ordered series of informal inter-actions. Rather like coffee breaks or 'ciggy' breaks they provided rest pauses and accentuated progress points in the passage of time. However, their major significance was in initiating the physical and verbal inter-play that acted as a carry-over of interest and which linked up with the next time interruption.

The diversity of situated activity

There are similarities and differences in Roy's analysis as compared with Glaser and Strauss's study of awareness contexts. Both studies are to some extent concerned with recurrent and general features of in-teraction. With the example of awareness contexts, this tends to be reflected in a concern with the properties of interaction that cut across quite different social situations (espionage, death, family and so on). In Roy's analysis, on the other hand, the routine and recurrent nature of 'times' and 'themes' owes its existence very much to a defined situation with specific individuals. This is not to say that the way that Sammy, George and Ike developed routines and rituals to break the monotony of the working day is not something that can be found among other groups of workers in similar situations.

In this respect, there are two aspects of situated activity to which this kind of analysis draws attention. First, the contribution of the individuals concerned is such that each instance of similar activity will bear the unique imprint of the particular configuration of individuals involved. For example, although other groups of workers in similar situations may be found to construct routines and rituals in order to overcome the tedium of repetitive unskilled work, each situation will develop its own variations depending on the personalities of those involved and the resources at their disposal.

The second aspect of situated activity which has a bearing on its nature, and which is highlighted in the banana time example, is the nature of the setting. Although Roy is primarily concerned with the dynamics of the interaction in the clicking room and its consequences for the job satisfaction of workers, he is also very clear about the importance of the specific nature of the setting. The clicking room was relatively isolated from the rest of the factory and was cut off from contact with the managerial hierarchy. Thus the workers were free from hounding by foremen, personnel staff, experts or any other authority figures. This meant that a major source of ingroup solidarity usually available to factory workers, that is, ill-will towards management, was largely lacking. Also, the relative isolation of the room from other groups of workers meant that other important sources of ingroup solidarity, such as rivalry, competition and conflict with other work groups, were also missing. With this lack of influence from outside, the group was thrown back on its own resources in the development of informal forms of interaction.

Glaser and Strauss's and Roy's studies illustrate the diversity which studies of situated interaction can take while still concentrating their main attention on the dynamics and forms of such interaction. Broadly speaking, they highlight the way various aspects and forms of interaction are differently related to the settings in which they occur. The different kinds of awareness contexts tend to be applicable to a wide range of situations and settings (although specific instances or applications of them will generate their own unique features). On the other hand, the ways in which workers cope with tedium in work activities is applicable to a narrower range of settings. The very fact that these studies exemplify rather distinct relations between situated activity and the settings in which it occurs vividly highlights the importance of the setting in any analysis of situated activity. This reinforces my earlier point that a concentration on situated activity is always a matter of analytic and methodological emphasis rather than an indication of its empirical separation from matters of self, meaning and setting.

These studies also well illustrate some of the other principal features of situated activity. The participants in such activities are constantly engaged in monitoring their own behaviour in the light of the behaviour of the others and with a view to achieving certain objectives and intentions (Giddens 1984 has referred to this as 'strategic activity'). In order to do this they employ social skills and knowledge ranging from the basic requirements of language and communication, to the unwritten rules and guidelines that govern the way people deal with each other on a face-to-face basis (such as keeping proper conversational distance and maintaining a certain level of eye contact). All these skills and forms of knowledgeability are organized around (and help to define) the meanings that the activities have for the participants and the understandings they have of the situations they are in. The notion of situated activity includes all these strategic elements of individual behaviour and attempts to capture how these meanings and understandings emerge, and are modified or reaffirmed in the situations under scrutiny.

Another aspect of social life which is linked at certain times and places with situated activity, but which cuts across it and also connects with issues of self, meaning and setting, is what John Lofland has referred to as styles of 'participation'. This refers to the ways in which participants 'vary in the manner in which they forge careers and adapt to settings' (1971: 31). For instance Garabedian (1963) in a study of socialization processes in prison identified five types of participant: the square John; right guy; politician; oulaw; and ding. Giallombardo (1966) found an equivalent set of types for female prisoners. All these participation types indicate how the individual adjusts and responds to the prison situation and how they interact with staff and other inmates.

A basic distinction between types of participation concerns whether the type is member identified or observer identified. The member-identified type of participation is one which is used routinely by members of the community in question and is usually expressed in terms of the everyday language of the group. Observer-identified types are ones constructed by sociologists in order to distinguish different career strategies and modes of adjustment to particular kinds of setting. For instance, J. Pahl and R. Pahl distinguish between different career types of managers in industry, such as 'the high flyer' 'the self-conscious career seeker' and 'the local jogger' (1971: 81–98). We shall return to the question of types of participation and career strategies in a general sense in the next section dealing with social setting. However, it needs to be emphasized here that to the extent that types of participation exist in particular communities, then interaction will be affected by them since they indicate key identities, motivations and meanings for participants.

Situated activity and the nature of the setting

For the moment, however, let us return to the question of the importance of various dimensions of the setting and how they interlace with situated activity. Let me illustrate this briefly with reference to my own research on the occupation of acting. Acting provides a sharp contrast to the work situation described by Roy both in terms of the demands it makes on participants and in terms of the continuity of their relationships. Obviously, there are aspects of any job that are dull and repetitive but by and large, and certainly in comparison to unskilled factory work, acting provides work that is intrinsically interesting and involving (although it must be borne in mind that for most of the time the majority of actors are unemployed).

As compared with Roy's factory workers whose main problem was boredom, actors, when working, are more prone to problems of over-involvement such as over-identification with their character and a consequent inability to 'shake off' the role after performance. Other examples of the problems posed by over-involvement are difficulty in handling the emotional demands of a role, or pressure from the director to achieve greater 'truth of performance', or even the emotional awkwardness created by the requirement to strike up levels of intimacy (albeit achieved by the contrived means of the actor's art) with a cast of relative strangers for the purposes of dramatic artifice.

Incidentally, these sorts of issues highlight the problem of the intrusion of occupational demands into the private lives (and selves) of practitioners of different occupations. For example, Barbour's (1985) study of social work students undergoing professional training in the UK points to the extent to which certain types of professions and organizations attempt to change the 'core self' of recruits. In so doing, they exert demands on practitioners which then tend to intrude into their non-occupational lives. For example, social work students were often asked by friends or members of the public to help solve problems, or found themselves analysing people and situations outside of the work situation. Barbour points out that the extent to which professions impinge on the non-work self varies according to the nature of the profession involved. Professions such as social work and psychiatry are relatively high in this regard while architecture and engineering are less intrusive. As we have seen, acting, for slightly different reasons, may pose similar problems in terms of over-involvement. Clearly, however, these kinds of occupations provide very different settings compared with those of factory workers.

Another feature of acting as an occupation that contrasts with Roy's study is the extent to which the participants are brought together in situated activity in the first place. The regular and continuous nature of the contacts between Roy's workers was, perhaps, one of the key elements in the development of their specific routines and rituals. The work and career situation of actors is normally quite different (the exceptions concern the quasi-permanent ensembles). Most work contracts in acting are short term (for the run of the show). Thus, even where actors are lucky enough to have a relative continuity of employment, they are constantly 'thrown' together with colleagues whom they see only on an intermittent basis, or with whom they have never worked before. The problems associated with a rapid turnover of colleagues are exacerbated by a career and work situation which provide no unambiguous signs or titles of career status in the occupation's labour market.

One adaptation to the problem of knowing 'how to behave' towards people about whom one has scant background knowledge (if any at all) is the use of camp language. Thus, irrespective of whether they know each other, and regardless of their gender and sexual inclinations, colleagues will address each other as 'darling' or 'love' and so on. I discussed some aspects of camp language in the previous chapter, but here I want to emphasize its provision of a 'safe' and neutral form of communication in interaction. Within its terms career egos may be co-cooned. It provides a quasi-emotional buffer against the vagaries of the acting labour market and the impersonal valuations of monetary worth expressed by job fee that constantly threaten to intrude into the highly personal milieu of acting. Other behavioural displays, particularly of effusive affection like touching and cuddling, provide adjuncts to the softness and protectiveness of camp banter and serve to buttress the security of actors in a milieu where there is always the constant threat to economic, status and emotional stability.

Checklist for field research

As with the previous section, let me conclude this one by summarizing the sorts of research questions that are implied by a focus on situated activity. These questions can be used as prompts or reminders in the formulation of research problems, hypotheses, concepts and frameworks in relation to specific topics or substantive areas;

1   Who is doing what, to whom, in this episode or strip of interaction? How are these things being achieved? Answers to these questions entail concentrating on the collective intentions and objectives of the participants (that is, as an interacting group rather than separately motivated individuals) and the forms of manipulation, persuasion and control that are being used.

2   Related to the above question is the further one: what are the recurrent features of the behaviour and interaction in this episode? That is, do patterns of behaviour or interaction emerge when observed over time?

3   What social functions do these patterns and forms of interaction serve? Expressed in another way, what social consequences do they produce? To what extent are these intended or unintended by the participants and are they aware of the unintended ones? For example, the intentions of the workers in Roy's study may have been to 'fool around' and engage in 'horseplay', and indeed on one level this was what was going on. However, as Roy so perceptively demonstrates, the underlying meaning or social consequence of this behaviour was to structure the passage of time in a monotonous job and make its performance more satisfying and palatable. At the same time the interaction served to enhance the solidarity and integration of the work group.

4   What forms of communication are being used? Are they verbal, non-verbal or both? Are they direct (accessible to everyone) or indirect (reserved for a select few) forms of communication? Are the communications presented in specific ways, for example through the use of irony, humour, banter of various kinds? Are there any special words or phrases or symbols being used (such as the camp language of actors, or the 'times' and 'themes' phraseology of Roy's workers)?

5   What aspects of the setting are pertinent to the analysis of particular episodes of activity? How do they influence the action?

   (a)   Do particular features of the setting 'intrude' upon the activity irrespective of the intentions of the participants? For example, the relative isolation of the clicking room from the rest of the factory allowed Roy's workers freer rein to develop their own routines and rituals. Similarly, various aspects of the career system in acting (such as the the short-term contract basis of work) creates interactional problems as a result of the high turnover of colleagues.

(b)   To what extent do participants draw on certain aspects of the setting to aid in the achievement of their objectives and intentions, as where doctors or patients manipulate different kinds of awareness contexts?

(c)   To what extent do the location, time-scale and spatial spread of the setting influence the activity? Clearly there are vast differences between a one-off encounter between strangers on a train, a temporary friendship struck up while on holiday, and the routine and regular meetings between work colleagues.

3   SOCIAL SETTING

As point 5 makes clear, after a certain juncture it is impossible to keep questions about situated activity separate from those about the setting in which it takes place. From the point of view of specific pieces of research, however, this divides into a number of related issues. The first concerns the extent to which particular pieces of fieldwork actually do concern themselves with the interweaving between situated activity and its setting (and the wider, macro context). Secondly, if the setting and context are allocated some role, how are they handled analytically? In many instances, the setting and context are treated in a residual way as fairly unimportant adjuncts to the main focus on events and activities. This often goes hand in hand with a perspective that tends to view settings (and to some extent context) as essentially indistinguishable from activity itself. That is, 'settings' are viewed simply as particular patterns of activity, and thus cannot be understood as a feature of social life that is, in any important way, different from activity itself.

I pointed out in chapter 4 that this is a characteristic feature of the grounded theory approach to fieldwork which draws primarily on an interactionist perspective. In so far as specific pieces of fieldwork have been influenced by this perspective then they will tend to take this view of the role of the setting and context of social activity. I want to stress that setting and context are more profitably thought of as rather different but *complementary* aspects of social life, and that, in principle, full and equal weighting should be given to each in field research. This is particularly important if the research is to throw light on general theoretical problems such as the relation between structure and agency and the nature of the links between macro and micro phenomena. I shall return to this topic at the end of this chapter.

Although, in principle, equal analytic weighting and attention should be given to both activity and its settings and contexts, it is not always possible to do so, for reasons of practicality, manageability of the research project, or whatever. In these cases it may be legitimate to give rather more emphasis to either activity itself, or its setting and context – that is, as long as it is understood that they are, in fact, complementary aspects of social life that are firmly bound together in the ongoing flux of social life. The point is that this sort of focusing in fieldwork should be deliberate and selective and not simply result from a tendency to see one aspect as more important than the other. Neither should it result from the mistaken belief that settings and contexts are nothing more than special types of activity (or even simply figments of the imagination of the researcher). This idea of selective focusing has a good deal in common with Giddens's notion of 'methodological bracketing' and I shall say more about this in the next chapter.

The concern to give weighting and attention to settings and contexts equal to that normally given in fieldwork to activities and events themselves is not simply the result of some idle yearning for completeness or inclusiveness. Although settings and contexts are always tightly intertwined with and dependent on each other, it is important to recognize that they have different characteristics and properties. I shall describe two of the most important of these and then go on to give some examples. The first concerns the *already established* character of settings and contexts. That is, they have an ongoing life that is identifiable apart from *specific* instances of situated activity, though the latter may in fact, be the subject of our research. However, it is important to stress that this established character is dependent on the more general activities that constitute the setting in the first place.

For example, although we are given no details by Roy, we must assume that beyond the clicking room where banana time and peach time were enacted everyday, there was a larger factory organisation. We must also assume that this organization would continue to operate irrespective of those particular participants and their specific routines and rituals. That is to say, if Sammy and George and Ike no longer worked in the factory, for whatever reasons, it may be the case that their routines and rituals would disappear along with themselves (although perhaps to be replaced by other workers who developed similar rituals). However, it would also be true to say that the organization of production in the factory and its hierarchies of responsibilities and authority would remain unperturbed.

So, while settings and contexts are always sustained by social activities in general, from the point of view of specific participants entering these settings they are experienced as already established forms of organization, with which they have to contend in various ways ('fit in', conform,

reject, resist, enjoy, 'use' and so on). Similarly, when specific participants move away from them, these settings and contexts generally remain substantially unchanged. Think, for example, of people leaving
hospital, of a person (or group) becoming unemployed or changing
jobs, or of even people entering and leaving a restaurant, a sports and
leisure centre, or a pub or cinema.

Specific participants, or groupings of them, experience the already
established character of settings and contexts for good sociological
reasons. In sociological terms, settings and contexts are in large part
made up of *reproduced* social relations. The problem of social reproduction concerns the question: how do whole societies, or their multi-
farious parts or elements, reproduce themselves over time in order to
maintain their continuity? Put in a rather over-simplified way in order
to make the point quickly, many sociologists would suggest that the
answer to this is that social forms are reproduced over time because
people generally replicate the habits, traditions, rules and stocks of
knowledge that sustain these social forms in the first place. In other
words, they continually put new life into the already established character
of the social forms that they enter into. It must be said immediately that
this does not imply that social forms are static and never change. On the
contrary, they are continually 'evolving' over different time spans and
in terms of a whole spectrum of scales of change due to the efforts of
people living within them. That is, social production is taking place at
the same time as social reproduction.

The exact degree to which one or the other of these predominates in
any particular case can be settled only by an empirical examination.
However, it is true to say that all social production or transformation
takes place only under certain conditions inherited from the past. These
conditions represent the 'already established' character of social forms
that have been produced and reproduced in the past. As such, these
reproduced relations entail forms of power and authority which deci-
sively influence social activity in these settings and contexts. Now let me
illustrate some of these characteristics with an examination of some
aspects of work settings. Two studies of the work situation of managers
in industry by Sofer (1970) and Burns and Stalker (1961) will serve this
purpose.

The organization as a work setting

Sofer's study was of managerial and technical specialists in two large UK
firms. The focus was on the mid-career problems of men aged 35–40 in

companies which displayed a bureaucratic form of organization. Among the characteristics that such organizations exhibit, those that concerned the men in Sofer's study were the grading of authority, skill and responsibility in terms of their work tasks and roles, the grading of rewards and benefits (that is, the provision of a career system), the stipulation of rules of procedure, and the documentation and monitoring of their performance. Bureaucratic companies such as these are hierarchically organized on the basis of status, authority and expertise and resemble a pyramidal structure with progressively fewer and fewer positions towards the top. It is in the context of this hierarchy of positions and the rewards associated with them (increments of pay, status, responsibility and power) that the managers work out their lives and careers.

One of the central elements in these companies was the existence of a central personnel department which kept systematic records on all personnel in the company (above a certain grade) with a view to their suitability for promotion when vacancies arose (Sofer 1970: 155–61). Such information was gathered on a regular yearly basis by the immediate superior of the employee and comprised a 'performance and potential' report and an 'appraisal' interview. The report contained an evaluation of the employee's performance in his present job, the appraiser commenting on such abilities as capacity to delegate, cooperation with colleagues, ambition and aggressiveness and so on. The report also contained an assessment of the employee's potential for higher responsibility and the expected management level that he would attain in a specified period of time. The contents of the report became the basis of the appraisal interview in which the employee was counselled on weaknesses and strong points, and in which he discussed his career aspirations.

Given the centrality of appraisal and career development in the company's scheme of things it was no surprise that promotion and the workings of the appraisal system were a central preoccupation with the managers themselves. The careers of the men in the sample (maximum age of 39) were based on the expectation of promotion, while they were also 'conscious of the narrowing of the managerial pyramid above them and of the implications for the diminution of opportunity' (Sofer 1970: 234–5). In this regard the men were particularly aware of and sensitive to the connection between age and grade as an indication of their prospects for attaining senior managerial rank. In direct contrast to the supposition that appraisal and its mechanisms would be regarded as an intrusion or invasion, the men actively wanted to be appraised and resented it if they were not appraised regularly or candidly (p. 254). Sofer suggests that this is for two reasons. First, the men want to be sure that they have not been lost sight of and are under continual consideration for vacancies, and second they wanted to find out 'how best to prepare for such vacancies' (ibid). In fact in all areas of management development, including training programmes, there was no complaint of being 'manipulated' or 'processed'.

Such evidence points to the formative influence that the characteristics of particular work settings have on the behaviour, attitudes and preoccupations of those who work within them, and forcibly demonstrates the connection between work settings and situated activity. While Sofer's study tended to concentrate solely on the work situation of managers, other studies have concentrated on the connection between work and other areas such as family life (Pahl and Pahl 1971, Rapoport and Rapoport 1971). Burns and Stalker's (1961) study of innovation higlights the fact that not all industrial firms operate with a rigid hierarchical management system. This, they imply, is more appropriate for enterprises operating under relatively stable market conditions and using an unchanging technology. Under rapidly changing circumstances (such as in the electronics industry) the management system may lack a clearly defined hierarchy and depend more on a continual redefinition of roles. Managers' responsibilities and tasks are coordinated through frequent meetings, and communications between them are regarded more as information and advice rather than instructions and commands. It is not important for our purposes to go into this in any more detail, the main point being that it is essential to know the exact patterning of social relationships that exists in particular work settings in order to understand specific instances of situated activity.

These examples illustrate well the 'established character' (the reproduced relations) of the work settings as they are experienced by the participants, and the forms of power and authority relations that underlie and give expression to this character. Such studies of managerial work and career situations have been complemented by studies of workers on the shop floor. Good examples are Edwards's (1979) analysis of the bureaucratic forms of worker control in factories (see the extended discusion of this study in chapter 8), and Blauner's (1964) analysis of the way in which different types of occupational technologies significantly influence workers' subjective feelings and attitudes.

Burawoy's (1979) ethnographic study of the labour process provides an interesting adjunct to Roy's study discussed in the section on situated activity. Burawoy's research was situated in the same factory studied previously by Roy. Burawoy utilizes a Marxian theoretical framework and is more clearly concerned with the way setting (factory) and context (capital–labour relations) influence activity (worker behaviour).

More specifically, he traces the way in which worker-led 'games' of 'making out' (maximizing bonuses by high levels of productivity) deflect attention away from worker–management conflicts over control of the labour process. In effect, productivity is increased through the self-organization of the workers 'games', thus making possible a relaxation of management control. Such worker 'games' have a parallel with the 'times' and 'themes' rituals noted by Roy in that they enabled time to pass more quickly. Not only did they provide the workers with bonus money but they 'eliminated much of the drudgery and boredom associated with industrial work' (1979: 89).

Other types of setting

Other studies highlight the importance of the established character of settings, including those other than work. For example, Goffman in his classic study *Asylums* (1968), illustrates the usefulness of the notion of a 'total institution' to characterize the way in which mental hospitals and prisons, for instance, control the meaningful world of the participants by excluding external meanings. The authority structure of such institutions has a decisive impact on the patterns of interaction within them. The personal identities of members are largely suppressed by the regime of the institution, and as a result they often withdraw from communication and social interaction. Longer periods of stay tend to generate other responses and forms of adaptation to the institution, such as 'working the system' or accepting the staff view of oneself.

Goffman's study alerts us to the fact that everyday life does not simply consist of work and work settings, although from the point of view of the staff of total institutions such as asylums, prisons, monasteries, boarding schools and so on they are experienced as work settings. However, everyday life is often bounded or intersected by the influence of organisations which are work settings for others. As customers or clients of particular organizations we may feel that their influence upon us may be transitory, but as members of such organizations their influence is more profound and far-reaching. It is the membership of, or prolonged participation in, particular kinds of setting that is of most significance to the field researcher. Many such settings may not be organized along the formal or distinctively patterned lines of the work settings we have so far considered. For example, the family is one such setting which has a less obviously patterned nature. However, as a number of studies have shown, families also exhibit certain distinctive features which have a bearing on a number of issues such as the nature and type of partnership bonds, physical and sexual abuse of children and adults (especially women), the extent and nature of links with extended kin, and so on (Bott 1957, Bell 1968).

Other kinds of setting are similar to the family in that they appear to lack any distinctive patterning or form of social organization. However, and as the example of the family shows, this may be for several related reasons. First, the social organization of the setting may lack the crystallized form that it takes in others because it is more informal, less public and its rules and norms less explicit (for example, various settings of 'deviant' forms of activity). Also, settings may lack crystallization in the sense that they are less concentrated in one location and include a number of cross-cutting patterns of organization. In this sense, the setting is physically and socially spread out. The career settings of many artistic and craft occupations are rather like this and I shall come back to these examples in a moment. Finally, for either of these reasons the social organization of a setting may be difficult to observe at first, or even second, sight. In this sense, the social relationships which underpin the particular setting and give it a distinctive form may remain largely hidden from the casual observer, or even a field researcher not trained or encouraged to see beyond the outward displays of behaviour and interaction.

Texts on fieldwork methods, particularly those emphasizing the use of qualitative data, have tended both to give rise to and perpetuate this situation by suggesting that the primary focus of interest for the researcher is on *behavioural events* of various kinds. For instance, Schatzman and Strauss (1973) suggest that there are three sorts of events that the researcher can observe: routine events that are part of the daily round of life (in a hospital, school and so forth); special events which are not routine but are none the less predictable; and untoward events such as emergencies and crises. Ideally, in fieldwork the researcher himself or herself is able to observe these events firsthand and to supplement this information with interviews with key informants or participants. This sort of emphasis, however, directs the researcher's attention towards the immediately observable features of settings: that is, the behaviour that constitutes the events themselves and the accounts of the participants. As a result, it shifts attention *away from* the organizational features of the setting, or in other words the pattern of reproduced social relations that underpins and influences the events.

This means, of course, that the less crytallized the settings are, the more likely it is that important features of the setting will be missed. In particular, the power and authority relations which always influence events in some way, but which are not always apparent from the events themselves, may be missed by a researcher geared to the description and analysis of the behaviour observed in events. A researcher who is not looking for hidden, or partially hidden, patterns of social relationships will not perceive and thus follow up clues in the observable data which could lead to their discovery.

Let me illustrate this possibility by focusing on the career setting in acting. A key feature of an individual's career in acting is that it is worked out between a number of different employers and employing organizations. This is because work contracts are generally for short periods, say for the making of a film or television show or, in live theatre, until the show or play closes. Since they are not generally tied to a single employer or employing organization, careers in acting reflect an individual's status in the occupation as a whole rather than in relation to a particular employer or organization (as in Sofer's study). Thus, career status in acting depends on which segment of the labour market the actor belongs to (the elite, the outer circle, or the mass), rather than on rank on a promotional ladder. As Stinchcombe (1959) has pointed out in relation to craft organization, careers in acting (as in other artistic careers) are influenced not by administrative regulation but by status in a structured labour market.

As can be appreciated, moving up the career hierarchy is an arduous process. Progress can be significantly helped or hindered by the activities of other occupational groups within the entertainment industry. These include agents or 'personal managers' who, as well as dealing with contracts, advise on artistic decisions. They also include casting directors and directors who are responsible for choosing actors and actresses for particular roles, and producers who are responsible for putting together the financial package and coordinating investors. The manner in which these groupings interrelate has a direct bearing on the career progress of particular actors as well as the way in which the labour market hierarchy is reproduced over time. The various balances of power and control that these groups exert over each other, and in particular over actors, cannot be underestimated. (I shall return to the question of power and research strategies in chapter 8.)

Power and the wider context

Understanding power and control as they operate in such an occupational setting requires that specific investigative strategies are adopted. Those strategies entailed in the observation of behavioural events and the collation of participants' accounts of these events need to be extended and supplemented in order to gain access to the mechanisms that drive these relationships. The uncrystallized, unfocused, informal and criss-crossing nature of these power and control relationships requires research strategies and analytic techniques which are not normally part and parcel of the fieldwork approach. In a broader sense, the existence of these sorts of phenomena require that fieldwork, and qualitative approaches in general, expand their conception of the nature of the empirical world that is under scrutiny. This is an important feature of settings that is often neglected in fieldwork approaches which are predominantly concerned with interaction, behaviour, meanings and accounts. It is not that these phenomena are not related to reproduced social relations, but rather that exclusive attention to the former cannot reveal much about the latter.

What goes for the analysis of the internal labour market of an occupation goes also for labour markets in general. For instance, to understand properly the experience of women at work we have to understand both the immediate setting of the work itself and its wider enmeshment in a system of gender segregation. Acker (1991), for instance, argues that work organizations are 'gendered' in so far as they house gendered hierarchies which are maintained through organizational controls. These are reflected in processes of sexual harassment, the relegation of the importance of childrearing and the penalization (or rewarding) of emotional labour, all of which are built into the structure of work organizations.

However, it is also important to understand the gendered nature of work organizations as a direct consequence of the wider context of gender relations which sees women concentrated in certain kinds of occupations (clerical, catering, sales, part-time work and so on, see Walby 1988). It is only in this context, and the even wider one of the power and control implicated in patriarchal relations in society in general, that we can properly understand, for instance, the nature of sexual harassment at work (Stanko 1988). As this kind of example makes clear, at certain junctures it becomes difficult, if not impossible, to separate out the effects of the immediate setting and the more macro variables such as patriarchal power relations, or class relations. Similarly, it is impossible to understand the way in which these wider, macro structures are reproduced over time unless we understand how the more micro processes feed into them.

The example of gender relations and occupations is a good one in that it vividly illustrates the manner in which immediate settings of activity (for example, work) are firmly connected to increasingly remote relations of domination and subordination in the wider social fabric.

The organization of occupations themselves and labour markets in general are also good examples of the intermediate social forms that transmit the influences of macro processes and factors into activity and its settings and back again. In this sense, macro processes feed into activity (and in some way 'make it happen') while the activity itself has the effect of reproducing these wider social relations. The extent to which aspects of setting and macro context penetrate the subjective worlds of people and vice versa should not be underestimated. For example, Cockburn's (1983) study of compositors as a male preserve in the printing industry in the UK emphasizes the importance of a macho gender identity (along with class and job segregation) in understanding the day-to-day realities of the labour process.

Checklist for field research

As we saw in relation to situated activity, the influence of the setting neatly dovetails with it and thus the checklist questions 5a, 5b, and 5c, on pages 88–9 are also pertinent to a more specific concentration on the setting. The following questions supplement this list and flow from the present discussion of the setting:

1   What is the nature of the setting? Is it enclosed and crystallized as in hospitals, factories, business and industrial organizations and religious communes, for instance? Or is it dispersed and comprised of several intersecting and cross-cutting forms of social organization as in acting and other artistic and craft occupations?

2   What are the typical forms of attachment and commitment that individuals have in these types of setting? Is it primarily pecuniary, as in some factory work which is simple and repetitive? Alternatively, what are the factors that provide people with a sense of pride or self-respect? Does the setting encourage spiritual fulfilment as in a religious commune? Do the activity and setting fulfil some creative need or skill as in music or art? Or do they fulfil (or thwart) an emotional need, as is the case in families? What level of emotional involvement does the setting demand of the participants?

3   What are the characteristic forms of power and authority in the setting? Is there a formal hierarchy of control? Do some groups and individuals control other groups and individuals? What resources underpin these relations of power and control? To what extent does conflict and tension characterize the setting? How are these things resolved, if they are indeed resolved? If they are not, what consequences does this have for social relationships in the setting?

4   To what extent do aspects of the wider macro context (gender, class, power, ethnic relations and politics) impinge on the setting and the manner in which it is organized?

4   THE MACRO CONTEXT

As I have just said, there is no rigid dividing line between settings and the wider macro features and processes that provide their context, and there are many social forms which straddle the two. Perhaps the main macro elements that have been used in sociological analysis are those concerning class, gender and ethnic relations. Of course, none of these can be seen as exclusively macro phenomena; they are also associated with typical forms of interpersonal relations (self and activity) as well as typical settings and forms of organization. However, the macro dimension of these factors concentrates the fieldworker's attention to the large-scale, society-wide distribution of resources in relation to the social group that happens to be the focus of analysis. Such 'resources' can be understood in terms of the allocation of material goods and services as well as of status, authority and power. For example, in the case of gender, women generally have less power than men in all spheres of life and, as we have seen, they are also segregated at work in terms of the less well paid jobs with lower status. Class and ethnic groups can be similarly analysed in terms of their possession of material and power resources.

Also, other less general kinds of group such as those concerned with business and economic interests can be analysed in this way, depending on their relevance to the problem in question. Thus various legally sanctioned forms of ownership and control, as well as market exchange, can be seen to be important factors. For example, in the acting profession, interlocking directorships and the ownership of various film, television and theatre companies, as well as different types of state intervention and regulation, are all macro features that provide the wider backdrop to actors' careers. That is, they represent the wider economic and social conditions of the occupation in general, and thus influence to some degree individuals' careers and work experiences. Another example of this can be found in Hochschild's (1983) study of air stewardesses, which demonstrates the importance of the wider context of economic competition between airlines for understanding company pressure towards 'emotional labour' among flight attendants. This study also highlights another effect of gender segregation, that is, the concentration of women in those jobs that require the performance of emotional labour such as nurses, social workers and teachers. (For further discussion of this research see next chapter.)

Other macro features that may be important for the analysis of particular forms of activity may be cultural (rather than material or structural) elements such as values and norms, codes of behaviour and linguistic forms that constitute the traditional fabric of particular societies or their subsectors. The characteristic they have in common with other macro elements is that they are aspects of the wider context in which situated activity takes place and which, to some extent, influences that activity. In this sense, the setting of activity performs a similar role, although it is typically much 'closer' to the action and, as I have already indicated, in some cases (such as the analysis of labour markets) it is difficult (and unecessary) to distinguish between setting and context.

As all these examples convey, there are several different types of macro contexts. This points to the fact that when our focal concern is with the analysis of a particular episode of activity, 'macro' phenomena cannot be understood simply in terms of their larger size or scale as compared with the smaller micro processes. In this regard, generality and distance (or 'remoteness') are also important variable features of macro phenomena. Thus, gender and class relations are very general in society, and hence are pertinent to a great many settings and situations. On the other hand, the relevance of forms of ownership in the entertainment industry, say, will be restricted to the analysis of certain occupational settings and work experiences. Similarly, some macro features seem to be closer to the action than others, in the sense of having a more immediate impact on particular forms of activity (for example, the labour market in acting). Once again, this indicates the interweaving of setting and context.

Checklist for field research

Concern with the macro contexts of social activity raises research issues which revolve around the following general questions;

1   What is the general distribution of power and resources in society as a whole that is most immediately relevant to the analysis of the activity that is the focus of the research? For example, how is patriarchal power, or the dominance of certain ethnic or class groupings in society at large, relevant to the analysis of discrimination or harassment on the street, in the family, at work and so on?

2   What values, ideas and ideologies encourage or discourage certain forms of behaviour?

3   What is the nature of the political, religious and economic situation relevant to the subject of the research? Remember, for example, the importance of the political and religious divisions in Ireland as a context for Brewer's (1990) analysis of the way the police talk about the danger from the threat of paramilitary violence.

5   THE HISTORICAL DIMENSION

I do not want to say much here about the historical element of fieldwork since I shall be dealing with it in detail in a later chapter. However, it must be said that in terms of the research map, history represents the temporal dimension through which all the other elements move. The important feature that needs to be highlighted at this juncture is the idea that all the elements of the map have their own distinctive emphases in relation to time. That is to say, self, situated activity, setting and context, as social processes, represent both different time-scales and 'units' of change. This is a fairly straightforward idea and follows from what has already been said about the elements themselves. That is, while all the elements are combined and interwoven in relation to particular empirical examples of social activity (represented in particular research projects or 'problems'), nevertheless they all possess distinctive characteristics and influences which demand slightly different analytic emphases.

Thus, the self element tends to focus on individuals' responses to the social situations in which they find themselves, while situated activity is rather more concerned with the dynamics of interaction, and so on. Given these differing emphases and properties of social life, it is no real surprise to suggest that each element moves through time with specific reference to these rather different properties. From the point of view of fieldwork, it is especially important to incorporate processes of change in the forms of power and domination. Such forms are normally thought of as macro phenomena (setting and context as I have defined them in terms of the resource map). In this sense, they should have the same attention paid to them as processes of interaction and self-presentation.

Equally clearly, it is of paramount importance to be aware of the different levels at which processes are taking place. This ensures that changes in one level (such as equal opportunities legislation affecting gender or race relations) are not confused with or wrongly generalized to other levels or areas (such as sexual or racial discrimination or harassment on the street or in the family or work). Related to this point is a central issue which concerns the execution of fieldwork studies. This is the necessity of distinguishing between the temporal spread and progress of interactional dynamics, and the larger and more emcompassing processes of institutional and structural change that provide their wider backdrop.

Although in some respects such a distinction may seem an obvious one to make, it has not always been recognized in fieldwork studies. Sometimes this is because the larger historical context has been ignored completely. At other times it results from the fact that interactional and historical dynamics have been assumed to have virtually the same form (see chapter 9). More generally, the major research question prompted by a historical focus is the question of how a particular feature of social life (defined, perhaps, in terms of the elements of the resource map) came to be the way it appears in the current investigation. Phrased differently, it asks what changes have taken place to this aspect of social life over a specified period of time?

The research map and the macro–micro problem

How do the elements identified in the research resource map relate to both the theoretical and empirical dimensions of the macro–micro problem in sociology? In general terms the resource map is designed to facilitate research which works across the macro–micro division, and thus represents an attempt to specify one way in which macro and micro analyses may be brought together. So far, my main concern has been to supplement, extend and where necessary modify fieldwork approaches which have concentrated their attention on the micro processes of social life to the virtual exclusion of important macro features. Equally, however, the resource map indicates the erroneous nature of exclusively 'macro' approaches to research which tend to deny or undervalue the importance of micro phenomena and the interpretive analysis of activity which is the main topic of fieldwork.

Although I have presented the resource map as a series of separable elements with their own properties (and associated research questions), I have also continually stressed their interconnected nature in relation to the analysis of specific research problems. In this regard, macro phenomena make no sense unless they are related to the social activities of individuals who reproduce them over time. Conversely, micro phenomena cannot be fully understood by exclusive reference to their 'internal dynamics', so to speak, they have to be seen to be conditioned by circumstances inherited from the past. In other words, micro phenomena have to be understood in relation to the influence of the institutions that provide their wider social context. In this respect macro and micro phenomena are inextricably bound together through the medium of social activity and thus the assertion of the priority of one over the other amounts to a 'phoney war' (Giddens 1984).

With regard to the main topic of this book (theory-generating fieldwork with a primary, although not exclusive, emphasis on qualitative data), this position on the macro–micro problem has the following implications. First, it rejects the proposition that macro-level phenomena are simply 'aggregations of micro experiences', and thus macro features can and should be 'translated' into micro terms (Collins 1981). As I have pointed out, any such 'dissolving' of elements into each other wrongly ignores the distinctive properties of different levels of social reality, and thus has the effect of producing empirical analyses which are imcomplete and lopsided.

Secondly, this view of fieldwork rejects the over-concentration on situated activity as the proper domain of observation and study which is a feature of interactionist and phenomenological perspectives in sociology. As a consequence, it is also set against the view that structural or macro concepts are peripheral to the concerns of field research. There are two variants of this view to be found in the literature. First, there is the idea that structural or macro concepts are 'legitimate' but only of secondary or minimal importance in qualitative analysis (Strauss 1987). In this sense, structural concepts are only to be brought in as adjuncts to the 'main' analysis of micro phenomena. The second, more extreme view is that macro or structural phenomena have no real or distinctive existence and thus their analysis is simply irrelevant. Both these views considerably undervalue the importance of structural or macro phenomena. It goes without saying that these views lead to a greatly weakened or even non-existent account of power and reproduced social relations in social analysis.

The undervaluing, or outright rejection of structural or macro concepts is, more often than not, associated with two further views. The first of these suggests that the use of macro or structural concepts in social analysis is a form of reification which wrongly characterizes social phenomena as being the products of essentially non-human forces, perhaps even of a religious or mystical kind. As I have described them in the resource map, macro phenomena are clearly the products of human activity. However, I have been at pains to point out that they also represent the (reproduced) conditions inherited from the past, under which human activity is played out. In this regard, the fear of reification is unwarranted and exaggerated, and serves only to constrict empirical research and blinker its potential field of vision.

Finally, most of the above ideas are also linked to the view that social analysis begins and ends with the examination of the interpretive capacities of the interactants and their deployment of the physical and social resources at their disposal (Collin and Young 1986). Without doubt, the interpretive work that individuals do to give direction and substance to social encounters is extremely important, but acknowledging this should not blind us to the part played by the wider social context of positions and locations in which the individual is embedded. Clearly these more encompassing social relations of domination and subordination play a significant role in constraining, as well as enabling, certain forms of behaviour and activity. It is therefore important that field research attempts to incorporate these features.

Conclusion: the research map and fieldwork

Summarizing the discussion in this chapter, we can say that there are two main ways in which the resource map is intended as an aid to fieldwork that has theory generation either as a principal or as a subsidiary aim. First, I have presented and described each of the elements in the map (self, situations, setting and context) in terms of clusterings of analytic and empirical characteristics which represent levels, or sectors, of social life and social organization. At the end of each section I suggested a number of research questions that are associated with each of the sectors (remembering, of course, that they overlap to varying degrees). These are the kinds of questions which have already been asked (although perhaps not explicitly or formally) in completed pieces of research which are associated with each of the sectors. As such, these questions can be used as starting points for new research.

In this respect, they represent a general set of questions that can be applied to any substantive area such as occupations and work, family, gender relations, sexual harassment, deviance, illness, doctor – patient interaction, organizations and so on. This would prompt various lines of thought on the particular area, which could then lead to more detailed and specifc research questions. For example, questions regarding the dynamics of situated activity (such as, who is doing what to whom and how is this being achieved) when applied to an observed instance of sexual harassment in a factory setting could lead to more specific enquiries. For instance, it raises questions such as how common this is, what specific forms it takes and how it affects the general climate of interpersonal relations in the factory. Similarly, questions concerning the setting (such as the nature of factory organization and the nature of power and authority relations) could lead to substantive questions about which groups control which others, and the nature of attachment and commitment of women workers. More macro questions concerning patriarchal forms of power in society in general may lead to questions about how they seep into and influence particular work settings.

In this sense, the cluster of general questions relevant to particular sectors may provide initial starting points for generating research problems, and suggest theoretical ideas or concepts that may prove useful in their analysis. Of course, I am not suggesting that they will necessarily prove useful, and neither am I implying that this resource map should, or can, be used in an inflexible way as a kind of conceptual straightjacket into which the data must be forced. Each substantive research topic or area will generate its own problems and thus, to some extent, will require forms of analysis and explanation that are specifically related to them.

The resource map, its elements and the general research questions they pose should simply be regarded as 'sensitizing devices' and should not be thought of collectively as a 'closed' conceptual framework. Instead they should be regarded as starting points, or ongoing facilitators, of theoretical thinking in relation to particular areas of fieldwork. In this sense they can be regarded as an aid to the development of more formal theoretical ideas which have a wider scope and relevance than the substantive area in which the current research is grounded.

The map is also intended to aid theory-generating fieldwork in terms of its relation to the macro – micro problem in sociology. As I pointed out in the previous section, the way in which the constituent elements of the resource map hang together can be understood as an attempt to specify *one way* in which macro and micro analyses may be integrated. I have attempted to give empirical flesh and form to different aspects normally referred to in 'macro' and 'micro' terms by treating them as 'levels' or 'sectors' of social life and social organization. In so doing, I have attempted to make a bridge between substantive problems of fieldwork and more general ('formal') theoretical issues. In this respect, I suggest that the benefit can, or should be, two-way. On the one hand, fieldwork accounts may be theoretically upgraded by contact with wider theoretical problems in sociology. On the other hand, these wider issues will be more robustly anchored in evidence and attain greater explanatory power as a consequence of some form of empirical 'application'.

To yield benefits from reflection on the macro–micro problem it is necessary, as I have already stressed, to bear in mind the importance of the organic nature of the resource map. In this sense it reflects the interdependent nature of macro and micro phenomena. This requires that we adopt a position seemingly contrary to that referred to above, where I stressed the relative independence of substantive problems. However, this is not contradictory and poses no real problems. The difference in emphasis reflects a difference in levels of analysis. All substantive areas and problems will pose unique problems relating to their particular circumstances. As a result, we would not expect a general or formal theory to account for these prior to research. On the other hand, all substantive problems or research topics will contain, or raise, general theoretical issues, such as the nature of activity or power, or the relative influence of micro and macro factors. However, it has to be remembered that such general theoretical issues can be discussed somewhat independently of specific substantive details.

It is in relation to the central question of the nature of social activity that we must understand macro and micro elements as deeply embedded in each other, even when we are dealing with specific substantive details. In this sense it is important not to treat the different elements of the resource map as separate domains of research interest which can be pursued independently of each other. For example, we should not concentrate on the internal dynamics of interaction (no matter how fascinating this may be) to the exclusion of the more macro elements. This would simply repeat the mistake of grounded theory and fieldwork and give us a partial or lopsided picture. Conversely, our interest in macro elements must not lead us into the characteristic error of structural or macro schools of thought (such as functionalism or structural Marxism). That is, we should not neglect the analysis of meaningful social activity and the way in which it is centrally involved in the formation and routinization of macro phenomena.

In the chapters that follow I shall be describing research strategies that attempt to give equal weight to both macro and micro elements in fieldwork. In this respect I shall be advocating a multistrategy approach, although a more 'rounded' version than that commonly referred to in the methods literature. The multistrategy approach is also designed to aid the development of theory as the fieldwork proceeds. That is, it represents a form of research which encourages 'grounded' theories (of a more inclusive kind than that envisaged by Glaser and Strauss) to emerge from the research process itself. This multistrategy approach attempts to create room for quantitative methods and data alongside the qualitative forms which tend to predominate in fieldwork. It is to this topic that the next chapter turns.

6

Data and Method in Multistrategy Research

Research strategy and fieldwork

The research map in the previous chapter is intended to stimulate questions which might provide useful starting points for research (as well as new directions for ongoing research). However, anyone who is contemplating a research project on a specific topic is immediately confronted with the following questions: What sort of information can I collect? What methods and strategies shall I use in order to gather the data? In relation to these questions, this chapter attempts to point the researcher in certain *specific* directions which are conducive to theory generation in fieldwork. In this sense, this chapter is not intended to be a general review or overview of methods and strategies of research. To begin to understand the specific directions in which I wish to point the reader, let us consider some of the important factors on which the answers to the above questions depend.

In general terms, the methods, data and strategies chosen by the researcher are determined by a number of considerations. These are:

1 The nature of the research problem or topic.
2 The research strategies, methods and data sources traditionally thought to be appropriate to a particular problem or topic.
3 The availability and accessibility of data.
4 The resources at the researcher's disposal (funding, time, equipment and assistance).

I mention them in no particular order of priority. In specific circumstances, certain of the above considerations will assume greater importance. At other times, and in different circumstances, other considerations will hold sway. While the adoption of specific strategies will be significantly influenced by 1, 3, and 4, it is important to note also that 2, the choice of strategy, will be in some measure independent of these other factors. That is, to some degree or other the researcher will *decide* which strategies to use on the basis that they are the best, or most appropriate, for the job at hand. Of course, as I have just said, the researcher's choice will be narrowed down by the nature of the problem, the accessibility of data and so on. Nonetheless, unlike factors 1, 3, and 4, over which he or she has little or no control, the researcher has some control over the choice of specific strategies.

The focus of this chapter will be on strategies. I shall not be dealing with availability and accessibility of data, or the problems of resourcing. To a certain extent, such things impinge on choice of strategy in a straightforward manner. However, the relation between the nature of the research problem and strategy is rather more subtle. These two are closely linked through the issue of 'selective focusing' which I have touched on at several points in the preceding chapter, and which I discuss in detail further on.

My specific recommendation in this chapter will be for the researcher to adopt a multistrategy approach. This will be explained in more detail later, but principally involves making as many analytical 'cuts' into the data at one's disposal as possible. However, this must not be understood as a call for an 'anything goes' or eclectic approach. In fact, the multistrategy approach involves theoretical elements which encourage a disciplined attitude towards research strategy. That is, the multistrategy approach involves judgements about the nature of social life and society, and these imply certain things about the most appropriate ways of doing the research. The main theoretical elements which concern us here are those which are contained in, and represented by, the research map outlined in chapters 1 and 5. These are, first, the layered nature of social reality; second, the unfolding nature of social activity over time and space, and third, the integrated nature of macro and micro features of social life.

In combination, these three clearly reflect judgements about the most fruitful and valuable forms and strategies of research. The research map presupposes all these, but in particular it underlines the organic and integrated nature of its own elements (self, situated activity, setting, context and history). In this regard, it expresses the importance of strategies of research which explicitly attend to the links between macro and micro aspects of social life, without undervaluing or overstressing either of them. Clearly, these theoretical elements shift the notion of multistrategy research away from an 'anything goes' eclecticism. However, in so doing, the multistrategy approach does not 'impose' a theory on the data being researched. In other words, while allowing theory to *emerge* from the data itself, it does so in the context of the more general theoretical assumptions about the nature of the links between macro and micro aspects, suggested above.

The multistrategy approach, therefore, has two principal aims which, on the surface, may *appear* to be contradictory. First, it is 'open' to as many strategies and analytic cuts of the data as possible, in order to produce robust and firmly grounded theory. Secondly, this 'openness' of the approach is tempered by an overarching vision of the relations between macro and micro elements. In this sense, the most appropriate and productive research strategies are those which incorporate this vision. Therefore, the multistrategy approach should not be misinterpreted as anarchic or eclectic. Rather, it should be understood as a form of 'disciplined flexibility'.

In the rest of this chapter I shall spell out in more detail what is entailed in the multistrategy approach. In particular, I shall concentrate on the following topics and issues. First, I shall argue that using this kind of approach in fieldwork requires that qualitative and quantitative data be viewed as complementary to each other. Although the use of qualitative data and forms of analysis is an essential requirement of field research, they should be complemented, wherever possible, by quantitative data and forms of measurement. In particular, I stress the use of quantitative data as an ingredient in the generation of theory. The discussion also focuses on the flexibility of research design and process in the multistrategy approach, as well as issues of validity, density of theoretical and empirical coverage, and selective focusing. The chapter ends with a detailed discussion of an example of empirical research, and a summary of the main features of the multistrategy approach.

Quantitative and qualitative forms of analysis

Before looking at this issue in terms of the use of specific types of method in social research, let me briefly review several ideas on the relation between quantitative and qualitative analysis. First, there has been a division among sociologists. These have been those who favour quantitative data and analysis on the basis that they are more 'scientific'. This, as we have seen in chapter 2, was the view espoused by Merton (although he did not reject completely the use of qualitative data) in his notion of middle-range theory. As Giddens (1984: 329-30) has pointed out, this favouring of quantitative data has often been coupled with the view that macro analysis is primary in sociology. Conversely, those who advocate qualitative analysis have often been hostile to the use of quantitative data on the grounds that the data 'impose a fixity on social life that it does not have' and thus they have emphasized the primacy of micro analysis.

Thus the division between quantitative and qualitative analysis has tended to parallel the macro–micro division. To some extent this distinction also persists in the debate about whether the social sciences are 'hard' sciences which attempt to uncover law-like generalizations about social conduct (positivism), or whether they should use a more humanistic approach which is more in accord with the meaningful character of social activity. Certainly, many of the theoretical schools that have influenced fieldwork method have taken this latter view, and have suggested that qualitative analysis and data are better able to capture the the 'emergent' nature of meaning in the fieldwork process.

I share with a number of writers the view that this division should and can be overcome (see, for instance, Silverman 1985, Hammersley 1985 and 1990, Bryman 1988). In my view the division is false, and has helped to perpetuate the sterile game of defence and attack between advocates of macro versus micro sociology. However, in order to break down this barrier it is not enough simply to join them together without presenting explicit reasons why this should be so. Indeed, a number of researchers have used qualitative and quantitative analysis in conjunction with each other, usually in the form of fixed-choice questionnaires which include some open-ended questions or which are followed up with some in-depth interviews. Now although such work is often well executed and presents us with important data on particular substantive problems, it is usually less than informative on the issue of the relation between macro and micro phenomena and how links are to be forged between them. Unless it is made explicit in what sense the conjoint use of quantitative and qualitative data works to undermine the false division between macro and micro phenomena, then there is no reason to suppose that it will contribute towards breaking down the barrier.

As we have seen, the middle-range theory approach to research has tended to endorse the use of quantitative data and is most apt in relation to theory-testing research. Grounded theory, on the other hand, has stressed the primacy of qualitative analysis and the importance of a theory-generating approach. Given that the principal interest of this book is with theory-generating fieldwork, let us see how the use of quantitative analysis and data can contribute to such research. However, let me first say how my approach differs from that of other qualitative researchers who have found a place for quantitative data.

A number of writers have noted that elementary forms of counting can add to the accuracy and strength of findings based on qualitative data and analysis. For instance, Silverman (1985) has suggested that qualitative studies often rely on only a few selected examples, and the critical reader is left wondering to what extent these examples have been selected because they support the researcher's argument. Silverman argues that simple counting techniques can give a sense of the whole body of data from which such examples are drawn, and provide a check on the accuracy of the researcher's impressions of the data. In this sense, simple methods of counting can deepen and extend qualitative analysis (p. 140).

For example, Silverman used a largely qualitative analysis in his study of doctor and patient behaviour in British oncology clinics both in the National Health Service and the private sector. His impression from the qualitative data was that the private clinics encouraged a more 'personalized' service and allowed patients more control over their treatment and the setting. However, Silverman also recorded some crude quantitative data on such things as the length of consultations, the degree of patient participation in the consultations, whether treatment dates were fixed at the patient's convenience, the amount of small-talk in the consultations. Although this kind of crude quantitative data did not allow any real test of his claims, it did provide a useful check on 'over-enthusiastic claims about the degree of difference between NHS and private clinics', as well as providing evidence of the direction of the difference. In this sense, suggests Silverman, both types of data can inform each kind of analysis.

Miles and Huberman (1984) also note that forms of counting can be an essential way of verifying impressions that have been formed on an intuitive basis, or on the basis of what 'seems' to be the case in observations or interviews. For instance, in a study of school improvements projects they expected that innovation would be related to upward career moves. Their early impression from the data was that this was correct. However, after counting up the number of job moves involved, they found that only 35 per cent of job-related shifts were upward ones. So, for Silverman and for Miles and Huberman, the use of such quantitative measures provides an essential check on the tendency for researchers to 'see' confirming instances much more easily than disconfirming ones (see also Nisbett and Ross 1980).

Without doubt this is an important role for quantitative analysis in the context of research that is primarily qualitative. However, I want to suggest that while useful, and in some cases essential, this is an unecessarily restricted role. In this respect, quantitative data can be more positively harnessed to the goal of theory generation in fieldwork. It does not have to be confined simply to the confirmation or

A   *Documentary materials*
     Official and government statistics
     Historical documents
     Diaries, letters, biographies, autobiographies

B   *Questionnaire surveys*

C   *Interviewing*
     Fixed-choice
     Semi-structured
     Informal

D   *Observation*
     Participant
     Non-participant

Figure 6.1   Methods of data collection in field research.

disconfirmation of findings or hypotheses that have already emerged through qualitative analysis. In order for quantitative data to play a more expanded role, they have to be seen to have a potentially complementary rather than a merely supplementary part to play in the emergence of theoretical ideas.

In this sense, quantitative components can be understood as satellites around the central axis of qualitative fieldwork, filling out and suggesting concepts and theoretical ideas as they emerge from the research. There are two related aspects to this. First, as part of a multistrategy approach which aims to interweave both macro and micro elements, then quantitative data should be drawn upon as a resource where necessary, to complement findings from qualitative research. Second, such an approach in itself will facilitate the development of grounded theory. Let me try to illustrate this first point by relating the research map of the previous chapter to the general array of methods and data available in social research.

Figure 6.1 summarizes the most common forms of method and data sources. Most methods are capable of producing both quantitative and qualitative data depending on whether a strictly interpretive or strictly numerical technique is used. However, it is also true that some methods or sources of data tend to be associated more with certain forms of analysis. The common pairing of participant observation with qualitative analysis is perhaps the most striking example of this. Let us now relate these methods and data sources to the research map. Clearly, fieldwork is based on the assumption that the meanings that people employ in their activities are of central importance to any attempt to understand or analyse this activity. It also rests on the assumption that the very nature of meaning as a fluid, emergent and interpretive phenomenon makes it impossible to grasp through the exclusive use of quantitative analysis. Thus, in this sense, qualitative strategies of description, interpretation, the use of hunches, intuition and insights are thought to be primary in fieldwork.

As we have seen, for some qualitative researchers simple methods of counting can be employed *after* qualitative analysis to act as rough checks (in a battery of checks) on the patterns that our qualitative analysis has indicated. To an extent I would want to go along with this idea. First, I can see no objection to the use of counting as a checking mechanism, although, as I have already said, I do not think the use of quantitative materials has to be limited in this way. Secondly, I agree with the fundamental idea that the analysis of social activity must rest on a bedrock of interpretive work in order to elucidate the meaning(s) of the activity for the people involved. Given that it is only qualitative methods that can do this in a satisfactory way, then fieldwork must employ them in a central role. However, social activity itself is inextricably bound up with the settings and contexts in which it takes place and, as we have seen, these elements of social organization have properties which distinguish them from the micro world of interaction. That is to say, features conventionally thought of as macro are also integrally involved with a rounded understanding of any episode of social activity, and must therefore be included in the analysis.

This is where my recommendations part company from those of the qualitative researchers mentioned above. A concentration on the equal importance of institutional or macro features in the constitution of social activity also demands that quantitative data which can be used to describe and characterize macro phenomena must also be brought into the analysis in a complementary fashion. This departs from qualitative research (even that which includes simple counting) in so far as the quantitative elements here refer to macro phenomena and are not restricted to the counting of observable *behavioural* events. Thus 'macro' quantitative data refer to aggregations of individuals in specific social circumstances such as the distribution of a population in terms of different occupational categories or in types of labour market.

It is important to point out that I am not implying that macro phenomena are exclusively defined in quantitative terms. I am simply saying that some aspects of macro phenomena can be expressed in quantitative terms, and that these should be called on, wherever possible, to complement fieldwork of a primarily qualitative nature. In other respects,

		Qualitative	Quantitative
HISTORY	CONTEXT	Theoretical/interpretive characterizations	Demographic characteristics
	SETTING		Traditional quantitative data
	SITUATED ACTIVITY	Importance of qualitative data from observations and interviews	Simple forms of counting
	SELF		

Figure 6.2   Qualitative and quantitative analysis in multistrategy research.

macro phenomena have to be identified in an interpretive sense and thus have to be expressed in qualitative terms. For instance, 'patriarchy' or aspects of the class, ethnic or economic context of forms of activity are often defined or dealt with in qualitative terms by various authors. Indeed, it may be said that some of the most important aspects of macro processes, such as the operation of power, have to be expressed in these fundamentally theoretical, and thus qualitative terms.

Nonetheless, quantitative forms of measurement may provide useful indications of the shape or parameters of macro processes. For example, the number of women concentrated in certain types of occupations gives us some indication of the workings of patriarchal power in the labour market. As this example makes clear, macro phenomena not only have a greater numerical spread than have micro phenomena but they are also reflected by a more durable distribution of power resources, and a restriction of access to these resources. Thus the dominance of patriarchal power in society at large is supported by the restriction of the access of women to positions of power in society by the discriminatory activities of men. Similarly, we could use quantitative measures of aspects of the setting of activity, for example, the degree of specialization in an organization, the number of women in positions of power in an occupation or a specific place of work, and so on. These are all macro or institutional elements that will be important to a rounded understanding of a specific strip of situated activity.

In general then, if we view a multistrategy approach to fieldwork in terms of the elements outlined in the research map, we can see in figure 6.2 moving from the micro elements at the base up towards the macro features, that there is a shift in emphasis in the kinds of analysis and data that are pertinent to different layers of social organization. Investigation of self and situated behaviour is best conducted by the use of classical forms of qualitative research, such as participant and non-participant observation, semi-structured interviewing and so on, because these topics demand some ethnographic, interpretive account of the meaningful world of the individuals involved.

I acknowledge that this view would be resisted by those who argue that behavioural phenomena can be more reliably measured in terms of statistical correlations between experimentally controlled variables, although I find this claim to be unconvincing. In this respect, I side with the humanist forms of social analysis which insist that the experiential and meaningful dimension of human behaviour can only be properly grasped by non-quantitative means. Qualitative data on self and situated activity may afterwards be supplemented by various forms of counting to indicate, for instance, the generality of a finding across different settings or locales, as in the Silverman and the Miles and Huberman examples. However, this kind of data will be defined by the experiential world of those being studied, as reflected in the initial qualitative analysis.

As we move up towards the macro or institutional elements of the setting and context, the primacy of qualitative analysis of forms of interaction becomes less and less important. This is because, although the meaningful, experiential world is deeply interwoven with them, macro phenomena are not defined entirely in these terms. In this respect, there is a more even spread between qualitative and quantitative analyses and data. As I have already implied, macro phenomena can be characterized in a number of ways, in the abstract terms of power and domination, as distributions of resources, constraint and so on, and not only as aggregations of individuals defined in certain ways (occupation, gender) and described in numerical terms. Thus either form of data or analysis will be relevant if it has a direct bearing on the situated activity under the research focus.

Types of method and sources of data in fieldwork

Relating figure 6.1 to this spread of applicability, let me briefly mention in slightly more detail the kinds of methods and data relevant to the analysis of the different layers of social organization. As I have said, the analysis of self and situated activity demands the primacy of qualitative methods. These include various forms of observation, ranging from 'complete' participant observation where the analyst merges her or his identity with those whom she or he is studying, through varying degrees of 'closeness', to simple 'uninvolved' observations (see Gold 1958). This kind of data can be recorded in different ways, for example by video recording ('free' or through a one-way screen) or by written notes which are produced either at the time of the observations or very soon after. The exact form of the observations and the means of data recording will depend on the practical problems posed by the circumstances of the research. For instance, a researcher investigating the ways in which children think and act cannot pretend to be a child, and thus cannot attain full participant observer status. Similarly, investigation of the ways in which terminally ill patients interact with their families demands that the researcher be particularly sympathetic, while not intruding too far into sensitive or personal issues.

The various forms of observation may be supplemented by other methods such as semi-structured or informal interviewing in which subjects are questioned about various aspects of their observed behaviour, such as the way they dealt with a situation as it arose. These interviewing techniques can also be used independently of observed events, although the objective is still the same: to get the person to talk about the meanings their social experiences have for them. Diaries can also record valuable qualitative information about the degree and type of contact that people have with each other in various kinds of settings. (Diaries, of course, can also be a source of quantitative data such as the incidence and type of event that a subject is experiencing, as they have been used in the analysis of individuals' movements in and out of labour markets, see Ashton and Sung 1989.)

Observation, semi-structured interviewing (as opposed to fixed choice or formal interviewing) and diaries are all efficient means of obtaining qualitative information on the fabric and dynamics of situated activity, either as it happens or shortly thereafter. However, as attention is concentrated more on the consequences of particular social experiences for the selves and identities of individuals, the less the researcher is concerned with the dynamics of situated activity, and the more he or she is drawn towards an interest in biographical information. In this respect, the researcher will focus less on giving an account of the texture of interaction in observed events that took place in the immediate past, and more on a specific person's recollections, perceptions and feelings about their social experiences over extended periods of time. This, of course, may require a person's 'reconstruction' of particular situations, events or behaviour through memory and recall. Since the researcher cannot check these recollections against his or her own observations, this has to be done either by comparing it with others' accounts or by discerning the presence or absence of inconsistencies in the overall pattern of the subject's account.

However, this kind of cross-checking will only be necessary in certain kinds of historical research where it is important to establish certain 'objective' facts of the matter. Normally, an emphasis on biography would require that the researcher simply record the subject's feelings and responses to events and situations rather than attempt to reconstruct an accurate picture of what 'actually happened' in particular circumstances. Semi-structured and informal interviews are, perhaps, the best means of obtaining this kind of information, since they allow subjects themselves to define the significance of events in their lives. However, diaries recording subjects' feelings and thoughts during the period of relevance to the research are also valuable documentary sources for this kind of information.

Let us turn our attention to the macro elements of setting and context. Although, as I have said, macro phenomena are defined partly in qualitative (theoretical) terms, for the purposes of fieldwork the main sources of empirical data relevant to these phenomena will be gleaned from documentary and survey analyses. This would be used to depict those large-scale aspects of social organization that have a direct bearing on the social activity in question. Predominantly, though not exclusively, this data will be of a quantitative kind summarizing such things as the distribution of ownership and control of various resources like property or productive units, commodities, services and so on. This would also include statistical data on the distribution of individuals in occupational, class, gender and ethnic groupings, revealing the basic contours of particular forms of power and domination on a society-wide basis.

The analysis of government documents and parliamentary papers as well as private business audits and sponsored surveys will also yield valuable quantitative (as well as qualitative) information (see Scott 1990). This may involve survey data of a primary (undertaken for the current research project) or secondary kind (produced originally for some other purpose, for example government census data). In so far as fieldwork has as its centre of attention the analysis of specific forms of activity, then there is no pressing need to produce survey data specifically tailored to the objectives of the research. This would only be a requirement in research which concentrated on institutional analysis and bracketed the analysis of activity. Thus survey research which has been undertaken for other purposes, and perhaps even by non-sociologists, can be used as a resource for qualitative fieldwork.

As we move towards the more specific and 'close-in' settings of activity, sociologically designed survey research may yield more data that has an obvious and immediate theoretical relevance. However, this by no means rules out the use of survey research undertaken by non-sociologists working within the research area. (My own research on actors utilized surveys carried out by the Arts Council and the actors' trades union Equity, in order to build up an impression of the demography of the labour market in acting.) Also, the very close links and overlaps between the analysis of settings and situated activities requires some kind of close dialogue between quantitative and qualitative material at this point. It is precisely at this juncture that the analysis of quantitative material can help in the formulation of grounded theory. I shall give some examples of this in the next section.

Before that, let us finally and briefly mention the historical dimension. In chapter 9 I shall argue in more detail that a historical dimension should be a more frequent accompaniment to fieldwork in order that greater depth is achieved, particularly with respect to the analysis of settings and contexts. In this sense, a historical dimension will greatly enhance an appreciation of the way in which forms of power and domination have been incorporated into the structural features of settings and contexts, as a consequence of various forms of social development. A detailed and meticulous historical analysis is not a requirement here; we simply need a 'sense' of, or an 'approximate' indication of, the relevant historical factors. Such a 'blocking in' of historical material will add contextual depth to the analysis, and thus will subserve and feed into the generation of theoretical ideas about the contemporary situation.

Given that detailed historical research will not be of pivotal importance to the fieldwork, it is not necessary to use the primary sources that 'serious' historians or social historians use such as state documents concerned with diplomatic and constitutional matters (Scott 1990), or biographies or diaries written by those involved in the events which are the subject of investigation. Of course, if such sources are at hand and relevant, then there is definitely no prohibition on their use. However, for most purposes secondary sources, particularly historians' accounts, will suffice. (See chapter 9 for a discussion of some of the problems associated with using secondary sources.)

Quantitative data and grounded theory

As I explained before, quantitative data must be used as part of a general multistrategy approach in fieldwork in order to tackle the question of macro–micro linkages. In this sense, quantitative data must be treated on equal terms with qualitative data when it comes to establishing the connections between situated activity and the reproduced social relations embedded in the settings and contexts in which activity unfolds. A further consequence of the complementary use of quantitative data in a multistrategy approach of this sort is its role in the development of grounded theory. Let me give an illustration of what I mean by this by using an example from my research on actors' careers.

In the first phase of the research I was working on two broad methodological fronts. First, I was conducting semi-structured interviews with actors about various aspects of their careers. From these it became obvious that agents and casting directors were highly influential in shaping careers, and so I began conducting semi-structured interviews with them as well. Around the same time, I became aware of a survey of employment and incomes about to be conducted by the actors' union. From an analysis of this data, and by comparing it with a similar survey completed seven years before, I discovered that the labour market in acting seemed to consist of a threefold, segmented structure representing an economic and status hierarchy. This comprised a large group of actors (80 per cent) at the base of the hierarchy, a middle-income segment (15 per cent), and an elite of 'stars' (5 per cent) at the apex.

During the course of the research I began to link the data from these surveys with the data from the qualitative interviews. Gradually, this provided a comprehensive picture of the nature and workings of the labour market in acting. The complementarity of the two sources of data was an emergent feature of the research process and was by no means obvious or straightforward. In this sense, theoretical interpretations of what each source of data 'meant' depended on the reciprocal influence of the other sources and the coordination of their analyses. The quantitative data suggested an economic dimension to the labour market and a rather stable structure of segments. The qualitative material indicated the kind of social processes that were involved in the establishment and maintenance of the stratified labour market.

I reconstructed the work routines of agents and casting directors and traced their interconnections. A picture began to emerge of the way in which these career intermediaries channel and control the interchange of individuals (actors) between labour market segments, via their control over the allocation of work and, thus, careers. The top agencies and casting directors have regular working relations and between them allocate the bulk of the work available (and thus the top acting jobs). It became apparent that those actors in the upper two segments got the lion's share of the available work on a recurrent basis and this, in fact, tended to perpetuate the segmentation of the labour market.

Of course, a few new actors and actresses rise to the top every so often but, by and large, those who are already successful continue to be so not only because of their talents, but because they occupy such advantageous positions in the network of contacts for job opportunities.

This tendency towards a 'status quo' is reinforced for a number of reasons. For example, relations between casting directors and the top agencies continue to be regular because of the reliability of the agent's actor clients, the ease of negotiating fees and the pervasiveness of the 'star system'. These all have the effect of reinforcing the 'gatekeeper' function of the career intermediaries. Thus access to the upper segments of the labour market is relatively closed to those at the bottom, while the position for those in the upper segments is stabilized.

This example shows how substantive theory can emerge out of the intersecting influences of quantitative and qualitative data. The two types of data can continually feed into one another in a complementary sense, rather than simply using quantitative data as a check or restraint on over-enthusiastic claims derived from qualitative analysis. Also, it is this kind of area, where there is a close interweaving between the analysis of settings and the activities which serve to reproduce them, that can most benefit from the combined use of quantitative and qualitative data as a means of generating grounded theory. In principle, this gives the fieldworker greater scope for the development of grounded theory. This is because it not only deals with the particular substantive area in question (in the above example, acting) but also says something of a formal nature about the operation of power and control in labour markets. In turn, such theoretical elements may be used in the elaboration of even more general theory about the nature of power and social control themselves. (I shall take up this theme in chapter 8.)

Mutiple strategy field research

Having said something about the relation between quantitative and qualitative data, the types of methods and data sources, and theory-generating strategies of relevance to this kind of fieldwork, I want now to say something more about the nature of multistrategy research as I envisage it. The term 'multiple strategies' has been used by others, notably Burgess (1984), and overlaps with a number of other terms such as 'triangulation' (Denzin 1970), 'combined operations' (Stacey 1969) and 'mixed strategies' (Douglas 1976). While my particular version has obvious links with these others, there are also significant differences.

Most of these terms refer to the use of a number of different methods or data or theories (usually substantive theory), primarily as a means of checking the validity of findings. However, my notion of multistrategy research refers to integrated combinations of all of these, specifically as they relate to the question of macro–micro linkages. As a corollary, it is directed primarily towards the development of grounded theory. By this, I do not mean to suggest that multistrategy research is not concerned with questions of validity and generality, but rather that it is not exclusively concerned with such things. We can see the other points of overlap and difference by dealing with a number of subissues.

Flexibility of design and process in research

Any research which is aimed at discovery (rather than confirmation or verification of findings by other researchers) needs to be both systematic and flexible. It needs to be systematic in order that the chances of discovery are maximized and not left solely to luck or 'happy accidents'. However, it also needs to be flexible so that it can respond to the unanticipated problems and detours that will almost inevitably accompany exploratory research (Douglas 1976, Glaser and Strauss 1967). My version of multistrategy fieldwork attempts to embrace both these aspects.

That is, the systematic element will be provided by the initial research design based on integrated aspects of the resource map, methods and data collection. (These, in turn, will be influenced by practical issues like accessibility of data, the nature and circumstances of the research, funding and so on.) The flexible component will inhere in the ability to reorganize and reformulate this initial design in the light of the emergence of unanticipated analytic problems thrown up by the data. In this way, any research which is oriented towards discovery and theory construction must be sensitive to the relevatory potential of the research process itself.

Triangulation as a validity check

A number of writers have used combinations of methods and data as a means of confirming or disconfirming a finding or hypothesis initially produced by the use of one particular method. For example, in-depth interviews may be used to check patterns or findings generated through participant observation, or simple forms of counting may check the generality of a qualitative insight (as in the Silverman example above). Thus, if the use of other methods turns up the same finding or result, then it is confirmed. If it does not, then the initial finding may be discarded as an artifact or aberration caused by the method used. Denzin (1970) has distinguished between different types of triangulation: data, investigator, theory and methodological forms of triangulation. Although these refer to different aspects of research, they all have the same function of 'testing' the reliability, validity and generality of findings. By its very nature, my version of multistrategy research has 'triangulation' built into it. However, this is not its only, or its primary role.

Density of empirical coverage

In order to facilitate the emergence of concepts and theoretical ideas relating to macro–micro linkages, it is important to cover the empirical area in question as intensively as possible. The multistrategy approach encourages the maximum utilization of the data at one's disposal by producing greater density of coverage of the area. In this sense, the question of density overlaps with the question of validity. The denser one's empirical coverage, the surer one can be of the validity of the findings. However, it also has two further advantages. First, it increases the possibility of emergent theory by more intensive trawling and sifting of the data. Secondly, greater density of coverage means that in the end, findings will be anchored in more robust interpretations and explanations of the empirical area in question.

Density of analytic viewpoints

This is basically the other side of the coin of density of empirical coverage. The multistrategy approach not only encourages an intense trawl and sifting of the empirical data, it also encourages a density of analytic viewpoints on this data. Different methods and methodological traditions contain within them different perspectives which allow the researcher using them to see empirical reality in slightly different ways. This is even more the case for different theoretical and analytic traditions or approaches.

Let us be clear here about what is being suggested. I am referring to the 'openness' of the multistrategy approach which I mentioned at the beginning of this chapter. That is, it allows as many analytic viewpoints on the data as are feasible and appropriate in order to stimulate grounded theory. This could take the form of the employment of different methods and techniques. Alternatively, it could involve the 'borrowing' of theoretical perspectives or particular concepts to help in the formulation of theory which emerges from the research. This type of strategy is reflected in Bloor and McIntosh's (1990) study of client resistance in health visiting and therapeutic communities. In this study the researchers applied some of Foucault's ideas about power and surveillance in order to develop their own typology of client resistance.

Such borrowing from general theory, or the application of perspectives drawn from wider frameworks, is simply in order to stimulate independent theorising concerned with the immediate research. Although the multistrategy approach encourages as many analytic viewpoints as possible to achieve density of analytic and empirical coverage, it does not therefore endorse an 'anything goes' approach. As I said at the beginning of the chapter, grounded theory is 'allowed' to emerge only in the context of more general theoretical assumptions about the nature of the links between macro and micro features of social life.

Bearing this qualification in mind, we can say that the multistrategy approach has built into it a multiplicity of perpectives on empirical data. To understand how these perspectives result from the way in which different methods or conceptual frameworks 'cut into' the data, let us employ the metaphor of a scalpel knife cutting into some object or material such as plant or animal tissue or even a mineral deposit. When such a knife cuts into the object it reveals a cross-section of the object patterned in a specific way. In a sense, the way in which the scalpel blade has revealed the inner substance of the object gives us a 'true' or 'accurate' picture. However, if further cuts are made into the object, all at different angles, then we know from experience that very often they will reveal differently patterned cross-sections.

This is because our perspective on the same object has changed by varying the angle of the cutting edge and the point of incision. In the same way, different research strategies (methodological or analytic) 'cut into' the data from different angles to reveal a variety of 'slices' of the research site. Thus, the accumulation of perspectives will add to the picture that was originally revealed. The truth or accuracy of that picture will be filled out, elaborated on, contoured, textured and so on. It is not that the original picture was fundamentally wrong, but rather that it was partial and thus not the whole truth.

Selective focusing in multistrategy fieldwork

The whole thrust of the approach I have been recommending has been one in which there is an attempt to make as many methodological and analytic cuts as possible in order to achieve a dense empirical coverage and thus to produce maximum yield in terms of emergent theory. In the next section, I shall present a detailed empirical example which conforms in most respects to this model of multistrategy research. However, in a sense this model has to be seen as a working template, or resource, which can be used more completely or less completely in particular pieces of research. This is because it will not always be possible, or even feasible, to achieve an evenness of emphasis across all the potential elements involved.

There are two aspects to this. First, it may not be possible, for various reasons, to employ the full range of methods and data sources applicable to a particular empirical research problem. In this case, the researcher can only use what is possible and available in the circumstances. Secondly, in relation to the elements of the resource map (the layers of social organization), it is possible to engage in selective focusing, whereby the researcher gives primary emphasis to particular elements of the map. It is crucially important to note that this is simply a matter of *emphasis*, and should not be taken to endorse a form of selection which entirely excludes the other elements. It simply means that, relatively speaking, more concentrated and detailed attention may be directed at, say, describing and accounting for the dynamics of activity than is directed at the setting, context or the implications for identity. We have already encountered empirical studies which display such characteristics in the previous chapter. While in principle multistrategy research should display equal attention to macro and micro concerns, selective focusing may be necessary for several reasons.

First, there may be a limited type or amount of data available, either because of restricted access or because of research budget constraints, or a combination of the two. Second, the nature of the initial research problem may be such that it requires selective focusing. This may be complicated by the influence of the funding source on the formulation of the research problem and the details of its execution. For example, a funding agency may require a focus on the social-psychological problems associated with drug dependency, which would in turn tend to limit research concern to the area of self and situated activity. The nature of the research problem, the circumstances of the research site and the constraints of funding are all factors which may justify a relatively greater emphasis on one element of the resource map. However, it must constantly be borne in mind that such selective focusing must only take place against the background of a wider appreciation of both macro and micro dimensions.

An empirical example of multistrategy research

Hochschild's *The Managed Heart* (1983) is neither a conscious attempt to develop a multistrategy approach to research nor an explicit attempt to relate a substantive area to the macro–micro problem. Nevertheless, in my view it does implicitly highlight and illustrate many of the themes and recommendations that I have developed in this and the previous chapter. Hochschild's study focuses on 'emotional labour', 'the management of feeling to create a publicly observable facial and bodily display' (p. 7), which is sold for a wage in the context of occupational activities. In particular, Hochschild centres attention on flight attendants as an occupational group from which emotional labour is typically required, that is, a middle-class service occupation which has a predominantly female workforce.

Flight attendants are required by airline companies to 'manage' their emotions in order to deal with 'difficult' passengers as well as to provide a calm and secure atmosphere for the flying public. Hochschild explores a number of dimensions and consequences of emotional labour, including its class, gender and occupational basis, its utilization by companies in order to project certain kinds of commercial image, and the relation between private feeling states and public displays of emotion.

Hochschild drew on two principal sources to illustrate her ideas. The first was a questionnaire survey of 261 students which inquired into the way emotional management varied by gender and social class. Although this information did not feed directly into her study of flight attendants, it did so indirectly by suggesting relevant contextual aspects of gender and class on emotion management in the private sphere. The second main data source came from a study of the flight attendants' world. Hochschild observed flight attendant training classes, she talked with trainers and students and interviewed airline officials. She also sat in on recruitment interviews and conducted open-ended interviews with flight attendants. This was supplemented by the study and use of company documents to support various arguments. She buttresses her study of the commercial uses of emotional labour by drawing on census data to analyse its distribution across a variety of occupations and their gender constituents.

In these respects, Hochschild uses qualitative and quantitative data in a complementary fashion to illustrate the intertwining of macro and micro elements. Thus the main analysis of flight attendants' emotional labour (corresponding to self and situated activity in the research map) is based on qualitative data (observation and open-ended interviews). However, Hochschild also traces the manner in which situated aspects of emotional labour intermesh with the more formalized aspects of the setting (the airline company) and the macro context (class, gender and occupation). She did this by using a combination of qualitative data (open-ended interviews, documentary analysis, observations) and quantitative data (questionnaire survey, census statistics). The flexible use of a fairly wide range of methods allows for a density of empirical and analytic coverage. This is reaffirmed in her analysis and findings.

One of the central themes of the book is an exploration of the way in which company requirements concerning emotion management are assimilated by flight attendants (mainly via training courses), and how these intersect and coexist with their 'real' or spontaneous feelings. The psychological costs of over-identification with the job, such as emotional 'burnout', and the way in which flight attendants distinguish between and deal with real and false aspects of self are all subsidiary themes and concepts which surround this core issue. Clearly, Hochschild is concerned here with the relation between self, forms of activity and a particular occupational setting. However, she does this by means of an analysis which dovetails the influences and effects of both macro and micro processes. This is accomplished by constantly shuttling to and fro between the analysis of macro variables (gender, class, occupation, company organization, occupational training programmes, forms of hierarchical control) and variables more grounded in everyday activities (emotion management, forms of interaction with passengers, colleagues and superiors, sense of self, and so on).

At the widest point, Hochschild deals with what are traditionally thought of as macro issues of social structure such as the nature of the occupational structure and the varying demands it makes on emotional labour at different points in it, especially the service sector. Associated with this, she analyses the class and gender basis of emotional labour (mainly middle-class, but predominantly female). She also analyses the kinds of contradictions and power inequalities that are involved (middle classes have power in relation to the working classes, but women are in a subordinate position in relation to men). Hochschild also highlights what she calls the 'commercialization of feeling' as exemplified in the approach of airline companies to their, mostly women, employees. In this sense, companies 'organize the way in which public-contact workers manage emotion' (p. 192), and thus 'the company's purposes insinuate themselves into the way workers are asked to interpret their own feelings' (p. 193).

Although she does not use the same terminology, Hochschild implicitly deals with the company setting as the mediation between the mutual influences of macro structural elements and the micro world of personal and interpersonal public contact. This is, in other words, the arena in which forms of company control and constraint over workers intersect with situational factors of a personal and interpersonal nature. In this sense, Hochschild implicitly endorses the proposition that macro and micro elements are tied together through the productive and reproductive effects of social activity.

That is, Hochschild seems to embrace a theoretical position which gives equal weighting to both macro and micro features, but at the same time does not unwittingly assert the primacy of either. Although she does not spend a great deal of time on a formal discussion of her theoretical position, her scattered comments lead me to believe that she adopts a position which is broadly commensurate with the one I have enunciated so far in this book. In particular, she draws on writers from interactionist schools of thought (especially Goffman), while at the same time being critical of their lack of attention to institutional analysis. Thus at one point she says that Goffman has gone as far as he could go with his emphasis on situated activity and the 'display' of emotion.

She goes on to say that, on the one hand, we now need a theory of emotion which allows us to talk of 'a prior notion of self with a developed inner life' (1983: 216) so that we can fill out what Goffman himself characterizes as his study of 'moments and their men, not men and their moments' (1967). Hochschild rightly points out that such a theoretical preoccupation may have its virtues, but it most definitely has its limitations. On the other hand, we also need a theory 'that allows us to see how institutions – such as corporations – control us not simply through surveillance of our behaviour, but also through surveillance of our feelings' (1983: 218). In short, Hochschild is saying that we need both psychological and institutional dimensions to complement Goffman's (1983) concern with the 'interaction order' and its emphasis on performances and presentations of self. Hochschild's general analytic framework is not identical with mine, nor is it as closely concerned with the formal linkages between macro and micro elements. Nevertheless, it is entirely consistent with both the theoretical thrust of the resource map and my version of multistrategy research.

Conclusion: key issues in the multistrategy approach

1   The use of qualitative analysis and data is a central requirement of field research which endeavours to give an account of the social activities taking place in some bounded social world. In other words, ethnographic material is needed to understand properly the social activities taking place in, for example, in an occupational group, some aspect of street life, interaction in a coffee bar, and so on.

2   However, a multistrategy approach actively encourages the use of quantitative data and forms of measurement in order to complement the central core of qualitative analysis. This may include both simple and sophisticated forms of counting which may act as a check on the insights derived from qualitative analysis.

3   Quantitative data and forms of analysis should also play a part in

generating grounded theory. In particular, quantitative data on macro processes can be linked with qualitative data on situated activities in order to generate substantive theory. This was the case with the analysis of acting careers. Here quantitative data on labour market characteristics was combined with qualitative information on the work routines of career intermediaries, to produce substantive theory about career processes.

4   The multistrategy approach encourages the researcher to make as many methodological and analytic 'cuts' into the data as possible, where this is theoretically warranted. That is, where these cuts throw light on the interlocks and linkages between macro and micro aspects of social life. Expressed more negatively, this rules out forms of research which endeavour to reduce the analysis solely to one or the other of these levels.

5   Multiple cuts enable the research and the researcher to respond flexibly to unforeseen problems and aspects of the research. Also, they act as a validity check through 'triangulation'. Finally, they increase the possibility of producing grounded theory which is empirically dense and robust.

6   In principle, the methodological and analytic cuts should attend to all the 'layers' or elements described in the research map in chapter 5. Hochschild's study of flight attendants is a good example of this kind of comprehensive analysis. However, for a number of reasons it is not always possible or feasible to attend to them all with equal emphasis. In such cases, a form of selective focusing will be necessary. However, again, selective focusing is conditioned by the need to attend in an explicit way to the mutual influences of macro and micro features in the research.

7

Research Strategy and Theory Building

This chapter considers the general problem of how to begin to develop theory in the context of a particular research topic or area. I examine three rather different ways in which the process of theory development can proceed in tandem with the research process itself. First, I consider the use of background or 'sensitizing' concepts. Using the concept of career as a prime example, I detail the way in which such concepts may help in the initial organization of data and may also aid the emergence of theoretical concepts and ideas. Second, I discuss the development and use of typological models as aids to comparative analysis in grounded theory methodology. Finally, I shall look briefly at the way in which the process of sampling in qualitative research can facilitate the emergence of grounded theory.

Getting started: the use of background concepts

Field researchers who are interested in generating theory from their research are typically uncertain when starting their research. They do not have a clear idea of 'where it's going' in theoretical terms. One way of alleviating uncertainty and anxiety is to use 'sensitizing' or 'background' concepts. Such concepts provide provisional pointers to relevancies in the data without imposing a 'closed net' on the research as a whole. That is, they provide useful starting points for theory building but do not necessarily remain important to the analysis as it unfolds. In this sense, the importance of the concept may recede progressively as the research produces newly emergent concepts which may prove to be more useful or relevant. On the other hand, the initial concept may prove to be of lasting value and, in fact, grow in importance during the research.

In relation to the multistrategy approach outlined in the previous chapter, the main requirement of a background concept is that it is 'two-sided', that is, capable of referring to both the subjective and objective aspects of the social world. I shall illustrate this in detail with the concept of career in the next section. However, other concepts possess this characteristic and have been used in as means of organizing research data. Hochschild's (1983) study discussed near the end of the previous chapter utilizes the concept of 'emotional labour' as a way of integrating the analysis of data from a diversity of sources. Emotional labour has precisely the duality of reference required. On the one hand, it refers to the types of feelings that are experienced by women, in particular, in the performance of certain kinds of jobs. On the other hand, it refers to segments of the occupational structure which demand forms of emotional labour.

Nijsmans (1991) study of a counselling institute in the UK utilizes the concept of 'organizational morality' as a way of organizing data on the day-to-day practices observed in the institute. Again, such a concept refers to subjective aspects of activity (such as counsellors' care to observe informal 'rules' about time, space and money) as well as more objective features of the institute, such as its 'patterned regularities' which constitute a 'structure' of principles, rules and daily practices (p. 17). There are other examples of concepts which may be used in this way, such as Foucault's notions of 'power' and 'surveillance', used by Bloor and McIntosh (1990) in their study of health visiting and therapeutic communities in Glasgow.

However, there is another aspect or dimension which not all two-sided concepts possess, but which can further enhance their utility as sensitizing or background concepts. This is the notion of process, or the passage of activity and institutions through time and space. Again, the concept of career fits the bill admirably in this respect. There are others which possess this quality, such as 'status passage' or 'configuration', but which tend to be rather abstract and restricted in their empirical applicability. Finnegan's (1989) ethnographic study of musicians and 'music-making practices' in an English town uses the concept of 'musical worlds', which is in many ways similar to that of career. In this respect, people tend to use musical worlds (classical, rock and pop, jazz, folk and so on) as 'pathways in urban living', as a means for the expression of personal and collective values.

'Career' as a background concept

The twin virtues of the concept of career stem from its theoretical relevance and the breadth of its empirical applicability. The empirical scope of the concept derives from its use outside as well as inside the context of work and occupations. Thus various writers have called attention to its general usefulness in analysing definable stages or phases of activity which people go through in a step-by-step fashion on the way to some end-point or goal or series of goals (Roth 1963: 94). In this respect, a number of writers have stressed the usefulness of 'career' in the analysis of connected sequences of activity such as those of illness or deviance, or marriage or various forms of interpersonal relationships (Goffman 1968, Glaser and Strauss 1971, Stebbins 1970b). However, before I look at its empirical scope in more detail, let me draw attention to its theoretical relevance since these two things are closely connected.

As I suggested in chapter 5, it has been noted that the concept of career spans both objective and subjective aspects of social life (Hughes 1937: 413, Goffman 1968, Stebbins 1970a). However, it has not always been recognized that this in itself also makes the concept uniquely suited to addressing the theoretical problems of the links between macro and micro phenomena and the relation between institutional and interpretive aspects of activity. This is because the concept of career has been used mainly by writers of an interactionist persuasion, who have by and large neglected the systematic character of the objective (macro, institutional) properties of career in favour of its subjective and interactional characteristics. However, if one goes beyond the limited focus imposed by this perspective, it is clear that the two-sided nature of career makes it a conceptual tool which can straddle both sides of the macro–micro division and thus can potentially be a force working to secure their eventual synthesis.

In this regard the most important modification required in order to break from the restrictions imposed by the interactionist perspective would be to widen the notion of power implicit in it. Thus power as domination, as a group resource which is unevenly distributed throughout the social structure, should be brought to bear on the concept of career. The idea of power as an underlying, potential influence on behaviour based on the group possession of particular resources needs to be brought in to complement the interactionist notion of power as the actual, observable control of behaviour. This institutional dimension to the distribution and use of power should play a much more significant part in the analysis of career processes. (I concentrate in detail on the analysis of power in field research in chapter 8.)

There are additional features that need to be attached to the concept of career in order for it to serve the needs of the wider conception of fieldwork advocated in this book. However, these further modifications would, in fact, be required by the more encompassing notion of power to which I have just alluded. These will become obvious as the arguments of this and the following chapters unfold. (I have also indicated the general direction and substance of these changes in the critical discussion of the grounded theory approach to fieldwork in chapter 4.) Given that these modifications are made to the concept of career, then its existing emphasis on social processes in time and space would be better able to tie together the elements of the resource map as I have described them (self, situated activity, setting and context).

That is to say, career analysis could be used to indicate the way in which these elements are connected in time and space. This refers back to an earlier point which stressed that social activity has to be understood as possessing a 'horizontal' dimension. This traces the variable pathways through social situations, settings and contexts that are taken by individuals (and groups) in their interactions and relations with others. Given the above-mentioned amendment of the notion of power, then the career perspective could capture the transitions and interrelations between personal and institutional power as they are arranged along the dimensions of time and space. (It must be noted here that the application of the career concept to historical analysis needs to take careful consideration of the nature of the different time elements and units of change involved – see chapter 9.)

There is one more theoretical property of career which is of paramount importance. In fact, this property is implicit in the other aspects of the career concept which I have already touched on. I have suggested that the concept of career is potentially capable of addressing certain problems in social analysis. In particular, it could help to overcome certain divisions such as that between macro and micro analysis and between interpretive and institutional analysis ('interactionist' or 'structural' sociology). This is because, as I have said, the concept of career is capable of reaching into both objective and subjective aspects of social life.

In these senses, the concept uniquely expresses the intertwining of individual experience and the collective forces that constitute what we generally mean by the term 'society'. Thus, career is a step towards overcoming the false distinction implicit in the old argument about the 'individual versus society'. This has given rise to such statements as 'there is no such thing as society, only individuals', and the opposite but equally erroneous view that 'social forces are the true reality and that the notion of the individual is a myth.' Carefully used, the concept of career enables the social researcher to chart the interpenetration of individual and social forces without undermining the distinctive reality of either, or their contribution to social processes.

Career: the occupational context

Turning away from a more abstract consideration of its virtues, let us now consider the empirical utility of the concept of career. As I have said, one of its great strengths in this regard is its applicability to a broad range of empirical phenomena, beyond the exclusively occupational sphere. However, before examining its non-occupational relevance it is worth considering the breadth of its scope within this area. In this regard, much sociological usage has rejected the lay stereotype of career as relating to success in high status occupations, like the professions. Thus the concept may be used in relation to all forms of occupational involvement from high to low status occupations and without any assumption that it necessarily implies upward movement through an officially defined hierarchy of power and status. Career movements may be downward (as in demotion or some other reversal of fortune) or lateral (as in moving to another job with equal pay and status), as well as upwards on a ladder of success and power. Similarly, 'success' may be defined by the participants themselves as something other than that defined in official terms. Thus Becker (1952) found that teachers in public schools in Chicago defined a successful career move as one that took them away from the slum areas to more salubrious neighbourhoods, rather than one which involved promotion as such. In a related sense, Thomas (1989) has discussed the coping strategies of blue-collar workers which help them to deal with the limitations inherent in blue-collar careers.

Apart from its lack of restriction to elite occupations, sociologically the concept of career has been used in a number of different ways to depict the occupational involvements of individuals. First, it has been used to give some account of the 'work histories' of individuals or groups. Willensky (1961) has used the concept of career in this sense to analyse the total work lives (including changes or discontinuities in work involvements) of older or retired workers in terms of whether they have been 'orderly' or 'disorderly' (see also Nicholson and West 1989). Other forms of work history have concentrated on a much smaller time-spans. For example, Ashton et al. (1990) have examined the types of labour market involvements of young workers in the UK (including periods of both employment and unemployment) a few years after leaving school. Both these types of work history (lifetime and short-range) can be examined using quantitative as well as qualitative data.

Another kind of research focus on careers has been the concentration on the typical experiences of practitioners within one occupational setting. This sort of research attempts to give an account of what it is like to be a member of a particular occupational group and the kinds of career problems that arise over time. The Chicago wing of the symbolic interactionist school has produced quite an array of studies of this kind: for example, Hearn and Stoll (1975) on cocktail waitresses, Gold (1952) on janitors, Becker (1963) on jazz musicians, Faulkner (1973) on orchestral musicians, Geer (1968) and Becker (1952) on school-teachers, Glaser (1964) on organizational scientists, and so on. There have also been a number of career studies outside of this tradition, typically focusing on careers within organizations such as managerial careers (Sofer 1970, Pahl and Pahl 1971, Grusky 1963).

However, one has to be careful not to be drawn into the assumption that all occupational careers take place within a continuous organizational context. Some occupations are organized such that careers are worked out on a freelance, market-defined basis. Occupational practitioners such as actors, singers ('pop' to opera), artists (painters, sculptors), writers and some journalists, for example, work in this kind of context where employment contracts are generally of a short-term kind, usually for the duration of a play or film or for the production of a 'work' (or a number of works) such as a book.

Other practitioners, such as those in professional sports like football or baseball, may be contracted to teams or clubs on a longer-term basis (say two or three seasons), but are also free to renegotiate terms as contracts terminate. In market-defined contexts such as these, practitioners are not following career paths that have been specifically designed by powerful people in the employing organization (as they are in managerial, civil service or military careers, for example), and this fact makes the nature of the career setting and the practitioner's experience very different. (I shall elaborate on this example in the following section on the use of typologies in field research.)

The wider context: multiple careers

Turning to its non-occupational usages, the concept of career is relevant to a diversity of areas, but in particular it has been applied in relation to the area of deviance and crime, including drug dependence, shoplifting, delinquency and criminal lifestyles in general. Very often these studies focus on the way in which the deviant or criminal activities have unfolded over time, the kinds of identity changes in the 'deviant' that have accompanied them, and the sorts of circumstances that keep people 'entrapped' or positively committed to such activities (see Stebbins 1970b). Similarly, the area of illness has received a certain amount of attention from a career perspective with studies of hospitalized tuberculosis patients (Roth 1963), terminal cancer patients (Glaser and Strauss 1965), and children with polio (Davis 1963).

The topic of illness careers brings into sharp relief the fact that any one person is more than likely undergoing several different careers at the same time, for example someone with a relatively successful occupational career may also experience recurrent bouts of illness, or one debilitating illness that requires hospitalization. At the same time, people have important personal relationships with partners, spouses or family members that have 'careers' of their own. That is, such relationships go through various stages and, as a result, will either be enhanced or set back by them. Clearly, these multiple careers will interact with and affect each other, as when a marriage or partnership is put under strain by an illness or an addiction to drugs or just overwork. Although the researcher will typically be focusing only on one 'career' during a restricted time period, it is important to bear in mind the multiple involvements of individuals and how they influence the focal career.

An important aspect of the notion of multiple careers is the idea that individuals are variably involved with social organizations and institutions when we consider their activities over time and space. One of the great advantages of the career perspective is that it enables the researcher to trace the interweaving of individual activity and group and institutional involvement as various strands of activity unfold and terminate during the course of social life. A good example of a piece of social research which draws together the themes of multiple careers, deviance, illness and variable social involvements is the study by Lemert (1962) of paranoia as a form of mental illness.

Lemert suggests that the paranoid response (an individual's belief that others are out to make life difficult for, or even harm him or her) begins with a person's loss or threatened loss of status which has led to a dramatic change in life circumstances. This may be the actual loss of a job or threatened unemployment, or may involve the incurring of a mutilating or stigmatizing injury. Whatever it is, the sudden and dramatic loss of status has the effect of making the person irritable and difficult to get on with in relation to his or her work colleagues, family or neighbours. The individual develops a reputation for being 'difficult', and other people start to withdraw from communication or avoid contact with the person. The individual senses that other people are talking behind his or her back and forming coalitions designed to minimize contact and involvement.

This barrier to communication simply fuels the paranoid person's need to obtain feedback from other people, and thus he or she begins to engage in even more severe anti-social behaviour in an effort to elicit a response from former colleagues, friends and family. The increasingly aggressive and accusatory ('I know you're all against me') nature of paranoid behaviour is taken by others as further evidence of illness, and so the individual becomes trapped in a spiral of ever-increasing isolation and more extreme paranoiac reactions. Committal proceedings may be taken against the individual and this may end up with involuntary hospitalization. In this kind of situation the individual may feel driven into a corner and given no other option than to accept the label of mental illness (Scheff 1966). Feelings of alienation and isolation may be further exacerbated where (former) friends, colleagues and family were responsible for initiating committal proceedings. In this sense the individual experiences a 'funnel of betrayal' during the course of what Goffman (1968) calls the 'moral career' of the mentally ill person.

This example vividly highlights the way the career of paranoia traces the group and institutional attachments and detachments of the individual over a particular stretch of time. It also exemplifies how the notion of career ties together the elements of the resource map in a dynamic, processual manner. That is, the changing identity of the paranoid individual (becoming more and more anti-social, aggressive and insulting, resulting in the full-blown belief in a 'plot' by others to discredit or destroy them) is related through situated activity (patronizing evasion, spurious interaction, collusive behaviour) to various settings and contexts (home, work, neighbourhood, hospital and legal institutions). Lemert's analysis also demonstrates how these elements are related to each other in time and space in a number of different ways. For example, they can be understood as overlaying (or partially overlaying) each other, or as standing in some kind of sequential relationship with each other. In this respect the individual's experience takes on a multidimensional character.

As this kind of general application of the career perspective indicates, it is useful as a background, 'sensitizing' concept for an extremely wide diversity of social phenomena. Most strands of activity can be shown to pass through successive stages on the way towards some definable endpoint. Thus the career framework may be fruitful in suggesting further and more specific concepts and theoretical propositions which can be measured against (although not in any simplistic manner) the data collected in field research. If sufficient attention is given over to rectifying the deficiencies and limitations of the concept in terms of the way it has often been used (lack of attention to structural aspects of setting and context, constricted notion of power and so on), then the concept of career can be a useful analytic background to field research. In this respect it closely ties in with the concerns of the research resource map outlined in chapter 5, and in particular its attempt to overcome some of the problems stemming from the macro–micro division in social analysis and research.

Getting started: the use of typologies

Another way of alleviating the anxiety that can attend the start of theory-generating research is to aim for an explicit analytic objective such as the construction of typologies. These are models or types of social phenomena that constitute the research topic, such as different political parties, forms of interaction, types of suicide or types of setting. By aiming to construct a typology, the researcher works with a clear analytic objective in mind (to construct a certain kind of typology), without knowing exactly what this will look like in the end in terms of its content and form. In this sense, the typology will significantly influence the emergent theory of the research. As compared with the use of a background or sensitizing concept, typology-building organizes data as a projected outcome of the research rather than as an initial means of 'pegging' the data to a conceptual framework.

Comparative analysis, typologies and theoretical sampling

As I think I have indicated throughout this book, I feel that Glaser and Strauss's vision of grounded theory, while in need of some crucial amendments and additions, is both path-breaking and an extremely valuable guide to field research. One of the great strengths of their methodological recommendations in this regard is their emphasis on the comparative analysis of data as a means of generating theoretical ideas and categories, and the closely associated idea that the researcher's data sample is directed by the theory that is evolving from the research. Before I go on to look at these in greater detail, let me say something about my overall objectives in this section. Generally, I want to endorse Glaser and Strauss's ideas in this regard, but I also want to extend their terms of reference so as to make comparative analysis and theoretical sampling a more flexible resource for field research.

My main point revolves around the use of typologies. While the grounded theory approach as it stands does not preclude the development of typologies, this is certainly given no particular prominence. I argue that more often than not the development of typologies can aid the formulation of grounded theory. Further, I argue that the grounded theory approach as it stands is more conducive to the development of action typologies (that is, relating to self and situated activity in the resource map). Conversely it is less relevant to the development of 'structural' (or macro) typologies (relating to setting and context), and I argue that this imbalance should be redressed by emphasizing the role of structural typologies.

How does the use of typological analysis relate to Glaser & Strauss's ideas about comparative analysis and theoretical sampling, and what do all these things mean in straightforward terms? In *Qualitative Analysis for Social Scientists* (1987: 14–17), Strauss offers a very simple empirical example that demonstrates both comparative analysis and theoretical sampling. The example is drawn from a study that was concerned with whether and how the use of machines in hospitals affects the interaction between staff and patients (Strauss et al. 1985). A basic category, that of 'machine–body connections', registers the basic observation that there are many types of machines connected to sick persons.

A further distinction is made between machines where the connection is external to the skin of the patient and those where the connection is internal (through various orifices). This distinction leads to questions about whether, or in what sense, the internal connections are uncomfortable or dangerous and what sorts of consequences these things have for interactions between personnel and patient. Did they bargain with each other? Was the patient warned of the difficulties? What tactics or techniques are used by the personnel to minimize or prevent disconnection?

These directed inquiries born out of the emerging categories and the hypotheses thrown up by them lead to theoretical sampling whereby the researcher, after previous analysis, is 'seeking samples of population, events, activities guided by his or her emerging (if still primitive) theory' (1987, p. 16). This sampling is directly linked to making comparisons in terms of the basic categories and distinctions of the emergent theory. Thus the researchers may compare machine connections that are comfortable with those that are not. They could also compare what happens when a dangerous disconnection occurs (as in a power blackout) versus a non-dangerous disconnection.

Strauss suggests that the researcher can sample even more widely by thinking about safety or discomfort with respect to other machines outside the hospital setting – whether body-connected or not. Machines such as 'x-ray equipment, airplanes, toasters, lawnmowers, or the body-shaking power tools manipulated by men who are employed to break up cement on street surfaces'. Such general comparisons are in the service of developing theory about medical machinery, so that this 'out' sampling links with the 'in' sampling of hospital comparisons.

It can be seen that theoretical sampling implies constant comparisons between the data uncovered in the research and other examples of maximal and minimal difference (Glaser and Strauss 1967). Such comparisons will force the researcher to ask questions about whether observed events or activities are different or the same as the ones they are compared with, and why, and thus will help to clarify analytic distinctions in the emergent theory. If we see potential comparisons as ranged along a continuum between maximal and minimal difference (as in the distinction between various types of hospital machines versus a variety of non-hospital machines), then we can see that this could be developed into a series of models or types representing the whole range actually available. The typology of 'awareness contexts' that surround terminal patients in hospital developed by Glaser and Strauss (1965) is a good example of just such a typology.

Grounded theory and the use of typologies

Surprisingly, however, in their general methodological recommendations Glaser and Strauss make very little of the notion of typology building as an aid to the evolution of grounded theory. Perhaps this is because they see typologies, as in the one of awareness contexts, solely as an end-product of fieldwork rather than as a continual and organic feature of the research process. However, this is not clear because they neither deny nor endorse the importance of typology building with regard to the emergence of grounded theory. Furthermore, in the context of grounded theory as Glaser and Strauss envisage it, the latitude for typology building would seem to stretch only to 'action' typologies (such as awareness contexts in social interaction). Clearly, action typologies attempt to depict various dimensions of self and situated activity, whereas 'structural' typologies are concerned with macro features of setting and context.

This emphasis on action typologies is for two main reasons. First, when it does attend to structural features, grounded theory tends to focus on the ones closest to the focal activities and events that are being researched, and thus tends to neglect the influence of seemingly more remote macro features which may have important and largely unobservable effects on the (observable) events and activities. Secondly, although Strauss (1987: 78–81) in particular has noted the importance of thinking both structurally and interactionally and attempting to link the two, in effect the interactional dimension is accorded priority over the structural dimension. This is because in Strauss's view the terms for the inclusion of relevant structural factors are set by the data on observed events and activities which have already been collected. Thus structural factors are brought into the analysis only when they are seen (observed) to have some direct effect on the interactional data. This, of course, rules out the effects of structural factors which are not necessarily visible in the data and cannot be immediately detected.

For instance, structural constraints often act in ways that significantly influence the direction and substance of activity prior to the observed activity itself. For example, specific circumstances of a class or gender type will rule out some activities while ruling in others. This is evidenced in the constraints which work against women entering public bars on their own (or walking alone in the inner city late at night), and in the way economic privations of working-class life prevent the pursuit of expensive hobbies or leisure activities. Such constraints are not manifest in observed events or activities themselves. Nonetheless, they significantly influence these activities by restricting the choices of the individuals concerned. The influence of such structural factors will be missed by the researcher if they are not directly given in the observed data.

This is all by way of saying that if interactional and structural data are to be properly married in research analysis, then the macro properties of settings and contexts must be treated in a systematic manner. Moreover, they must be regarded as phenomena *in their own right*, in order not to be treated as residual or marginal to the 'main story', so to speak. In this respect, settings and contexts must be regarded as patterns of already reproduced relations which stretch away in time and space from the micro encounters which take place within them (and which continuously work to reproduce them in the present).

Both the established character of macro features and the fact that activities always take place within definable settings and contexts means that the researcher must automatically assume that these factors will have some effect on activity and that therefore it will be a matter of understanding as much about as many of them as possible. It is only by making this assumption of equitable influence that the mutual implication of action and structure, macro and micro, can be properly registered in social research and preserved in its methodological procedures.

Interactional and structural typologies

This seeming 'diversion' has been necessary to buttress the point that even if the grounded theory approach were to attend to the role of

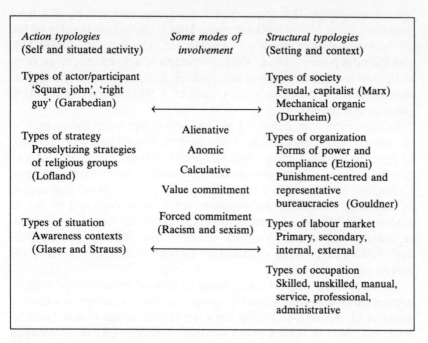

Action typologies (Self and situated activity)	Some modes of involvement	Structural typologies (Setting and context)
Types of actor/participant 'Square john', 'right guy' (Garabedian)	←———————————→	Types of society Feudal, capitalist (Marx) Mechanical organic (Durkheim)
Types of strategy Proselytizing strategies of religious groups (Lofland)	Alienative Anomic Calculative Value commitment	Types of organization Forms of power and compliance (Etzioni) Punishment-centred and representative bureaucracies (Gouldner)
Types of situation Awareness contexts (Glaser and Strauss)	Forced commitment (Racism and sexism) ←———————————→	Types of labour market Primary, secondary, internal, external
		Types of occupation Skilled, unskilled, manual, service, professional, administrative

Figure 7.1   Typologies and social research.

typologies in field research, it would result in a tendency to emphasize what I have called action typologies at the expense of structural typologies. Certainly I would endorse the idea that action typologies are an important adjunct to the evolution of grounded theory and I would encourage their use whenever possible and appropriate. However, my argument has been to suggest that structural typologies are of equal importance. Further, I have suggested that because of the (perhaps unwitting) priority accorded to interactional data in the general framework of grounded theory (and interactionism and phenomenology in general), then the importance of structural typologies to comparative analysis and theoretical sampling is in danger of being overlooked.

Let me now give some examples of action and structural typologies in general before going on to detail the way in which structural typologies can help in the formulation of grounded theory. Figure 7.1 gives an indication of the variety of phenomena involved. As with the macro–micro distinction in general, that between action and structural typologies must not be regarded as 'hard and clean', so to speak, because the phenomena to which they refer overlap and intertwine to a considerable extent. However, as I have indicated previously, action typologies tend to emphasize the domains of self and situated activity as I have described them in the resource map. That is, they largely refer to the internal dynamics of interaction and the individual's relation to it. This also includes perceptual and strategic aspects of activity that result from either the individual's unique biographical circumstances or from their membership of particular groups, such as a religious cult or an occupational community.

In this respect, as figure 7.1 shows, action typologies cover quite a diversity of social phenomena. For example, they include types of actor or types of 'participant' in particular social settings. These, in turn, can be subdivided into member-identified types and observer-identified types. Examples of the former are the 'role types' of prison inmates that appear in Garabedian's (1963) study (square johns, right guys and so on) or Unruh's (1979) types of participation in social worlds (strangers, tourists, regulars and insiders). Examples of observer-identified types are Pahl and Pahl's (1971) types of manager careers (the highflyer, the local jogger and so on).

Action typologies also include classifications of typical behavioural or communicative strategies used in social situations. This covers a diverse range of phenomena including Brewer's (1990) 'forms of talk' used by RUC members in talking about job-related danger (the skills, fatalism and routinization vocabularies); or Lyn Lofland's (1966) modes of entering a public establishment; through to risk and non-risk behaviour among rent boys and prostitutes (McKeganey et al. 1990); and types of client resistance to professional surveillance (Bloor and McIntosh 1990).

Moving on to structural typologies we see that the emphasis shifts towards describing the structural or macro features of settings and contexts rather than interactional dynamics. Structural typologies are also variable, particularly in terms of their generality and the scope and inclusiveness of the form of social organization to which they refer. Thus at the highest level of generality there are classifications of societal types as found in the work of Karl Marx, Émile Durkheim and Max Weber ('feudal', 'capitalist', 'ancient' and so on). At a more intermediate level the area of 'formal organization' has been the focus of many classifications and types. For example, Etzioni (1961) classifies organizational power in terms of three forms: coercive, remunerative and normative. Gouldner (1954) distinguishes between 'punishment-centred' and 'representative' forms of bureaucracy (see Clegg and Dunkerly 1980 for an extended review). There are also typologies of occupations (professional, semi-professional, service, skilled, unskilled and so on) or labour markets (primary, secondary, internal and external) – Krekel 1980, Kalleberg 1983, Layder 1976 and Freidson 1982 have relevant discussions.

It should also be noted that figure 7.1 indicates that there are specific social concepts that directly represent some of (clearly not all) the interrelations between action and structural typologies. These I have referred to as types of social relations or modes of social involvement. These refer to the ways in which individuals are connected to specific kinds of social organization such as occupational communities, prisons, hospitals and so on. In this sense, they depict the substance and content of the typical social relations and forms of attachment that exist between individuals and the social environments in which they find themselves.

Such relations have been variously described in the literature as alienative, calculative, privatized, anomic, value committed, continuance committed and so forth. I do not want to go into these here, I merely mention them for the sake of completeness to indicate that such concepts represent analytic and empirically researchable links between macro and micro processes. Thus they can be seen as bridges linking the two main sorts of typologies that are the subject of the present discussion. (Some aspects of the topics of social relations and modes of involvement in field research are raised in the next chapter.)

To return to the discussion of structural typologies, I want to suggest that those concerned with intermediate forms of organization (occupations, labour markets, formal organizations) are of particular importance for field researchers, especially in connection with grounded theory. This is because it is these forms of social organization that mediate between macro or structural features of society and the interpersonal micro processes of daily life. As 'mediators' they embody, and in a sense 'distribute', the effects of settings and contexts on activity at the same time as conveying and registering the effects of social activity (ranging from far-reaching transformative effects to basically reproductive ones) on the the macro features.

As I have said, the construction of action typologies can be an important feature in the development of grounded theory. However, it is because intermediate forms of organization mediate the mutual influences of macro and micro phenomena that structural typologies take on an increased importance. In this sense, the construction of structural typologies (or the use of already existing ones) in conjunction with conventional field research can valuably feed into, and thus enhance, the process of comparative analysis and theoretical sampling. This is especially the case since Glaser and Strauss envisage comparative analysis and theoretical sampling as forming an essential part of the grounded theory approach. Let me illustrate this with a fairly detailed example.

An example: a typology of occupational careers

My own research on the occupation of acting and actors' careers was prompted by the general questions of how the occupation is organized and what are the typical career experiences of actors (I include both men and women actors in this term). This rather general starting point was necessary since there had been very little work done on acting. Thus the research was exploratory rather than of the theory-testing type, or concerned with the relationships between predetermined variables. I used a combination of documentary research, survey analysis and semi-structured interviews with actors and other members of the entertainment industry (agents, directors, casting directors, producers). However, by taking seriously Glaser and Strauss's notion of comparative analysis and theoretical sampling it soon became clear that my focus needed to be widened.

That is, in order to understand the links between the career experiences of actors and the organization of the occupation, I needed to know how the structural features of the occupation and career in acting differed from or were similar to other occupational careers. In effect, this was applying Glaser and Strauss's notion of comparing one's focal group both with other similar ones and with ones that were quite dissimilar. In this respect the distinct features of the occupation of acting could only be defined and clarified in comparison with other types of occupational careers. By reviewing the research literature on occupational careers I began to construct a preliminary typology. I found that there were quite a number of studies of 'traditional' or conventional careers such as those in management or the professions, especially those which had an organizational setting, but very few on careers which had a short-term contract (or freelance) basis. This discovery reaffirmed my interest in the occupation of acting as a research focus since it underlined its importance as a piece of exploratory research.

Thus my interest in applying the constant comparative method (and the grounded theory approach in general) had led me to the idea of constructing a (structural) typology in conjunction with a fieldwork investigation into the substantive area of acting. The development of a progressively more refined structural typology and the emergence of substantive theory about the occupation and career in acting proceeded hand in hand throughout the whole research process. Both analytic activities provided stimuli for each other and aided the emergence of theoretical categories relevant to both. However, before providing illustrations of this, let me indicate how these ideas relate to the general approach of grounded theory.

Theoretical sampling and the use of typologies

I believe that the form of 'dual input' into the research process described above expands and enhances the basic parameters of grounded theory. This is because it makes comparative analysis more systematic and creates a more flexible approach to theoretical sampling. However, to adopt this position requires that some of the basic premises of grounded theory are questioned and reformulated. First, Glaser and Strauss's approach places by far the greater emphasis on the development of theory from ongoing fieldwork, rather than through 'ungrounded' or 'speculative' theorizing. That is, theory is developed through a continuous dialogue between the gathering of data and the comparative method, which in turn informs the emergence of theoretical categories and dimensions.

Further sampling of the data is guided by these emergent theoretical ideas and this ensures that there is a direct and continuous tie between data gathering and the evolving theory. Also feeding into this process is what Strauss refers to as the researcher's 'experiential data', that is, data 'in the head' drawn from 'the researcher's personal research, and literature-reading experiences' (Strauss 1987: 21). In this manner, extant grounded theories which are to be found in the general sociological literature will enter into the research process. However, by developing a typological model (in this case, of the structural characteristics of the career in acting) in parallel with an ongoing fieldwork project, one can enhance the quality of two of the central objectives of the grounded theory approach.

First, the increased span of the research domain enhances the exploratory potential of the research by spreading, and thus increasing, its empirical penetration. Second, by allowing a dual theoretical input into the research process one increases the theoretical density of the emerging theory. This is entirely in accord with Strauss's view that because of the complex nature of reality, grounded theory must be conceptually dense (with many concepts, and many linkages among them) in order to avoid 'simplistic rendering of the phenomena under study' (1987: 10). By allowing the theoretical feedback encouraged by the parallel development of a typological model, one is allowing an extra theoretical resource to enter into the research calculation.

To their credit Glaser and Strauss are committed to the idea of developing more formal or general theory. However, at the same time they tend to restrict its terms of reference by suggesting that it is grounded in and corresponds to a particular area of sociological interest 'such as stigma, formal organization or socialization' (Strauss 1987: 242). This is confirmed by their insistence that when the focus is on formal or general theory, 'then the comparative analysis should be made among different kinds of substantive cases and their theories, *which fall within the formal area* (p. 242). In relation to the example of my research into acting this meant comparing and contrasting actors' careers with other occupational careers (from gravediggers to government administrators), since they all fall within the formal area of careers.

Using multiple resources

However, it is clear (and an interest in structural typology will only confirm this) that a focal interest in occupational careers intersects with a number of other formal sociological areas. For example, labour market and labour process analysis, class and status stratification, formal organizations, occupational structure and power and domination and so on. It is also clear that this intersection with other areas means an analytic meeting with a number of extant theories that are attached to these areas. An interest in developing typological models as an adjunct to substantive fieldwork makes it apparent that some kind of dialogue with these other theories is required in order to do justice to the empirical overlapping inherent in the research. In this sense, grounded theory must be sufficiently flexible to allow this kind of dialogue, especially with theory stemming from other traditions and perspectives.

Having suggested the ways in which the grounded theory approach must be expanded and amended in order to include the benefits accruing from an interest in structural typology, let me now briefly describe how the twin elements of my own research derived mutual benefit. As I said, my initial interest in developing grounded theory about the career and occupational organization of acting led me to ask comparative questions. For example, how does acting compare with careers which seem to be very different such as in management, the military, technical areas, the civil service and so on? Are there any senses in which they are the same? How do they differ from the careers of lawyers or doctors? In what sense are they similar to the careers of singers, dancers, novelists and artists? Immersion in the empirical data culled from pilot interviews with actors pointed me towards some of the relevant information, such as the importance of agents and casting directors or the regularity of unemployment in acting careers. However, I could not relate this to an overall framework or perspective without being drawn into comparisons with other careers.

It is true that in a specific sense Glaser and Strauss's method encourages the researcher to make these sorts of comparisons. For example, this is necessary in order to encourage the generation of hypotheses and to direct the focus of further sampling. That is, to provide answers to questions: Who next shall I interview? What documentary material exists, and what do I need to look at? However, the grounded theory approach tends to encourage researchers to do this in a rather loose way, as they go along, by applying experiential data (data 'in the head' from research experience or reading) in order to make comparisons. This has the advantage that it does not interrupt the continuous dialogue between collected data and emergent theory. On the other hand, it has the disadvantage that the comparative process may well be rather unsystematic, with the researcher 'plucking' comparisons out of the air, in a rather unordered fashion. This is where the development of typological models provides a record of the comparative dimensions that are of most pertinence to the emergent theory. Thus the emergent theory is more systematically (and therefore more closely) related to the comparative process.

This is why I was led towards the development of a typology of occupational careers after collecting initial interview data on actors' careers. I wanted to build up a systematic picture of the structural properties of careers like those in acting and this necessitated the development of an overall framework in which different types of occupational career could be situated. The provisional typology was developed from a review of the existing research literature on careers. As I indicated, there was a fair amount of material on people in conventional middle-class careers such as managers and professionals, but little on careers like acting where 'naked' market forces seemed to define career progress. This review of secondary sources suggested certain concepts and categories such as 'career appraisal', age–grade synchronism' and the centrally important issue of control over occupations, work and careers. Armed with these initial ideas, but also conscious of the gap in information about market-defined careers, I returned to the interview and documentary data on actors' careers and sampled around the concepts, categories and issues raised by the provisional typology, particularly the issue of power and control over the career structure.

Substantive and formal theory

From this point on in the research, there was constant switching of analytic attention between the substantive area of acting and the typology. As ideas emerged from the substantive area, they would feed into the progressively more refined and elaborated typology. In turn, the comparative frame of reference of the typology suggested ideas about the substantive area. The central category of control as a distinguishing feature of careers emerged in this fashion. As I say, the issue of power and control over the career emerged as part of the provisional typology but as yet I had no idea about how to characterize these things in relation to actors' careers. The substantive analysis of the role of agents, casting directors and producers in actors' careers clarified this for me, and yielded the category of 'shared control'. This notion refers to the fact that career mobility (success or failure in the career) is determined by a mixture of influences, including audience reaction to performances and critics' pronouncements about the quality of such performances.

However, the most influential people in actors' careers are those who channel and control access to work opportunities in the profession. These are employers (owners and producers of film, television and theatrical enterprises), agents, who 'manage' actors' careers and provide work contacts and job information, and casting directors, who decide which actors get which roles in particular productions. To some extent the functions and activities of these groups of personnel overlap. However, the way in which control over the careers of actors is shared (though not necessarily intentionally) is typical of careers in open-market contexts. In this sense, the career situation can be characterized as a balance of power between competing interest groups in the career.

Although the notion of shared control accurately depicts the career situation of actors (and other freelance or market-defined careerists), it only makes complete sense when understood alongside the forms of power and control which characterize the other types of career. That is, shared control in market-defined careers has to be viewed in the context of 'employer control' in bureaucratic careers and 'collegial control' in professional careers. These are the three basic types (along with a number of subtypes and mixed types) which constitute the structural typology. In this way, the central category of control was intrinsically related to the emergent substantive theory about the career in acting (the nature of casting decisions, the nature of agency work, the subjective experience of the career and so on), as well as to the emergent structural typology. The same applied to the other structural properties, such as the different forms of appraisal, the nature of the status structure and the internal labour market and so on.

I think it can be appreciated from this example that the construction of a typological model not only increases empirical penetration and coverage but also adds significantly to the theoretical resources that may be called on in fieldwork. In addition, such model building gives the researcher a flexible (because of its cumulative nature) but none the less reliable benchmark against which particular comparisons can be measured and evaluated. In sum, typological construction is one way in which the comparative method and the theoretical sampling that derives from it can be rendered orderly and systematic. Moreover, these are not the only 'benefits' that accrue from such a research strategy. The whole emphasis on the importance of structural typologies (as against action typologies) is designed to highlight the way in which the grounded theory approach needs to concern itself more with the structural features of social life that are inscribed in the settings and contexts of social activity. An emphasis on structural typology is one way in which a preoccupation with the interactional data that tends to preponderate in field research can be turned towards a confrontation with structural issues of power, domination and control in social life. It is to these themes that the discussion in the following chapter will turn.

Conclusion: some guidelines for field research

Let me conclude by summarizing the main issues dealt with in this chapter. In general I have concentrated on proposing strategies which are intended to aid the process of theory building in field research.

1   First, I dealt with the use of background or sensitizing concepts. These can provide useful, although sometimes provisional, means of ordering data. They allow the researcher to grapple with the broad parameters of his or her data in the initial phases of fieldwork. The main requirement of such concepts is that they have a 'dual reference'; that is, they refer to both objective and subjective phases or aspects of social life.

2   I used the concept of career as a prime example and argued that its usefulness is basically twofold. First, if the concept is carefully used (in a way that goes beyond the limitations imposed on it by previous usages) then it is theoretically suited to research which cuts across the macro–micro divide. Second, coupled with its theoretical versatility, it has an extremely wide empirical scope. Particularly important here is the fact that the concept can trace subjective and objective aspects of social life over time and space.

3   However, the use of any background concept (including 'career') is not meant to be a lead weight that attaches itself to the analysis come what may. In this sense, such concepts are merely 'sensitizing' or 'orienting' devices that may be suggestive of lines of inquiry or modes of explanation. If, during any phase of research, it becomes apparent that the concept is no longer performing this function, or is simply irrelevant

to the problem or issues at hand, then it should be phased out as an analytic reference point.

4   Developing typological models alongside the conventional collection of fieldwork data can be a useful aid to the generation of grounded theory. Again, my point is not that such a strategy must *inevitably* accompany fieldwork (clearly such an enterprise would be irrelevant to some research problems), but that where it is appropriate and feasible, it can expand both the empirical and theoretical scope of the research.

5   In particular, I have emphasized the importance of developing 'structural' typologies which concentrate on the nature of the settings and contexts of activity. This is in order to balance the emphasis on interactional typologies in fieldwork influenced by the grounded theory approach. Interactional typologies emphasize the dynamics of situated activity and the strategies that participants use in their dealings with others. A focus on structural typologies forces the researcher to confront empirical issues that are normally thought to be the province of macro sociology. This also encourages dialogue with analytic styles other than the ones enshrined in the grounded theory approach.

6   The construction of typologies is not only important as a means of generating theoretical and empirical descriptions of phenomena such as forms of interaction, types of careers, political parties, religious organizations, and so on. The typologies also provide systematic benchmarks for comparative analysis and theoretical sampling, both of which are central features of grounded theory methodology.

8

Investigating Power, Commitment and Constraint

Dealing with power in field research

It is unusual for texts about methods or research strategies to discuss the study of power relations. In a sense, this is puzzling since according to many scholars power is a generic feature of social life whose influence is not limited to the sphere of institutional politics and large-scale social change but also reaches into the most mundane features of daily life. The diversity of forms of power, its ever-present character and its ubiquitous nature require that researchers are equipped to deal with it on a routine basis. This is most pressingly the case for those engaged in the kind of middle-range research that I am concerned with in this book. However, most approaches to qualitative methods, including grounded theory, have tended to sideline the issue at the same time as implicitly endorsing a micro view of power which either ignores completely or significantly undervalues the importance of a macro-structural dimension to power. However, it is also true to say that within the micro perspective there is a fairly wide range of views.

At one extreme there is a radically subjectivist strand of social analysis which insists that structural phenomena (like power) are fictive creations of over-zealous sociologists and have no place in the analysis of human behaviour (Benson 1974, Blumer 1969). On the other hand, there are those like Glaser and Strauss who acknowledge the existence of a structural realm, but who tend to concentrate their attention on power in interactional terms as a result of a close-in (and thus myopic) focus on action, meaning and negotiating strategies. In so far as it does not deny the existence of a structural (macro) realm, it almost goes without saying that Glaser and Strauss's view, despite its shortcomings, has greater merit with regard to the problem of overcoming the macro–micro division in social analysis and research. However, there still remains the significant problem of the foreshortening of focus of the interactionist perspective, which has the effect of encouraging researchers to identify and deal with particular aspects of power relations at the same time as it tends to obscure and disregard others.

In the discussion that follows I shall avoid, as far as possible, the labyrinthine literature on power (see Clegg 1989 for a general discussion). In order to go directly to the research issues of importance in this context, I must of necessity skirt round many of the contentious issues and problems associated with the debate on power. For present purposes, I simply want first to identify those aspects of power that are emphasized and those that are neglected by interactionist perspectives. Having isolated the dimensions of power that are regularly overlooked, I shall then present some examples of power and control in the labour process which illustrate the importance of these dimensions for field research in these areas.

This will involve spelling out what it is that researchers using a grounded theory approach should look out for in the analysis of power relations, in order that their emergent theories adequately reflect the macro institutional realities that embed these phenomena. This is then followed by a brief discussion and illustration of the 'dialectic of control' (Giddens 1984), as it applies to this kind of research. The second part of the chapter will then turn to the question of the relation between power and constraint and how this impinges on field research. Finally, the discussion turns towards the question of the nature and type of involvements that fashion the interconnections between people and particular social settings.

The interactionist approach to power

First, let us deal with the question of the kind of power phenomena that interactionism and grounded theory tend to emphasize. A paper by Luckenbill (1979) is very useful in this regard since it is an attempt to develop a conception of power consistent with the symbolic interactionist perspective. Luckenbill insists that power 'is a meaningful activity which two or more individuals do together as a unit' (p. 107). In a power relationship the source of power exercises greater control over the behaviour of the 'target', but there is mutual and intentional adjustments between them in respect of this imbalance. However, these processes of adjustment and negotiation are characterized by a conflict of interest, that is 'a conflict over what is considered best for the participants in the matter at hand' (p. 102).

My point is not that there is nothing of value in this view of power, but rather that its research use is somewhat limited because of its restricted applicability to particular empirical forms of power and power relations. In short, this view of power is more useful in analysing concrete power relations between people where there is overt conflict or tension between the parties, and in situations characterized by 'active' forms of resistance and coercion. Such is the case with armed robbery, an example given by Luckenbill, or the kind of status conflict identified by Gold (1964) between janitors and their tenants over the issue of garbage collection. However, many forms of power and control do not conform to this active and overt model and, as one might imagine, these tend to be the ones that characterize the macro elements of settings and contexts. In this sense, power is often dormant or latent and is built into the the structural features of settings. Thus, forms of power *underlie* or underpin the observable dealings between people. These power relations are the result of historical processes through which have emerged forms of domination and control based on the group possession (including ownership) of valued resources.

To understand these indirect structural forms of power and control and how they combine and interrelate with the more direct interactional forms, we as field researchers working primarily with qualitative data have to do two things. First, we have to widen the interactionist vocabulary for describing power relations. Secondly, thus armed, we must adopt research strategies geared to detecting the wider range of phenomena thus identified. Importantly, it must be borne in mind that macro-structural forms of power often exhibit a low level of visibility. Thus the researcher who is geared solely to observing the more overt aspects of interaction, such as interpersonal or intergroup conflict, may tend to overlook the underlying, more remote and impersonal forms that are inscribed in the settings and contexts of activity. Similarly, structural forms of power represent patterns of domination which are not easily characterized as exhibiting a continuously active mode. It is more pertinent to understand these forms as both dormant and active at different points in time and in different circumstances. Perhaps the best way of understanding these differences is by looking at a few examples.

Power and control in occupations and the labour process

Edwards's (1979) study of the development of different forms of employer control over the labour process in work organizations in the

USA, highlights the importance of a historical dimension in the analysis of power relations from a macro perspective. (Foucault's work (1977) on the emergence of disciplinary forms of power, among other forms, also underlines the centrality of the historical dimension.) In particular, Edwards's study centres on the emergence of 'structural' forms of control over the labour process, which gradually displaced the original 'simple' or 'personal' forms which characterized the workplace in early capitalism. At the end of the nineteenth century and the beginning of the twentieth, because of the relatively small size of firms, control over the workforce in industry was based on the direct personal control of the entrepreneur. Although such personal ties between the owners of firms and their workers often resulted in arbitrariness and favouritism, they also engendered bonds of loyalty in workers.

As the firms expanded in size to reach a wider market, entrepreneurial control was gradually displaced by hierarchical control whereby the 'right to exercise some power had to be delegated to hired bosses' (Edwards 1979: 30). However, as Edwards points out, hierarchical control did not alter the form in which capitalist power was exercised because, in essence, foreman–worker relations in the extended firm were based on the same type of power as capitalist–worker relations in the small entrepreneurial firm. In Edwards's words the 'work tasks were organized and controlled by the continuous, direct, ad hoc, and arbitrary instructions of the foreman' (p. 33). This kind of system increased the visibility of unequal power relations, making it easier for the supervisor to enforce the compliance of the workforce through the power to punish or fire workers. These two 'simple' forms of control are not only of historical importance, they survive in the 'peripheral' economy of the present day (mainly retail and wholesale trades, light manufacturing). However, according to Edwards, at the turn of the century such control ran into trouble because of the increasing size of the firm's workforce and the organized resistance of workers.

Edwards's argument is that structural forms of control were developed in order to overcome the problems encountered by the simple, direct forms. Edwards identifies two forms of structural control: technical control and bureaucratic control. Although technical control preceded the emergence of the bureaucratic form (1945 onwards), and although the latter has subsequently become the dominant form of control, technical control (as with the simple forms) still persists to some extent in conjunction with the bureaucratic form. I want to concentrate on bureaucratic control as Edwards describes it, but first let me briefly describe the main elements of the technical type.

What the technical and bureaucratic types have in common is that they displace the locus of power away from the direct intervention of authority figures (owners, managers, foremen and supervisors) and invest it in the very structure of work itself. Thus, instead of the open exercise of authority, power becomes an invisible part of the work environment. In technical control this transmutation occurs through the deliberate design and use of technology as a means of disciplining the workforce and exacting its compliance. A particularly effective type of technical control is possible in certain industries where continuous-flow production is possible, as in meat packing, textiles and car assembly. Such continuous-flow methods ensure the pace and direction of work without the intervention of foremen or supervisors (and drastically reducing the need for them). In this kind of situation there are no direct personal confrontations, and conflict is mediated by the technology itself. More recently, the use of computer technology has extended this potential for managerial control 'behind the scenes'.

Edwards argues that for what he calls the 'monopoly corporations' (which include single-seller and few-seller markets), technical control proved inadequate by itself and was thus combined with another form of structural control: bureaucratic control. In this type, control becomes embedded in the social and organizational structure of the firm and, as such, is built into the job categories, work rules, promotion and discipline procedures, wage scales, definitions of responsibilities and so on. As with technical control, the overt exercise of power becomes much less important in this type. Instead, the influence of power and control makes itself felt indirectly through the silent machinery of bureaucratic organization.

Thus, although the machinery of control intrudes into the lives of the workers, the operation of power within that machinery is rendered virtually invisible. Perhaps the major element of bureaucratic control is its utilization of, and dependence on, a finely graded division and stratification of the workforce. Edwards cites the example of Polaroid, ranked 230 on the 1977 rating of top industrial corporations by *Fortune* magazine. In Polaroid there was a distinction between salaried and non-salaried staff; and the latter were divided into 18 'job families', within each of which there were between 15 and 30 grades of work. Overall there were some 300 job titles. In addition, there was a pay scheme which consisted of 14 levels, and within each of these there were seven pay steps. This bureaucratic stratification of the workforce meant that there were 2,100 individual slots for 6,397 hourly workers.

Within this system of stratification the depersonalization of control over workers is effectively brought about in conjunction with elaborate job descriptions and the regular appraisals and evaluations based on these descriptions and 'objective rules' of promotion. Edwards argues that workers' cooperation and compliance is enforced by the provision of positive incentives for 'proper' behaviour as opposed to the punishment of 'bad' behaviour. For example, the pay steps establish a clear reward of up to 30 per cent higher pay for those who obey the rules and cooperate. Bureaucratic control reduces the workers' ability to create a workaday culture, it is 'a totalitarian regime demanding not only a hard days work but also the worker's demeanour and affections' (Edwards 1979: 148). Thus the 'good' worker is one who has a 'rules orientation' (that is, one who is a regular and punctual attender) and has the habits of predictability, dependability and reliability and so on. Edwards points out that in this way bureaucratic control rewards behaviour relevant simply to the work itself, and thus represents an *indirect* path to the intensification of work.

Asking research questions about structural power

I have dealt with Edwards's study at some length because it amply demonstrates the points I made earlier about the way power is characterized. First, it vividly illustrates the importance of understanding power relations in a historical context. In this case, it also illustrates the developmental shift from simple forms of control which depend on direct interpersonal contacts (the emphasis in interactionism), to structural forms. Structural power is institutionalized and this has the effect of making power appear to emanate from the formal organization itself. Clearly an approach which concentrates on the direct, active and mutually adjustive relations between two or more people may overlook this form of power. The researcher must be sensitive to the existence of partly hidden, social relations of control embedded in the setting and context of such firms and which lie behind the upfront interactions between workers and authority figures.

Also, many of the other features of power which are emphasized in the grounded theory approach, and the interactionist perspective in general, tend to skew the researcher's attention away from important aspects of power in this kind of setting. Thus, the concern with the meaningful and intentional nature of power relations has the effect of encouraging the researcher to 'home in' on observable activities and relationships. However, this is at the expense of asking questions of a structural type, such as questions as to how worker compliance is secured through the operation of promotion and appraisal procedures. Without doubt, such procedures and structural arrangements do have

meaning for workers and such things may well figure in their deliberations and intentions. However, it is wrong to characterize the power
relationship itself in this way since it is not a face-to-face relationship.
Rather, it is one which is mediated by the impersonal rules and regu-
lations of the work setting. In this example it is also clear that one is
dealing with relations of domination and subordination of a class nature
which have been fashioned through a historical process of struggle. Such
aspects of the general power relation between employers and workers
represent even more remote contextual aspects of control and they are
implicit in the contractual basis of work.

Similarly, although a conflict of interest may characterize the relation
between workers and bosses, and this may at times manifest itself in
such things as strikes, lock-outs or working to rule, it would be wrong
to seize on the notion of overt conflict as a defining feature of power
relations. As Edwards's material makes eminently clear, the great advantage of structural forms of control for those who do the controlling
is that it replaces direct personal confrontation and an emphasis on
punitive sanctions with a set of positive incentives to encourage worker
conformity and compliance. In this sense, structural control cannot be
understood simply as 'operating on' workers from above, so to speak;
rather it becomes an aspect of workers' consciousness, their 'demeanour and affections', as part of a self-imposed discipline.

In a sense, Edwards's study complements Sofer's (1970) study of
industrial managers which I discussed in chapter 5. Although the class
and status position of workers and managers is very different, many
other aspects such as the promotional hierarchy and regular appraisals
are the same. In this respect, the purchase that the mechanisms of
bureaucratic control have on practitioners' aspirations, attitudes and
general orientations is reflected in the managers' willingness to be appraised. In discussing Sofer's study I pointed out that the careers of
managers in bureaucratic organizations give a good indication of the
'established' character of reproduced social relations and practices that
typify social settings.

The way in which structural forms of power and control become
embodied in the consciousness and subjective responses of practitioners
gives us a clue as to how power and control relations that characterize
certain kinds of settings are reproduced over time. These should, and
can be, legitimate focuses and topics of social research undertaken from
a grounded theory or qualitative fieldwork point of view. Yet this is
rarely so since such approaches tend to marginalize or obscure the
structural dimensions of power and the discussion of wider theoretical
topics like social reproduction. As I have said, one reason for the

interactionists' lack of attention to the structural dimension is their tendency to treat power as if it necessarily involved active, direct relations between two or more people. Empirical studies like those of Edwards, of Sofer and of Hochschild (1983) have produced a plethora of evidence to suggest that many types of power and control relations are indirect, impersonal and remote. None the less, such relations lay claim to a large part of the person's psychological demeanour.

Other configurations of power

There are yet other types and configurations of power relations in the occupational sphere which are rather different from those applying to perhaps the commoner or more widespread areas of the labour process. These are apt to be overlooked if approached from an interactionist or grounded theory perspective. In this respect, the partly hidden or poorly visible features of power relations are not a result of the specific nature of the organization of certain settings. In fact, they result from the lack of a unified, crystallized or focused setting. The problem for the researcher in these settings is not only where to look for key powerholders and key areas in which power and control operate, but also how to represent such configurations in terms of emergent theory and concepts. (Incidently, I say 'operate' here deliberately in order to capture the sense in which power relations may influence activity without there necessarily being instances of the actual exercise of power – as in structural control.)

Examples of this kind of situation can be found in craft-like occupations where practitioners' careers are worked out in terms of demand and supply of their skills or services on the basis of the operation of an occupation-wide labour market, as opposed to the 'internal' markets of particular firms or organizations (Stinchcombe 1959). 'Artistic' careers such as writing (including journalism), painting, sculpture, acting, singing (from 'pop' to opera), as well as many professional sports careers (football, baseball, tennis, athletics), are all of this nature, although the details often vary. As Kanter points out (1989: 512), in these careers upward movement 'depends upon establishing an external marketplace value that is reputation based'.

In this sense, there is greater mobility between employers and employing organizations, and this creates room for the operation of career 'intermediaries' such as agents, personal managers, promoters and dealers. The job of these intermediaries is to hunt out or sift through work offers, create career opportunities, negotiate contracts, 'plan' careers, develop contact networks and generally counsel their clients. The influence of agents or personal managers is greatest at two key junctures of the career. The first is at the point where the individual is trying to break through into the more successful core of the occupation. The second key point is when initial success has made the individual's career more complicated in terms of deciding between job offers, negotiating fees for personal appearances and keeping the career 'moving' in the right direction.

Clearly these intermediaries (including the public following and critics) are extremely important to an understanding of the organization of such occupations and the development of careers. However, it is not always clear how such intermediaries exert their influence and how their occupational basis intersects with those of their clients. That is to say, we are dealing here with a network of power interdependencies which is crucial to the question of control over career mobility. We are dealing with relationships that are implicated in both interactional and structural forms of power as well as their interweaving influences. As such, because the grounded theory approach accords primacy to interactional data, it tends to give more analytic weight to this level and thus underestimates the influence of the structural components. The problem of overlooking or simply not recognizing such phenomena is compounded by the fact that these power configurations are generally of a low level of visibility. In addition, they are often 'dormant' (behind the scenes) rather than active (up-front), and regularly involve a coalescence of interests (as well as competitive and conflictual ones).

Moreover, although the degree to which the work of different kinds of intermediaries overlaps is essentially a question to be decided by empirical investigation, researchers should always be sensitive to this possibility since it highlights the relevance of the above problem of visibility. This is because the power configurations involved do not constitute a readily recognizable organizational form in the sense that we normally think of it. Thus they lack the crystallization that results from formally defined connections and conduits. They also lack an overall rule or normative structure which would 'map' the terrain of social influence and draw together the rather disparate constituent elements.

A good example of this is provided by the stratified labour market in acting and the interrelations between the different intermediaries involved in its reproduction over time. For example, the interests and powers of agents and casting directors coalesce in relation to the allocation of work for actors. Their combined influence performs a gatekeeping function which controls the career mobility of actors and has the unintended consequence of reaffirming the status hierarchy among actors. Thus the configuration of power and control elements involves a number of intersecting and overlapping labour markets and status hierarchies (the controlling group of agencies, casting personnel and various kinds of employers, such as producers, directors, entrepreneurs, impresarios and so on). In terms of the occupation and career of acting, these cross-cutting occupational networks, their interlocking nature and their combined influence on actors' career mobility must be regarded as a distinct layer of social organization that both embodies and mediates structural forms of power and control.

The dialectic of control

Giddens (1982, 1984) has drawn attention to what he calls the 'dialectic of control' in power relations. This notion involves two key elements. The first centres on the idea that all human beings possess some power in the form of their ability to transform, to some extent, the circumstances in which they find themselves. It is this ability to respond to the social environment and to manipulate it in some way that is a basic human characteristic. The second element follows from this and points to the fact that although it is usually one person or a group who dominates in a power relationship, the subordinate party always has *some* power (by way of the manipulation of resources at their disposal) which enables them (in varying degrees) to counter or offset the power of the dominant party. Thus a baby can manipulate the emotions of its parents by crying in order to gain attention, or a prisoner can engage in hunger strikes or dirty protests in order to put pressure on the authorities.

As these examples show, subordinate parties certainly do not always have enough in the way of resources at their disposal to transform entirely the basis of their subordination (although clearly at other times they do, as in revolutionary situations). None the less, they always have *some* resources to work with. Thus it is wrong to characterize power relations as if they involved a relation between those who have power and those who are literally powerless. There is always a shifting balance between the parties concerned. I believe that this notion of a dialectic of control is a useful way of understanding the dynamics of power relations, and can be harnessed to an approach which emphasizes a grounded theory methodology. In this respect, I believe that the idea of a dialectic of control (and Giddens's wider 'theory of structuration' from which it derives) is consistent with the previous discussion emphasizing the interplay between structural and interactional dimensions of power.

Certainly it is a useful counterbalance to the idea that structural power simply flows from the 'top down', and alerts the researcher to the ways in which subordinates attempt to deflect, cushion or radically subvert the ongoing forms of control to which they are subject. This is also consistent with Foucault's (1977) idea that power has a 'capillary' form in that it does not derive from some central institution or person, but circulates throughout the whole of society down to the seemingly most trivial micro practices. From a historical perspective, too, it is important to understand the ways in which the balance of power in such relationships has shifted or been transformed over time. (Giddens 1982 gives the example of the development of worker rights through forms of protest, collective action and the wider evolution of citizenship rights.)

However, I think it is worth pointing out that the dialectic of control can take on slightly different characteristics depending on whether we are dealing with power relations between individuals or between groups. It is true that there is always an overlap between what are, in other words, interactional and structural dimensions of power. In this sense, interactional forms of power are always played out under the auspices of some wider institutional backdrop (setting and context), in the same way that institutions are given life by the very activities that they influence. However, this mutual overlapping and interweaving should not obscure the differences of emphasis that appear when the research focus shifts from one level to the other.

A good example of this is the relationship between actors and career intermediaries (and the same applies to the other freelance careers mentioned before). In order to understand the different kinds of social processes that are taking place in the analysis of careers, it is important to distinguish two levels at which this relationship exists. On the one hand, there are specific 'individualized' relationships between particular actors and their agents. On ther other hand, there is the general, occupation-wide relationship between actors as a group and agents (as a group) in their capacity as career 'intermediaries' (which they hold in conjunction with casting personnel). In this respect, a dialectic of control operates for each relationship to some extent independently of the other.

For instance, over the period of an actor's career the balance of power between actor and agent may vary considerably. At the start of the career, while the actor is 'unknown', the agent has more control and influence over the actor. However, the actor may become a famous star during the course of the career, shifting the balance of power in the direction of the actor. During the course of time the public popularity of the actor may wane and again tilt the power back towards the agent. However, the waxing and waning of dependence in this specific actor–agent relationship, although it is related to the general power position of actors and agents, does not necessarily conform to the general dialectic of control between actors and agents as collectivities. Thus the diminution of an agent's power over his or her client as a result of the client's success has no bearing on the general capacities of agents (and casting directors) to operate as 'gatekeepers' to the career success of actors in general.

Similarly, the agents' basis of power in the labour market for actors (contacts and information about work opportunities, the expertise in contract negotiation, counselling and 'career development' skills) is not affected by the uneven spread of control they have over specific clients within their general clientele. The continuities and discontinuities in the power and control relation between actors and agents as occupational collectivities is something which has to be understood in terms of the collective activities of both groups over an extended period of time. This includes such phenomena as the actors' trade union's attempts to secure a minimum wage, the market nature of the career, the ability of agents to impose a code of ethics and to maintain their monopoly on work contacts and information (itself buttressed by their position as intermediaries in an 'open market'), and so on. Thus, while the notion of a dialectic of control is a useful adjunct to this kind of analysis, it is essential to bear in mind that there may be a number of cross-cutting and overlapping 'dialectics' to be considered. This merely highlights the more general point that although interactional and structural forms of power are intrinsically related, they are not always related in the same way, and thus the same empirical or methodological emphases may not apply.

Power, constraint and commitment

Grounded theory, and qualitative aproaches in general, have tended to ignore the concept of constraint as a topic or focus of research. This is, perhaps, because the concept has been largely associated with approaches which have emphasized the primary importance of the influence of structural or macro features on social activity and which have, as a result, undervalued individual creativity in the social process. That is, schools of theory such as functionalism or structural Marxism have tended to see constraint entirely in structural terms as an external limitation on freedom of action. In this sense, people act in terms of the 'demands' or 'expectations' that are imposed on them by society. Of course, to interactionist schools of thought (particularly those influenced by the work of Herbert Blumer), such structural approaches miss out the constructed elements of social behaviour. On this view, the individual acts on the basis of the social meanings and interpretations that arise out of interaction. Here the emphasis is on the freedom of individuals creatively to construct their activities rather than on their submission to socially acceptable patterns of behaviour 'imposed' on them.

There have been notable exceptions to this general interactionist stance, particularly the work of Turner (1962, 1981) and Stryker (1981) who have attempted to incorporate some notion of structural constraint into a symbolic interactionist mould. In my view these efforts are to be applauded since they dislodge the idea that constraint should be exclusively identified with determinism, and also attempt to break down the barriers between macro and micro analyses. Such approaches add to rather than restrict the theoretical resources available to empirical researchers, and in that sense are concordant with the aim of expanding the terms of grounded theory.

In so far as the question of constraint concentrates attention on the connection between social activity and its social environment, then it must become a key element in understanding the way in which macro and micro elements are interwoven in social processes. I have argued that this question cannot be resolved simply in theoretical terms, and thus empirical inquiry must be brought to bear upon it. However, the process has to be two-way, with theory responding to empirical inquiry and research drawing on general theory (as well as theory grounded in the current research project). In this sense, the concept of constraint has to be brought in from the 'cold' of exclusively abstract theoretical discussion and made to serve the interests of research as well as theory.

In this respect Giddens's theoretical work is also of importance since it is an attempt to overcome the division between macro and micro analyses. Giddens's framework (structuration theory) attempts to give equal weight to interactional and structural phenomena in the analysis of constraint. (In this respect it has an advantage over Turner's and Stryker's formulations which tend to absorb the notion of constraint into an interactionist framework.) Giddens insists that constraints are not impersonal forces which compel people to act without their being able to do anything about them (1984: 181). In this sense, constraints only operate through the motives and intentions of people and are thus inherently tied to their freedom to act.

In this manner, structural elements (like constraints) are involved in activity at the same time and in the same way that activity contributes to the reproduction of these structural elements. Social reality is double-edged, and thus the notion of constraint as a limitation on activity imposed by social institutions must be coupled with the idea of 'enablement'. This refers to the fact that these very institutions provide the resources which allow and enable people to do the things they do in social life. A good example of this is language. The grammar, syntax and vocabulary of the language we use imposes on us certain rules concerning sentence construction, word order, general modes of expression and so on, and in this sense constrains our behaviour. However, at the same time, language is a resource which enables us to communicate and create an infinite number of the most elaborate and subtle of messages. In this sense, language facilitates our interactions with others and enlarges our freedom within the social sphere.

Clearly, Giddens's emphasis on the dual nature of constraint and enablement and the way constraints only operate through the motives and intentions of people is an important corrective to those structural approaches which tend to exclude these elements. From an empirical point of view it poses a number of interesting questions about the nature of constraints in particular settings and contexts, and how and in what sense they influence the behaviour and activities that take place within these settings. Both Giddens himself (1984, 1990) and a number of other authors (Preiss and Ehrlich 1966, Turner 1962, Layder 1981, 1987) have noted the possibility of the empirical variability of constraints in terms of their compelling or coercive nature, the extent and inclusiveness of their influence, and the manner in which they are experienced by people.

Turner (1962), for instance, has noted that behaviour in formal organizational contexts (such as that described in Edwards's and Sofer's studies) is more rigidly prescribed than in informal contexts such as the family or relations between friends. Turner suggests that there is more latitude for the creative responses of people in these latter kinds of setting because there is less formal definition of obligations and responsibilities. This suggests a number of interesting empirical questions concerning the nature and types of constraints across a whole spectrum of different types of settings and contexts – for example, different types of organizations and occupations, encounters on the street, encounters between males and females, relations between family members, and so on. Other empirical questions concern the extent to which constraints are experienced as more or less compelling, how inclusive they are and the sorts of strategies people adopt in order to stave off their intrusion into their lives. Goffman's (1968) analysis of the 'underlife' of a mental hospital is a good example of how such informal and 'unofficial' activities provide a means of subverting and cushioning the effects of an authoritarian regime in it's attempts to control the inmate's identity.

By addressing these sorts of questions, field research can connect with general theoretical problems in a mutually beneficial way. Thus some reference to the above issues associated with the notion of constraint could be built into research 'designs' which are otherwise based on approaches which emphasize the emergence of theory. That is to say, the emergent theory could be conceived of as a running dialogue with constraint issues in which the researcher constantly asks questions about what the data and emergent theory reveal about the nature of constraint, the degree of compulsion or inclusiveness involved, and so on.

Although there is a sense in which the empirical ramifications of constraint can be treated in their own right, it is also true that they cannot be separated completely from the question of power and control. Clearly power or lack of power is related to the ability of groups or individuals to overcome, or deal with, the consequences of certain kinds of constraints and to carve out areas of freedom for themselves. In this respect, the kind of power that individuals and groups have in certain settings and contexts is crucially important to understanding the nature of the tie between the individual and her or his social environment. It is to the nature of this tie that I now wish to turn since this again highlights the interpenetration of macro and micro aspects of social reality.

An illustration: occupational commitment and involvement

First, I shall examine some studies of occupational commitment since they highlight the subtlety of social constraints and the interplay between power, activity and structure in fashioning the social bonds between individuals and the settings in which they find themselves. The studies I shall examine have been developed around Becker's (1960) concept of commitment which was originally designed to address the question of why and how people become consistently attached to particular 'lines of activity'. People are committed to such lines of activity to the extent that they are unable to relinquish the activity despite pressure to do so. Why, for instance, do some people settle for relative failure or modest success in particular occupations rather than try their hand at something else?

Becker argues that there are two main sources of this type of commitment. The first concerns the satisfactions and rewards that the individual gains from remaining in a particular occupation, such as pride in the status that follows from attaining promotion, or recognition of one's contribution or achievements by colleagues. The second source derives from the individual's assessment of the penalties involved should he or she want to change tack. Becker gives as an example of this the person who remains in an unfulfilling job because the rules governing the firm's pension fund would mean that he or she is unable to leave without losing a considerable amount of money. Stated in a rather different way, Becker's argument is that, over time, the individual accumulates 'valuables' associated with a particular line of activity which feed into his or her sense of identity or general personal satisfaction. The individual remains locked into a particular line of activity because he or she anticipates receiving more rewards of the kind that have already been gained, or fears losing what has already been achieved.

This is an interesting conception of the way individuals become caught up in social involvements through the subtle interplay of volition and constraint. However, Becker tends to emphasize the volitional elements – the way the individual makes intentional decisions – rather more than the way structural factors such as the power and status situation influence the range and types of choices available. This can be seen if we look at Geer's (1968) study of commitment in the teaching profession in the USA. Geer was intrigued by the finding that most teachers did not want to make teaching an uninterrupted lifelong career and attempted to account for this lack of commitment by applying some of Becker's ideas in her analysis of teaching as a career.

Geer asks the question of what kinds of career valuables are available to teachers, and how these compare with other professions. Compared with high-status professions like medicine and the law (where the process of commitment begins before the end of training), teachers enter a profession far from the top of the prestige ladder and this in itself reduces its potential as a career valuable. However, it is work-related issues that are most interesting in this regard. Unlike other professionals such as scientists, scholars and engineers, teachers are conveyers and transmitters rather than *creators* of knowledge. Whereas these other professionals can see the expanding basis of the knowledge that they have produced as a career valuable, this is not generally available to teachers.

Similarly, the cultivation and maintenance of a clientele is important for partnerships and solo practitioners in law and medicine, for instance. The acquisition of a good clientele 'makes possible a continuing sense of responsibility, pride and satisfaction' (Geer 1968). By contrast, teachers have a captive and low-status clientele – children – and thus they are deprived of the opportunity to establish useful and prestigious relationships during their daily work. Unlike professional athletes and creative artists, teachers have no public audience in terms of which they can measure their success, and thus this major career valuable is not available to them either. Likewise, teachers lack a wider audience of colleagues, something which is associated with scholars, scientists and professionals engaged in research. These colleagues who share interests and follow professional journals constitute a network that both binds the practitioner to the career and enables the career to expand beyond the confines of the local community.

Geer points out that even the traditional career valuable of promotion is of restricted relevance to teaching. Industrial and business organizations and government bureaucracies have a differentiated, hierarchical structure. For the careerist, the climbed rungs of the promotional ladder are looked on as investments of time and energy which are highly valued and difficult to abandon (as is borne out by Sofer's work mentioned before). The organization of schools is characterized by a two- or three-step hierarchy and relatively undifferentiated work; thus the number of positions is small compared with the number of people on the bottom rung of the ladder.

So, in terms of potential valuables related to the work and career itself, teaching is poorly endowed. Certainly, Geer's analysis points to the importance of the lack of structural characteristics which 'allow' people to become committed in the first place by making investments that are difficult to abandon. This problem becomes even more apparent as we move down the occupational (and social class) hierarchy of status and power. The question of why people remain in low-status occupations which have little in the way of intrinsic rewards or interest becomes difficult to answer in terms of the accumulation of valuables.

Forced or continuance commitment

Hearn and Stoll (1975) have noted this problem in their study of cocktail waitresses and have suggested that commitment to low-status occupations has to be understood in terms of a lack of feasible alternatives, rather than any real choice between one occupation and another. In this kind of situation individuals become entrapped in the occupation and thus their commitment is of a 'forced' or 'continuance' type, rather than a 'value' type. This directs our attention to the way structural or institutional factors shape the choices that individuals can make in these kinds of situations. As far as cocktail waitresses are concerned, Hearn and Stoll point out that their commitment changed over time from an initial value commitment (based on subjectively defined rewards), to a form of forced commitment (based on an awareness of the impossibility of a move).

The waitresses typically entered the occupation with positive feelings that it was the 'best' they could find and that it seemed to offer rewards other than simply money (such as the enjoyment of seeing people in periods of play and relaxation), although without doubt money was important. However, as time passed this initial enthusiasm was replaced by a recognition of the true reality of the work. In particular, the waitresses became aware of their subservient position in relation to management, bartenders and customers, and thus that they had little control over their work situation. Also, the anticipated enjoyment of seeing people in times of relaxation was more than offset by obnoxious drunkards, continual sexual harassment and 'superior' and disrespectful customers.

In fact, when it becomes apparent that there are few intrinsic rewards to be gained through the work, the goal of making money becomes a primary consideration. In this respect waitresses begin to rely on such strategies as lying to customers and even short-changing drunks as means to that end. (Note here the dialectic of control at work – the employment of whatever resources the waitresses have in order to gain some control in a situation in which they are relatively powerless.) As waitresses grow older and accrue more and more responsibilities, the alternatives to this kind of work become ever fewer. To the extent that finding another job would involve a financial loss that could not be tolerated given the persistent demands of feeding the family and educating children, then the waitresses are forced into continuing with the job.

So Hearn and Stoll's study illustrates the way in which an initial form of value commitment is transformed as the waitresses, experience reality shock. While they come to experience feelings of degradation, powerlessness and estrangement from the work, they are also entrapped by it and are forced to remain in a job with low status and few intrinsic rewards. Although this study concentrates on the experiences of the waitresses, it also brings to our attention the influence of the structural factors. It is important to incorporate the effects of phenomena such as occupation, class, power, status and gender (as well as the effects of ideology in the legitimation of power relations) when we are analysing subjective experience and types of social involvement. Similarly, Geer's analysis, depending as it does on a comparative frame of reference, forces us to attend to the structural variations that lead to different kinds or forms of commitment.

However, it is important to recognize that while these studies have the effect of underlining the importance of structural factors, it is also true that such factors remain peripheral to the main focus of analysis. This is because of the interactional frame of reference that is built into Becker's concept of commitment, as well as the general orientation of the studies themselves. In this sense, there is great emphasis on the way in which individuals become attached to lines of activity or enmeshed in forms of social involvement as a result of their intentional deliberations. Conversely there is rather less emphasis on the structural factors that provide the settings and contexts for individual experience and social activity. There is a great need for this type of analysis to incorporate structural factors such as power, class status, gender and so on as aspects of the reproduced social relations and practices that are inscribed in the settings and contexts in which activity takes place.

As I have said before, this requires that the researcher or analyst takes into account the different properties that characterize, on the one hand, the face-to-face nature of situated activity and, on the other, the relatively impersonal and established character of the social relations that stretch away from them in time and space. In this sense, setting and context represent the crystallization of social forms that have been reproduced over time by ongoing social activity. As such, structural forms infuse and inform social activity with a force equal to that involved in the processes through which social activity gives life and form to social structures.

From a research point of view it is not a matter of substituting an over-emphasis on situated activity for another, equally lopsided emphasis on reproduced social relations. Rather it is, as Giddens (1984) says, a matter of demonstrating how action and structure are implicated in each other. However, I have been at pains to point out that in order to do this the researcher must be sensitive to the different properties of interactional and structural elements in order to be able to give them appropriate analytic weight. This is particularly important in the case of the study of social constraint where there is a delicate interlacing of subjective experience and social environment, of intentional action and the limits of power.

The need for new strategies of research

Throughout this chapter I have tried to underline the importance of adding to the analysis a structural dimension of topics like power, commitment and constraint from the point of view of theory-generating fieldwork. To this end, I have also underscored the importance of dialogue between emergent theory and general theory. In this sense, my argument is a call for two sorts of research strategies to be added to the existing stock. First, forms of empirical research, particularly those influenced by an interactionist framework (such as grounded theory and qualitative research in general), should more readily borrow from theoretical debates centring on the relation between action and structure and the integration of macro and micro levels of analysis. Thus field research with a primary emphasis on emergent theory could be constructed as a running dialogue with general theoretical issues. In this manner, mutual benefits would accrue for both elements. Emergent theory would be more theoretically informed, and thus possess greater explanatory power, while aspects of general theory would benefit from research input by making its scope and domain of application empirically and evidentially more secure.

The second strategy derives from a call for general theory to more readily incorporate its concepts, axioms, propositions and so on into research designs, and thus more routinely subject them to the adjudication of research evidence. In this respect, general theoretical debates about macro–micro and action–structure links must connect more strongly and clearly with empirical work in this area. Only with this kind of empirical anchoring can general theoretical concepts and ideas be drawn out, elaborated, 'verified' and so on, thus allowing central issues and problems to be tackled in a more thorough and searching manner.

Guidelines for field research

Let me now summarize the main points of the chapter in a more concrete and practical manner as a set of 'guidelines' for field research. As with all the 'guidelines' in this book they should not be thought of in a rigid and formal way. They simply represent the sort of questions and strategies that the researcher *may* find useful for his or her own purposes.

1   The researcher should be aware of forms of power and control relations that operate 'behind the scenes' of the observable interactions of everyday life. Some forms of power and control are built into the settings and contexts of activity, like work or occupational organization. These power relations influence behaviour in a subtle manner and may not be fully revealed by the more overt exercises of power that can be readily observed in behaviour. It is true that many instances of power and control exhibit overt conflict or opposed interests between individuals and groups. However, structural forms of power are often covert in

nature, and characterized by a lack of conflict and an overlapping of interests. Moreover, structural forms of power involve relations of control which operate 'at a distance from the action', although they reach into the heart of such activity. In this sense, they cannot be researched simply by attending to the dynamics of self and situated activity. Some analysis of the reproduced relations of setting and context is also necessary.

2   Researchers must be aware that structural power is 'housed' in settings and contexts that vary considerably. Some types of structural power are housed in formal organizations (such as those in industry, education, medicine and so on). These forms of organization are crytallized, unified and are more 'obvious' by virtue of their visible patterning. As such, they present less of a challenge to the researcher than do forms of social organization that are more spread out and less obviously patterned and visible, such as the market organization of certain occupations.

3   The 'dialectic of control' is a useful conceptual tool for analysing power relations in field research. However, it must be borne in mind that different forms of the 'dialectic of control' may operate with respect to the distinction between structural and interactional aspects of power.

4   A useful starting point for emergent theory in fieldwork is to consider the empirical dimensions of social constraints in different kinds of settings and contexts, such as on the street, at work, in leisure activities. To what extent do these constraints 'demand' conformity? To what extent can they be flouted or manipulated by people in their everyday activities?

5   Another way to develop emergent theory which connects with more general theory is to consider the way people develop different types of commitment to, and involvement in, various social activities over time (jobs, careers, hobbies, emotional ties and so forth). This strategy brings together a concern with personal involvement in social activity with the analysis of structural constraints.

9

The Historical Dimension

The different meanings of history

Although I have mentioned the importance of the historical dimension in field research at various junctures, I have not so far given it the kind of attention it most definitely deserves. That forms of historical analysis should be accorded a central importance in contemporary, theory-generating research is a feature which is not usually emphasized in methods texts. If it is mentioned at all as part of the researcher's potential armoury of 'techniques', it is done in a purely nominal way which, in effect, simply draws attention to the fact that every research project or topic has a 'history' and that the researcher must be aware of it (see Burgess 1984). However, this raises the question of the varying meanings of the word 'history' in this context. Therefore, before proceeding to the core themes of this chapter, let us be clear about this issue.

There are a number of related notions of history that are of relevance here, but they are distinguishable in terms of the time-scale and the unit of analysis involved. For example, the notion of history as the 'history of a research project' mentioned above is clearly distinguishable from the conventional notion of history as a narrative succession of 'significant' events over large tracts of time, by virtue of its much smaller time-span and its reference to a specific research project. I shall refer to this notion of history as the 'internal' history of a research project. When I use the term history on its own I shall be referring to the more general conventional usage. However, even here it is useful to distinguish between what I shall call the 'proximate' (immediate) history of a social phenomenon, and its long-term history, and I shall employ these usages later in this chapter.

Unfortunately, this is not the end of the story. In chapter 1 I introduced the idea that different elements or layers of social life (represented in the research map) have their own 'histories'. That is, selves, situations, settings and contexts possess their 'own' time-scales and represent different units of analysis, as well as sharing the wider, narrative sweep of events denoted by the conventional notion of history. As I phrased it in chapter 1, it is useful to think of these smaller constituent 'histories' taking place 'inside' the larger narrative sweep of historical time which embraces them all. It is important to bear these different notions of history in mind in the following discussion. However, where I think it is necessary, I shall clearly signal the usage I am employing at any particular time.

Fieldwork and historical analysis

In this section of the chapter I want to concentrate on the role of historical analysis in the conventional sense in field research. I want to suggest that a historical dimension in this sense should have a more important role in fieldwork than is traditionally accorded to it in methods texts. However, I do not want to go to the opposite extreme and insist on its absolute necessity. While I believe that a historical analysis can add depth to research which focuses on short-term processes, I do not think that it is an absolute precondition of such analyses. There are several reasons for this which will become clearer as the discussion unfolds. However, one of the reasons is that very often fieldwork has different research objectives from developmental, comparative forms of sociological research. Thus fieldwork usually has a contemporary perspective on social life while these other forms of research, by definition, have a historical perspective.

Obviously, in the latter, tracing the historical antecedents of the social phenomenon that is being investigated is an absolute necessity. This could include tracing its origins. Clearly, in many such cases, for example the development of particular professions, we would be dealing with many centuries of occupational evolution. The question then arises as to whether all or only part of this evolutionary history is relevant to a particular research goal. If, for example the research goal were defined in terms of giving a detailed, historically informed account of the emergence of a particular occupational form then clearly there would not be much that could be left out of the analysis, since even periods when no significant changes took place would gain relevance. However, in sociological research, this exhaustive kind of analysis would be rare since from a sociological point of view it is only significant periods of social change or stability that are of moment.

Thus, right from the start, the sociological perspective would demand that the researcher be selective both about the periods and time-spans selected for scrutiny and the degree of factual detail required to support the arguments. In this sense, the exact parameters of historical data to be considered will be determined in large part by the nature of the problem that is being investigated. Clearly, accounting for the emergence of capitalist industrial society from the earliest human social groupings will demand much more in the way of data and spans of time studied than would accounting for the exclusionary practices of a particular professional group.

Fieldwork studies, in contrast, typically take a much narrower focus, and more often than not exclude a historical dimension. However, even if it were thought that some form of historical perspective would enhance the fieldwork, it would by its very nature require a more limited form of historical analysis. The focus on contemporary activities and short-term processes would mean that a long-term investigation of origins would rarely be required. Furthermore, depending on the nature of the research and its objectives, even this limited historical focus may be of less relevance.

For example, if the research topic was 'interaction in the classroom' and the data consisted mainly of observations of school-children inter-acting among themselves and with their teachers, then a general historical perspective on the teaching profession and schooling would be of du-bious relevance to the central concerns of the research. (Although it must be remembered here that the different 'histories' relating to the biographies and day-to day lives of both teachers and pupils would be relevant to classroom interaction.) Here we must bear in mind what was said in chapter 5 concerning the applicability of the research map. There I pointed out that the researcher will, and must, use both discretion and theoretical judgement in choosing which parts of the map will be of most use. The same principle is at work here; the researcher must de-cide whether a historical dimension will enhance the explanatory power of the framework employed in the research.

Let us dispense with the exceptions to the requirement of a historical dimension and concentrate on those that would benefit from such an analysis. In relation to the research map, the framework as a whole is most pertinent to those research problems or topics which include some reference to the intermediate forms of social organization that are exemplified in the study of occupations. However, even in this kind of research the question of what cut-off points to choose in one's review of the history of the phenomenon is still somewhat problematic. How far back do we need to go before we have given an adequate account?

Again, in a sense, this sort of question can only be answered in terms of the specific problem at hand. Are we attempting to give a causal account of the origins of a particular phenomenon, or are we simply trying to highlight particular features of its evolution?

From the point of view of our concern with theory-generating fieldwork it will be more likely that we are trying to do a bit of both. On the one hand, we would want to be rigorously selective about the periods we study, sticking only to those things that are absolutely essential to our research remit. On the other hand, we would want to say something about the succession of changes that have taken place and why they had occurred. The first thing to be remembered about this kind of fieldwork is that a historical dimension is meant to add *depth* to the analysis, not to become the primary focus. In this respect, a historical dimension is being employed as an *adjunct* to other forms of analysis and data collection. In this context a historical dimension is both a supplement and a complement to the analysis.

History and the nature of sociological analysis

It is necessary to view historical analysis as complementary to this kind of fieldwork for sound theoretical and empirical reasons. These reasons are often either ignored or obscured by those writers who advocate a form of 'historical sociology' without attending to the sorts of distinctions that I outlined at the beginning of this chapter. These writers often assume that all social analysis is historical in the sense of being intrinsically concerned with long-term processes of change (Elias 1978). Alternatively (or in conjunction) such writers assume that sociology is intrinsically historical because all social life concerns the analysis of 'processes in time' (Abrams 1982: 3). Held singly or in combination, these views mask important distinctions between elements of social life and their differing characteristics (as depicted in the research map).

Thus such authors tend to overlook, or at least seriously underestimate, the importance of the distinction between the historical forces that promote specific kinds of processes of social change, and the flux and dynamics that characterize everyday routine forms of behaviour and interaction. However, the erosion of this distinction obscures the unique characteristics that each of these processes possesses. This is where a distinction between macro and micro phenomena is again instructive and important for our overall understanding of social phenomena.

The micro world of everyday behaviour is indeed dynamic and processual in so far as it involves a multiplicity of human beings continually interpreting and reinterpreting the meanings of each other's behaviour, and cooperating or coming into conflict on this basis. However, although it is true that such interaction depends on the not inconsiderable social and cognitive skills of the people involved, much of the creativity produced in such processes remains specific to certain situations. Also, at times, it remains dependent on the presence or otherwise of particular people. That is, in these routine, everyday episodes, the processes of interaction produce their own dynamics and maintain their own localized domains of influence. Most crucially, they possess a personalized character, being based in the main on face-to-face encounters. The evanescent and transient character of these social processes contrasts quite markedly with the rather more far-reaching and impersonal processes of institutional or structural change that characterize the larger movements of history.

This is not to say that there is no connection between these two processes. Far from it. In fact, they are intertwined and mutually dependent on each other. While routine encounters produce their own emergent properties, they are also directly involved in the reproduction of the institutional forms which provide their backdrop, and which have been fashioned through a historical process. So both types of process are connected through the mutual dependence of micro and macro features of social life, a dependence which is 'carried' in the reproductive effects of routine encounters.

However, the main point I want to stress is that although they are locked together in this way, this must not blind us to the fact that these processes and 'levels' of social reality are, in other ways, independent of each other and, in fact, push in quite different directions. As I have already indicated, the routine encounters of everyday life are stamped by their transient nature, their tendency to 'fade away' as the people involved disperse and their paths begin to diverge. This is because such processes can only be sustained by the co-presence of those involved. As a consequence, these processes are also characterized by their personal, face-to-face nature and an indestructable bond with the specific situations in which they occur.

This latter indicates an extremely important difference in the two sorts of social process. The situation-specific tie of everyday encounters means that the time dimension associated with these processes is somewhat different from that associated with larger-scale processes. This is not simply a question of the 'length' of the strip of time involved; it has more to do with the 'quality' or the nature of the time to which we refer and which provides, as it were, the differing 'organizing principles' of the two processes. This is perhaps a difficult idea to come to terms with, inasmuch as we are so intimately bound up with the idea that time is a uniform phenomenon – the clock time with which we are so familiar.

This is potentially a very complicated issue, but I do not want to become embroiled in a debate which is largely tangential to the business at hand. The basic point is that the elapsing of time in situated encounters is marked off in terms of the unfolding of the encounter itself, and in this respect it is linked to the presence of particular people who impress a certain reality on those situations. Thus time passes in terms of the local creation and disappearence of successive umbrellas of meaning formed around the co-present encounters.

By contrast, in the context of wider structural changes, the elapsing of time has to be understood as something which marks out the emergence and eventual disappearance of social forms whose continuity both precedes and post-dates the succesive generations of individuals who come within their domain of influence. By their very definition (and if, indeed, they are to eventually reflect the traditions and routines of certain social groups), institutions must endure beyond the lifetimes of particular individuals and transcend particular situations and encounters. This more diffuse notion of time characterizes the organizing principle which underlies the wider institutional type of social process. The other distinguishing properties of institutional processes follow from this: their relative impersonality, and their independence from situated encounters. In this sense, there is a qualitative distinction between the two processes despite the connection forged between them by the reproductive activities of people in general.

It is because we are clearly dealing with two types of social process rather than a single uniform process that it is not possible to treat historical sociology and social analysis as if they were identical. Those who argue that sociology can only be, and indeed must be, historical in nature are thus dangerously close to an analytic mistake which can result in misleading research claims. In particular, it can lead to the implicit claim that a historical analysis of general social processes can give us an adequate framework for the development of research which has a contemporary focus and which relies heavily on observational data culled from situated interaction.

For example, Elias's (1978) analysis of the development of a personality type emphasizing internal (superego) control of behaviour from a previous type which lacked such controls – as a consequence of a civilising process general throughout western societies – is excellent as a general analysis of behavioural changes that occurred in tandem with various institutional changes. Indeed, this sort of framework may eventually be a source of initial hypotheses adding depth in a complementary sense to a research topic with a contemporary focus. However, in the absence of a clearly delineated appreciation of the quite distinct properties of situated encounters as compared with general institutional processes, there is always the possibility that such a general framework is seen to be sufficient in itself for the analysis of present-centred research drawing on situated data.

This danger is compounded in Elias's case by his insistence that there is no real distinction between the individual and society and that for all intents and purposes they should be seen to be part of the same phenomenon. Such a view obscures an important distinction between the formation of general personality types and the development of specific personalities through unique biographical circumstances. Overall, Elias's position masks significant differences between, on the one hand, general institutional change and situated encounters and, on the other, between general personality types and unique individuals. In this respect, Elias's framework appears to be rather more comprehensive than it really is.

However, when it comes to the analysis of research which draws on observational data from situated encounters, such general characterizations of the movement of history can never furnish us with anything other than provisional hypotheses and incidental contextual information. No matter how compelling and rich in historical fact such schemas are, they cannot supply us with contemporary situated data, or the conceptual equipment to analyse it. Obviously it would be absurd to argue that research with a contemporary focus could substitute for historical analysis. I hope I have indicated that the obverse is also a quite inadequate basis for social analysis.

We have to be sensitive to the profoundly significant differences in the properties of social reality that feed into different kinds of social processes. Only in this way can we understand the nature of the cooperative dialogue that can and should take place between the historical analysis of social processes and fieldwork that has a contemporary focus. I shall be going on to give an example (from the acting profession) of the sort of research that attempts to establish just such a dialogue but, before I do, I want to say something about the nature of the data and methods that are of use in this kind of historical research.

Data and method in historical analysis

The first thing to note in this regard is that, because our primary interest is in short-term research with a contemporary focus, our additional historical research does not require extensive use of primary sources. As a form of evidence that is going to add depth to our analysis in a supplementary manner, it is not encumbent upon us to search out new or original sources for our work. We have to bear in mind that the main burden of originality in the kind of research we are concerned with here will centre around the analysis of primary data drawn from a short-term time frame.

Of course, a historical dimension may contribute to the originality of the analysis and the theoretical ideas that are generated directly or indirectly through the research. However, this does not necessitate that our historical materials be newly discovered or original. This parameter, so to speak, has the effect of keeping the research within manageable and practicable proportions. What is of paramount importance is that we utilize as much relevant data as we can in order to achieve as rich an analysis as possible. In this respect, my concern is to encourage researchers to utilize the vast fund of reliable historical data already gathered by historians, biographers, archivists and diarists and available to us as secondary sources.

For all practical purposes and in the absence of any evidence to the contrary, we should treat this data as reliable, valid and as representative. (See Scott 1990 for a discussion of the authenticity, credibility, representativeness and meaning of documentary sources.) Of course, we must make checks on reliability and so on by examining several accounts of the same event or of the social conditions of the time. However, having done this, and also having satisfied ourselves that the sources are properly documented and cross-referenced where necessary, we may assume that we can draw freely on the data. As might be imagined, the problems for social analysis begin to arise in relation to the question of making forays into the data, making relevant selections and thus emerging with appropriate material. These problems arise, of course, because the historical narratives we are using as resources were not originally constructed with a sociological audience in mind. Our task is to determine which data, from a vast potential array, can best serve our purposes.

However, in one sense this problem is not unlike the one routinely facing the researcher collecting primary qualitative data through interviews or participant or non-participant observation or even documentary sources other than historical ones. (See Platt 1981 for a similar argument.) All these situations require two further stages of selection. In the first stage, while the researcher is in the data-gathering situation, he or she needs to be able to absorb the information as it presents itself. At the same time, the researcher needs to be able to recognize elements that are of relevance to either the emerging theoretical elements, or to the preconceived conceptual framework. However, even an experienced researcher would find it difficult to make all the appropriate data selection decisions at the point of collection. Thus the researcher will gather an amount of data that is far in excess of what will be needed eventually.

The second stage of selection will come as the researcher reviews the collected data, develops a set of coding categories, and orders the data in terms of them. This ordering will enable the researcher to make decisions about whether to concentrate attention on particular aspects of the data as important explanatory or illustrative resources. (Of course, it needs to be emphasized that the remaining data should not be discarded or destroyed since it may be of use at some future time.)

These same stages will be pertinent to the analysis of secondary historical data. The ability to recognize what is of relevance in these two stages will depend on familiarity with sociological issues, concepts and problems, as well as increasing experience of this kind of research. The main feature of historical materials that requires special attention derives from the fact that they are documentary sources. The fact that documents are a written source of data demands the ability to read in a rather special way. In this sense, the elements that are of most relevance may not be contained directly and obviously in the historical narrative itself. The narrative may have to be 'mined' and interrogated until it yields up the answers.

Developing theory from historical analysis: an example

To illustrate this and some of the other points I have talked about generally, I shall now focus on the example of the acting profession in Britain. In previous chapters I have discussed some of the research strategies I used to analyse the different aspects of the occupation of acting from a contemporary point of view. In the light of what I have said so far, we can ask: how would a historical dimension add depth to this analysis? To answer this question we need to return to the original concerns of the research. It will be remembered that my interests were quite specific in that they concentrated on certain questions rather than others. My primary interest was in how the occupation was organized and how this affected the general career situation of actors. It can be appreciated that this focus moved other potential questions to the periphery of research interest. Thus, the position of women in the profession or the exact class composition of the acting population were only of importance as they impinged on the focal interest.

The occupation and career were analysed in terms of the different elements of the research map: context, setting, self and situated activity. They represent different levels at which macro and micro aspects of social life intersect and interfuse with each other. It will be recalled that as one aspect of the analysis, I was developing a typology of career structures in order to situate the acting career in a comparative framework. It was felt that this typology would be suggestive of concepts and theoretical ideas pertinent to the analysis as a whole, and would complement any theoretical elements that emerged directly from the primary substantive research.

Let me now try to demonstrate how a historical dimension helped in the analysis of these areas of interest. It did this in two ways. First, it served as a check on the validity of the concepts, models and forms of evidence that I was using, while also enriching these things through the accumulation of an alternative kind of empirical data. By tracing the variable forms which the organization of the occupation had manifested throughout its history, I was able to engage in some fine tuning of the typology of contemporary career structures. In this respect, although my analysis of the secondary data from which I was constructing the typology did contain some historical material, especially in relation to the more bureaucratic forms of career, there was little if anything on the more open-market forms. Thus, historical material on acting would partly fill this gap and help me to say something about the way open-market types evolve.

The second area or direction in which a historical dimension could help was in enhancing the substantive analysis of the occupation of acting itself. In this sense, the proximate history of institutional and organizational change that the occupation had undergone would give greater insight into and more incisive analysis of the structure of the labour market. It would also throw light on the power position of career intermediaries by suggesting the kinds of processes that were involved in their evolution. In both these ways a historical dimension can add to the analytic resources from which one can subsequently generate more informed and sophisticated theory about career processes and structures.

The data that was at my disposal in order to 'block in' the antecedent forms of the occupation and career were basically of two types. One type was the accounts by professional historians or writers on the social history of acting. These mainly focused on particular periods, such as the Elizabethan era or the nineteenth century, and from the point of view of my own research they represented secondary sources of data. (Although, of course, they were based on original research.) The other type of data was that drawn from biographies and autobiographies of actors. Biographies have to be treated like the other secondary sources since they represent data that has already been 'worked on' or analysed from a specific point of view. However, the autobiographies could be regarded as primary data inasmuch as they had not been used for further analysis.

Blocking in sequences of change

The first analytic problem encountered was that of deciding what was the relevant span of time for the purposes of the study. A preliminary review of the material suggested that the first definite indications of a move towards the occupational organization of what were then wandering entertainers was reflected in the Act for Restraining Vagabonds in 1572. The fact that the time period involved was rather sizable posed the problem of whether to select a smaller period or attempt to cover it all. However, in order to make an informed decision on this it was necessary to have a rough idea of the whole sequence of changes involved so that periods of greater or lesser importance could be identified. Thus material was chosen to give a skeletal coverage of the main changes that had taken place within the whole period. Analysis of this material suggested that it could be broken up into four important subperiods within which the occupation and career could be seen to have taken on fairly distinct forms during its evolution towards the present market type.

In one sense, the dates that separate the subperiods are arbitrary in that social change does not often occur in the rather abrupt and 'discontinuous' manner that is suggested by such temporal markers. However, in another sense the dates were not arbitrary; they were chosen because they signalled significant changes in occupational practice. In three cases the dates indicated legislation which either initiated occupational changes, or simply reflected and legitimized changes that were already in train. In the fourth case the temporal marker (the end of World War I), was a purely analytic device used to distinguish a whole cluster of related changes which were taking place simultaneously and which had begun at roughly the same time.

The two focal dimensions of change of most relevance to my research were changes in the organizational form of the occupation and, since the two are related, the resulting differences in the career structure. It was with reference to these dimensions that a subsequent fourfold periodization was developed. By sifting through the historical materials and extracting core features and concepts, this mode of analysis yielded four distinct historical periods through which the occupation and career had passed. The next step was to develop sociological characterizations of these periods based on the perceived changes in the organization of the occupation and the career context. Of course, at this stage the characterizations were provisional in nature, but none the less they served to order the data in a way which would make the eventual identification of typological elements much easier.

This was the first stage in the analysis of the data and involved condensing the material as well as sorting it into provisional categories. As I hinted before, this sort of operation requires some prior knowledge of the relevant concepts and categories. This in turn not only requires a general sociological grasp of issues and concepts, but also demands a fairly detailed knowledge of the specific area in focus. In this case, knowledge of concepts, processes and properties germane to the analysis of careers was a precondition of being able to match particular pieces of data with the particular conceptual categories that appeared in the four 'characterizations'.

In my case, I had begun the analysis from a present-centred career perspective and was concerned to establish a comparative perspective in the form of a typology. This meant that I had extensively reviewed the secondary literature already, and therefore I had an intimate know-ledge of this area. Thus, I had prior knowledge of significant 'ordering' concepts and themes such as the nature of control over the career, typical career routes, forms and criteria of appraisal, types of social relationships, forms of occupational organization and so on. This prior knowledge allowed me to order the data in terms of a four-phase evo-lution of the occupation.

Perhaps the main motive that underlay my concern to develop his-torically informed typological models were questions as to how long the market type had been in place, and what forces had been involved in its development. The sequence of changes represented in the four-phase characterization of the evolution of the occupation and career allowed some purchase on these questions. So my intention was to try to ensure that the analysis of the historical data directly informed the develop-ment of models of preceding occupational forms underpinning the career system in acting. Further, and as a consequence, I wanted the analysis of the historical data to lead to the refinement and sharpening of the model of the contemporary career situation. In the long run, this in turn would feed back into the overall refinement of the general typo-logy of contemporary career structures. (See chapter 7.)

The four characterizations of the occupation and career that corre-sponded to the four phases of its social development can be summa-rized as follows:

Phase one

The earliest period between 1572 and 1642 witnessed the initial organization of a rather disparate group of wandering entertainers into an occupational group that was eventually to become the acting profession. The main features of the group at this time were the newly established feudalistic ties of dependence and noble patronage; the rudimentary emergence of a commercial market; the development of craft-like forms of organization and control over the career.

Phase two

The second phase begins after the Civil War of 1660 with the establishment of the Royal Patent Houses, and continues until 1843 when the Theatres Regulation Act was passed. This period saw the proliferation of diverse forms of theatrical activity: the rise of the provincial stock companies; the emergence of actors as salaried employees and the role of theatrical entrepreneur; the development of regularized career routes from the 'training grounds' of the stock companies to the metropolitan patent houses.

Phase three

The third phase covering the period 1843 to 1918 saw the consolidation of the commercial basis of the theatre after the Theatres Regulation Act abolished the monopoly of the patent houses and created the conditions for free trade. This stage also saw the emergence of a middle-class audience; the increased status of actors and the further consolidation of the influence of market forces in the career in the shape of the 'long run' and the consequent emergence of short-term contracts. Alongside these moves towards a progressively freer market, especially in the more commercial metropolitan area, there were pockets of regular employment provided by the permanent ensembles led by the 'actor-managers'.

Phase four

The final phase, from 1918 to the present, deals with a great number of changes and developments: the development of drama schools and an actors' trade union; the infusion of working-class actors into a predominantly middle-class occupation; the emergence of non-theatrical entrepreneurs and commercial touring systems; the consequent development of typecasting and the consolidation of the star system. At the same time, there was also a diversification of the market for acting skills in the shape of the emergence of two media, film and television, and an increase in the significance of agents and casting directors as career controllers. There was a development of state patronage to help finance quasi-permanent ensembles of actors; the emergence of the repertory movement in the provinces; the decline of actor-managements; and the depersonalization of work relationships, and the emergence of the casual-labour status of actors.

Although the above series of characterizations is based on a wealth of material, I do not propose to discuss detailed issues stemming from this material. In this sense, the characterizations have to be regarded as sociological 'summaries' of the periods in question, although it must be borne in mind that the summaries are related only to a limited number of issues concerning the occupational career context. As I have said, these characterizations are but the first stage in a continuing process of condensation of the historical data. They represent a 'sifting through' of a diversity of material in order to establish the broad parameters of the issues relating to the career context.

Identifying core elements

The 'analytic sifting' mentioned above renders the material more manageable from the point of view of identifying elements that will be important in the construction of typological models. The clarity achieved by the condensation allows a swifter targeting of important typological 'variables'. It is to the building of such typological models that our attention must now turn. Prior to outlining the above characterizations, I mentioned that in order to match data with relevant concepts and issues the analyst has first to possess, and then to apply, knowledge of the relevant concepts and so on to the analysis of data.

In this sense, one is taking a broad trawl of the data. By keeping the conceptual net as broad as possible, the analyst is keeping her or his options open. In this way, the analyst is letting the data fill out, reflect or elaborate on the broad framework of conceptual elements which act as background 'guidelines' to the analysis. Of course, these guidelines do act selectively in that they direct attention to particular aspects of the data at the expense of others. However, at this stage the analyst should ensure that the guidelines are applied in an undogmatic fashion. This in turn will ensure that the selective targeting that results from their application is regarded as negotiable. It is important, particularly at this stage, that the operation of the guidelines should merely afford 'suggestions' or 'possibilities' rather than non-negotiable directives. This kind of application will make it possible for unanticipated findings to be more easily assimilated by the analytic framework.

However, as analytic attention turns to the question of the construction of typological models, the broad trawl strategy becomes less relevant. The objectives now should be twofold: to focus in on key elements or variables, and to sift out all extraneous details. As far as the first objective is concerned, the problem is to reduce the conceptual elements involved by moving away from a general concern with *all* career-related concepts, variables, categories and so on, to a specific focus on a core group of them.

In so far as we are dealing with a typology and are thus interested in developing models, in this case of career structure types, then it is essential that the core concepts and variables be exclusively type-related. Specifically, this core group must represent the criteria by which the different types are distinguished from each other. In my case, the core criteria could be identified fairly readily since they had emerged from the prior work I had done on the development of a present-centred typology, and thus could be applied to the historical data.

Although this was the most appropriate strategy in this particular case, I do not want to suggest that analyses must always follow this sequence. If, for example, analysis is begun from a historical point of view, then the core criteria could not be imported from a parallel analysis of the contemporary situation. In such a case the core criteria would have to be derived from a sociological examination of the historical data. That is, the historical data would have to be measured against the relevant sociological literature on occupations and careers. In effect, this almost amounts to the construction of a rudimentary typology, a working model, while centrally involved in a somewhat different enterprise.

As this implies, such a strategy would make the task more difficult and 'messy' than it need be, and thus the former strategy is to be recommended. My point is, however, that while it is not absolutely essential to begin such an enterprise from a contemporary viewpoint, an examination of the historical data in and of itself would not furnish the analyst with the core criteria. One has to bring to the historical data a sociological sensibility cultivated by exposure to relevant secondary literature, in order to be able to impose on it an explanatory pattern.

Even if this recommended route is followed, the comments made in chapter 7 concerning the development of typologies alongside other theory-generating strategies are pertinent here. As I pointed out, in operation the different strategies are to some extent dependent on each other, and thus the development of theoretical elements from different sources will be going on simultaneously. In this respect, the additional utilization of a historical dimension is no different. That is, one of the central purposes of the historical examination is to add to, complement and otherwise supplement the other theory-generating sources deployed in the overall research strategy.

This implies that the historical material must, at least potentially, be able to influence the other theory-generating elements in a relatively independent manner. Specifically, in the case of the career structure types, the historical dimension has a crucial role to play in validating and refining the other theoretical elements, especially the typology. This role is buttressed by the fact that this kind of multiple strategy research will depend heavily on the uneven development of the separate components. In short, viewed in this light, the whole research process cannot be characterized as ordered and linear. Rather, it resembles a succession of direction changes in a shuttling or zig zagging pattern, back and forth between different data and theory sources or inputs. In essence, this means that core elements, while being core, must be open to revision in the light of emergent evidence and theory.

Typologies and the historical dimension

Let us return to the problem of the application of the core criteria to the four-phase characterization of the evolution of the occupation of acting. As I said earlier, in my case I could readily identify the core criteria. Notwithstanding what I have just said about the potential revisability of the core, the core criteria will in all probability be fairly abstract in character and this will facilitate their application and relevance to a wide variety of empirical phenomena. In one sense, this general applicability will create the flexibility that is implicit in the requirement that core criteria be potentially revisable.

Such is the case with the core criteria associated with the career structure types. In fact, these were four in number and can be expressed as follows;

1 Mode and agencies of control over the career structure.
2 Type of career context: the social organization of the occupation.
3 Dimensions of mobility and type of status system: labour markets & formal organization.
4 Type of appraisal and criteria involved: systematic and defined or dispositional and diffuse.

Perhaps not surprisingly, when these criteria are applied to the data contained in the four-phase characterizations, they yield four typological

Occupational control	Craft autonomy. Careers usually company-tied and based on seniority.
Employer control I	Transitional phase. Move away from craft autonomy towards commercial market (control mixed). Development of managerial component. Employee status of actors.
Employer control II	Full development of market principles. Restricted and regular career routes. Paternalistic companies.
Shared control	Control shared by employers and intermediaries (agents, casting directors, producers, critics). Proliferation of work media. Multiple career routes and impersonal market relations.

Figure 9.1 Career types in acting.

models of the career in acting. These are illustrated in figure 9.1. However, it will be immediately obvious that although four types are identified they could logically be reduced to three, in so far as one of them – Employer control I, – essentially represents a transitional phase. That is, it represents a cumulative process of development away from the internal control over career mobility derived from the craft autonomy of the occupation. It represents a move towards employer control as a result of the steady commercialization of acting and the rise of the theatrical entrepreneur. So the Employer control I phase represents a mixture of elements deriving both from previous feudalistic and craft-like forms of organization and from the embryonic capitalistic and commercial features that would eventually become dominant.

For our present purposes then, we are dealing essentially with three distinct types of career structure. First, there is a type based on internal occupational control, which in turn is based on craft autonomy. That is to say that it was the actors themselves (particularly in the form of senior members of acting companies) who controlled access to the occupation and thus a career in acting. This included a system of promotion within companies based on seniority. As I have already intimated, this was followed by a long period which witnessed the progressive establishment of a commercial market, a managerial component and employee status for the actors.

This long-drawn-out process eventually produced the second type of career structure based on (external) employer control, which in turn was related to and conditioned by the need for commercial success. The mobility context was such that although actors were nominally free to move between different theatres and employers as the demand for their services dictated, they were in practice limited to a restricted number of recognized and regularized career routes. This situation was also complicated by the existence of a number of permanent ensembles owned and led by actor-managers who paternalistically oversaw, and effectively controlled, the careers of those actors within their companies.

The third main type of career structure, and the one that has come to characterize the present situation, is based on shared control. This reflects both the dominant influence of intermediaries in the careers of actors today and the steady proliferation of work media and work locales that are available. Any remnants of employer paternalism have been replaced, in the main, by a diversity of impersonal relations between many possible employers. The multiplicity of potential career routes and the general complexity of the career in terms of the technical and psychological demands made on actors has added to the power of agents and casting directors as career intermediaries. As a result, the career context is one which is dominated by market factors and this is reflected in the segmentation of the labour market.

In relation to general research strategy, it can be appreciated that this resultant threefold typology literally adds another dimension to the analysis. The typology places the present career situation of actors in the context of prior forms in which market factors were influenced by different modes of occupational organization. In terms of the elements of the research map outlined earlier, the career setting mediates the two-way influences of the wider context and the social activities which are the stuff of day-to-day occupational life. In fact, this precisely characterizes the way in which the organization of the occupation in acting gives rise both to an overall career context or 'structure', and to a resulting pattern of typical career routes, career processes and subjective experiences.

Of course, I have only taken the analysis so far, in order to illustrate the way in which the predominant influence of the market on the present-day form of the career grew slowly out of the preceding forms. From the point of view of using historical analysis to complement other research and analytic strategies geared to present-centred research, this 'depth' of analysis is sufficient for this purpose. However, clearly the analysis of the emergence of the market could go much further, becoming a focus of interest which displaces the primary concern with the career context. This, of course, would then become another research project in its own right!

In relation to general theory-generating research strategy, the resultant typology also provided a check on the market-type model that I had used to depict the contemporary situation of actors. The initial model proved to be roughly accurate, although certain refinements could be added as a result of the historical check. The importance of the notion of 'shared control' was emphasized and the idea of the market having varying modes and levels of influence in the preceding occupational forms was also highlighted.

As far as the typology in general was concerned, the historical analysis impressed on me the fact of the enormous diversity of market influences mediated by occupational forms as a consequence of their historical evolution. Thus, in general terms, the typology began to possess analytic depth by beginning to furnish a temporal and processual context. Quite apart from the typology, the addition of a dynamic temporal dimension also contributed to the richness and density of the analysis of the contemporary form of the occupation. For example, it was possible to develop a temporal perspective on the emergence of the gatekeeping function of agents and casting personnel, and to appreciate how the changing class composition of the occupation has affected careers generally.

Macro processes and the analysis of settings

It must be pointed out that in the above example the historical sweep of data was in no sense exhaustive, and neither was it meant to be. With regard to the research sectors outlined in chapter 5, it may or may not be apparent that I concentrated on a particular slice of data. In this respect, the wider macro context took a definite back seat to my scrutiny of the occupational setting of acting. This, of course, was a strategic decision in terms of the initial design of the project since career structure was conceived to be directly related to these intermediate forms. However, it is also true that these intermediate forms are reciprocally related to wider macro features and processes and thus, in a sense, they have to be understood in relation to them. That is to say that these processes mutually reflect each other, and therefore this fact must register itself in our descriptions and analyses. However, the question of whether or to what extent the unravelling of this relation in empirical terms should be, or become, the central point of interest is rather a different question.

Let me put it another way. Clearly, the consolidation of market forces and their impingment on actors' careers had a definite connection with

wider social processes such as the emergence of an industrial bourgeoi-
sie, the development of industrial organization and commercial activity
in general. For example, it was no accident that the actor-managers
exerted authority over their actor employees in a paternalistic fashion
(see Harwood 1971) at a time when paternalistic forms of owner-
management were prominent in the industrial sphere (Dahrendorf 1967).
However, although these are intrinsically interesting parallels and connections, from the point of view of laying bare the organizational forms
that provide the career contexts of particular occupations, these connections are only of secondary interest. The point is that if they were
to become the primary interest, then in effect the research project would
itself be fundamentally transformed.

This is similar territory to that covered by the question of the extent
to which a historical analysis is a necessary adjunct to research with a
contemporary focus. Earlier I suggested that the role of a historical
dimension was to add analytic depth in a complementery fashion to
such research. This recommendation necessarily implies the rejection
of the point of view that sociological analysis *must* include a historical
dimension in the long-term, general sense. Of course, it must be recognized that all research is located in time and space, and thus the
'internal' history of a research project will automatically affect both the
conduct of the research and the explanatory accounts produced by
the research. However, there is no reason to accept the view that it is
necessary to have an explicit historical or developmental perspective in
the wider sense in order to grasp the dynamics of social processes contained within the more restricted scope of present-centred research.

The same kind of objection can be levelled at the contention that a
focus on macro process is somehow primary and must be a feature of
historical research into social processes. Although macro and intermediate features are undeniably interwoven with each other, there is no
need to suppose that the 'larger' questions have some sort of primacy.
The question of what level or slice of data one should concentrate on
is first and foremost a strategic question which will depend on the aims
and objectives of the research. Thus the particular question of whether
to unravel the interconnections between macro and intermediate phenomena must be adjudicated in relation to the central research interest.

In this sense, the question of macro processes in general (as well as
any interconnections) has to be bracketed out of the analysis while
concentration is fastened on to intermediate social forms and processes.
Much the same applies to the other research sectors (situated activity
and the self) in so far as they too become peripheral to current concerns. Again, it is not that these are not intrinsically interrelated with

each other and the 'larger' sectors, it is rather that they are bracketed out of the analysis for strategic and methodological reasons.

Situated activity and history

Situated activity poses a unique problem from the point of view of historical analysis, and this derives from the fact that the notion of 'situatedness' can refer to two distinct types of phenomena, with their corresponding empirical indicators. The first meaning associated with the notion of situated behaviour centres on the notion of co-presence. That is, face-to-face interaction between real, describable people. This sort of phenomenon can be described and analysed either in terms of direct observation, or by mechanical means such as a tape and/or video recorder. The crucial requirement is that a direct and exact record be kept of the events as they unfold, in order subsequently to reconstruct the events in analytic terms.

The second meaning of the term 'situated' refers to the way sociologists imaginatively reconstruct typical forms of behaviour in times past or for situations for which we have no direct access to observable behaviour. Max Weber's depiction of the 'Protestant ethic' and his analysis of how this influenced typical modes of economic conduct is an example of this kind of reconstruction (Weber 1930). In this sort of example it is clear that because there is no direct access to the activity or conduct that is of central interest, the status of the account produced by the sociologist will differ considerably from an account that has benefited from direct access to the emergent interaction.

Although the accounts are ostensibly about the same kind of subject matter, in fact they have different groundings. One is grounded in an actual concrete episode involving and dependent on the co-presence of specific people, while the other is grounded on typical forms of conduct imaginatively reconstructed from various documentary sources. It follows from this that the respective explanatory accounts produced on these different bases are not interchangeable. They are about different things and serve divergent purposes. Since most of the subject matter of historical analysis is located in the past, this provides an obvious obstacle to the development of accounts that are truly 'situated' and hence dependent on direct access to the phenomena. Therefore it is to be expected that the majority of accounts of activity and conduct in everyday situations will more closely approximate the reconstructed type (for example, historical accounts which purport to evoke 'daily life in the time of . . .'). Of course, in autobiographical accounts by people who were actually involved in the situations they are describing, one is apparently getting much closer to the real substance of the event than is possible, say, with secondary accounts such as biographies or documentary interpretations.

However, this seeming 'closeness' may be more apparent than real and should be treated with caution. There are two reasons for this. First, there is no way in which the veracity of the account can be checked and therefore we should allow for the fact that a person may gloss an account in a way which reflects a favourable impression of their own behaviour (see also Scott 1990: 174–85). Second, it must be remembered that we are interested in sociological accounts of situated activity and this requires that the perspective adopted has to be one which goes beyond the subjective responses of particular individuals and embraces the criss-crossing interactive effects which are 'group' emergents. It goes without saying that this sort of perspective is missing from the vast majority of historical, autobiographical accounts and thus they cannot be used as reliable data sources for this particular kind of work.

The notion of oral history derived from interviews with subjects who can remember particular epochs and events is seemingly another way round this problem. However, the difficulties associated with autobiographical accounts apply equally to oral history, since the fact that one is speaking to a living person does not ensure that this person will be any less disposed to recounting their exploits in a favourable light. Certainly the problem of perspective does not recede with oral history since the respondent would need to couch a personal account in terms of a group perspective in order to provide the sociologist with relevant data. Of course, if the whole point of the research is to establish imaginative reconstructions of typical conduct, then oral history may provide a rich fund of suggestive data, providing that we bear in mind the problems of recall and glossing.

Oral history plays its most crucial role in research when interviewees are asked to recall the atmosphere associated with particular epochs or their responses to events of national or public importance, where they were never directly involved on a face-to face basis. The data gathered in this manner is invaluable for the purposes of evoking the texture of particular periods and the important events of the time. The great advantage of having interviewees focus on these sorts of events is that the problems associated with ego protection and identity management are largely absent when this kind of recall is required. Of course, this has to do with the fact that the researcher is asking the respondents to talk about things which they have 'experienced' in a less personal sense than participation in a co-present encounter. Thus interviewees may readily provide reliable and genuinely informative data regarding their own (and others') feelings, say, about the war years, or royal occasions. However, it is important to bear in mind the background of the inform- ant in such cases – a royalist may describe a royal occasion differently from a republican.

So historical analysis poses unique and interesting problems for the study of situated behaviour. As far as personal identity and the self are concerned the problems appear to be less numerous and less intracta- ble. An obvious source of data here would be the very autobiographical accounts that provide such problems for the analysis of situated behav- iour. Although the person writing an account of their own life may wish to have themselves regarded in a particular way, a skilled and experi- enced researcher will be able to spot the most obvious of these pieces of 'embroidery'. Having located and registered the kind of slant or gloss that the writer wishes to convey, the researcher can then read the nar- rative critically in order to focus on the 'subplot' of actual events and experiences that constitute the life history of the author.

By skilfully reading 'through' the writer's attempts at impression management, the researcher can then use autobiographies as sources of data on the basic framework of events that provide an objective backdrop to the writer's subjective career. Such accounts will also furnish impor- tant information on the subjective career itself, since even if the author has attempted to disguise or omit certain things, what does get included will reflect felt emotions and personal experience. The main problem is to check the validity and accuracy of such accounts if at all possible by cross-checking with the known and otherwise documented facts of the matter. This can be done more readily in the case of public figures since it is more likely that secondary accounts of their lives and careers will exist in the shape of biographies. It is also more likely that famous personnages will have more to hide than autobiographers without much in the way of a public life, and thus the accounts of the latter will tend more often to be more reliable.

Coda: the historical option in field research

Apart from providing a summary of the main themes of this chapter, the following represent some reflections on the use of historical analysis in conjunction with field research.

1   Depth and validity of analysis

I have suggested that theory-generating research with a contemporary focus will very often benefit from the inclusion of a historical dimension.

This will provide the research with additional energy inputs both in the shape of a further data source that adds empirical depth to the analysis, and in the form of another potential source of concepts and theoretical ideas. At the same time, a historical dimension provides validity and reliability checks on both the substantive and formal theoretical elements that have already emerged from the actual field research.

2   Building models

I have illustrated these points with reference to the construction of a model of the sequence of changes involved in the development of the occupation and career in acting. In so doing, I developed a typology of the antecedent forms of the career context of acting which both complemented and added to the analytic depth of the typology of contemporary career structures which I had begun to develop in an earlier phase of the research. In this sense, the illustrative material was intended only to give a 'flavour' of the possibilities in this regard. Clearly there are a number of pathways and points of interest to follow in the case of historical research. However, I have attempted to indicate something of the range of possibilities in this respect by briefly discussing some of the issues associated with other starting points and focuses of interest.

3   History and social analysis

(a)   I have suggested that short-term (contemporary) social processes have their own properties and emergent features which cannot be captured adequately within a long-term developmental perspective. Thus I further argued that field research with a predominantly contemporary focus does not *necessarily* require a historical underpinning. This is because there are features of short-term social processes that can only be detected and adequately captured by field research which concentrates on contemporary, micro-scale social processes.

(b)   However, I did not use this as a point of departure for claiming that historical research has little use in general. On the contrary, I have argued for the integral importance of historical analysis in two respects. First, it is indispensable in so far as a research project is predicated on intrinsically historical problems, such as those implied in the questions of how and why such and such a phenomenon (say occupational organization or class structure) has come to take the form it presently takes. This kind of question of necessity requires investigation into the historical forms, events, processes and so on that preceded the particular phenomenon. It also requires a time-scale tailored to the specific problem at hand.

(c) By including a long-term historical component in the unfolding research design (which should necessarily include an appreciation of its 'internal' history), one is adding empirical and theoretical depth to the consequent analysis. This is because, although short-term and micro social processes possess their own partly independent properties, by the same token so do long-term and macro processes. In this sense, large-scale processes of social change covering an extended time period always leave their stamp on contemporary aspects of social life. By incorporating a historical dimension into field research, one is attempting to give some indication of the manner in which the past impresses itself on the present.

4 Bracketing and selective focusing

Another problem which impinges on the general issue of historical analysis is the question of to what extent it is necessary to try to untangle the relations between macro and micro features of social life while primarily engaged in the analysis of one particular aspect of social reality. I suggested that in order to maintain a concentrated focus on one layer of social reality (as with the occupational setting in acting), a feasible option would entail bracketing off the analysis of the other sectors while attention is fixed on the area of current interest.

It is important to note that this is a purely expedient strategy to make relevant data more easily accessible and to stabilize one's focus. It must always be remembered that in reality the different sectors are bound together in an organic unity, and that a singular focus of interest is a matter of emphasis and strategic convenience. In this regard the idea of bracketing does not express a claim about the underlying or fundamental character of social life, to the effect, for example, that it is composed of discrete and atomistic entities. But generally, when using historical analysis to complement or supplement present-centred research, the very objectives of the research will demand a restricted focus that will limit the amount of analytic attention that is devoted to broader theoretical and empirical questions of interest.

10

New Strategies: Some Reflections and a Practical Guide

In the first two sections of this chapter I discuss some rather general issues arising from the wider perspective I have employed in formulating these research strategies. In the opening section I discuss the general nature of the approach I develop and the objectives which I hope it will further. In particular, I call for more cooperation and dialogue between research methods and general theoretical issues. In the second section I address specifically the question of the connection between substantive theory, grounded in research, and general theory. In the final section I return to a more practical level of discussion and attempt to describe the main features of the approach I have developed in this book. In this sense, the later discussion is more in the form of a practical guide for field researchers who want to employ these strategies. It also serves as a summary of the main arguments of chapters 5 to 9.

The nature and uses of the new strategies

I have discussed the strategies of research outlined in this book in the context of a critical encounter with two influential perspectives: middle-range theory (MRT) and grounded theory (GT). These strategies attempt to overcome some of the principal weaknesses of MRT and GT while drawing on and incorporating their strengths. In this respect it might be true to say that I have tended to borrow rather more from the GT tradition in so far as my interests have been mainly concentrated on the problem of theory generation in research. However, as I have endeavoured to make plain, the MRT approach has much to offer in its attempt to construe social research in terms of a systematic and scientific framework. The main drawback with MRT in this respect is the rather inappropriate and rigid notion of science on which it rests. Indeed, the 'realist', multistrategy approach is underpinned by a rather different model of social science which, I feel, is more flexible as regards research strategies in general, and more conducive to theory construction in particular.

Notwithstanding their differences, both MRT and GT suffer from a lack of attention to several major issues which my approach attempts to address and incorporate within its terms of reference. These are: the macro–micro problem (and the associated problem of institutional versus interpretive analysis), the stratified nature of social life, the analysis of power, the historical dimension, and last but not least, the relation between general theory and research theory. All these problems are deeply interconnected and therefore, in many instances of research practice, it is impossible to disentangle their separate strands of influence. The question of the relevance of a historical dimension vividly highlights this, and at the same time underscores the major areas of weakness of MRT and GT as approaches to social research.

However, having defined my approach as an 'alternative' to these others, I do not intend that it should be seen as an entirely separate and new direction for social research. This would be quite contrary to the spirit of the arguments of this book. In this respect, the whole thrust of my discussion has been to engage in a cooperative dialogue with other research methods and traditions, as well as a cluster of theoretical issues. This 'cooperative' component has not been pursued for its own sake or to the exclusion of many points of conflict and disagreement between my approach and those with which it intersects. However, even when it was necessary to reject or bypass the received wisdom of other traditions and perspectives, the underlying premise of my arguments has been that social research must draw on a diversity of methodological and theoretical resources. I believe that only by attempting to draw together what would otherwise be regarded as antithetical or incompatible viewpoints or positions can social scientific knowledge advance. Alternatives which eschew dialogue and interchange of ideas constantly risk being parochial and insular.

It is in this context that I intend the book to be used as a resource for research which emphasizes the discovery or construction of concepts and theory. Thus, as I have said in relation to the research map in chapter 5, the approach as a whole should be seen as a resource which may prompt ideas on research strategy or on theoretical and empirical questions pertinent to the research at hand. In this sense, the book can be either an aid to initial research design, or it can be used in an ongoing, consultative manner to feed into a rolling project. The openness that accompanies this 'dialogical' stance endows it with a great deal of flexibility as a research tool. In this respect, the realist approach argues against false separations between types of data and research strategy. Thus, even though it could be argued that it is mainly of relevance to theory-generating qualitative research, it is also clear that this approach could be used in conjunction with research that is primarily quantitative and theory testing.

All in all, the book has attempted to be practical in nature by providing a fund of ideas about strategy which can be drawn on by a multiplicity of types and styles of research at different points in the research process. However, this flexibility of potential application is not the only characteristic which makes the book rather different from conventional 'methods' texts. Throughout I have underlined the extreme importance of theoretical themes and motifs. In this respect, I have attempted to cross the divide between research methods on the one hand, and social theory on the other (or, put differently, between general theory and research evidence). This is because I believe very strongly that the lack of dialogue between these two specialisms is one of the most important problems that the discipline of sociology has to face. I regard the approach set out in this book as a modest attempt to grapple with some aspects of this problem.

I have dealt with these issues on two broad fronts. The first has involved incorporating theoretical themes or ideas as part of the substantive framework of research strategy in general. Thus issues of power and history, the relation between activity and structure, the stratified nature of social life and so on are *integral* elements of the research strategies I have described. Secondly I have endeavoured to stimulate dialogue between theory and research specialisms by insisting on the close relation between general social theory and the substantive theorizing which forms an important part of research activity.

Before moving to the latter, let me say something about the first of these issues. Broadly speaking the realist approach can be defined in terms of those things that are missing from MRT and GT and cognate approaches. That is, it is defined in terms of a concern with the different layers of social life (self, situated activity, setting and context), and the dimensions of power and history that ramify through them, as central to the formulation of research strategy. These things are in themselves both theoretical and empirical in nature. That is, they can form part of an abstract conceptual argument and, at the same time, refer to real empirical phenomena. As such, they should figure in discussions of research methods and strategy. The fact that such concerns are generally missing from the many accounts of research practice that emanate from either MRT or GT is the result of one or both of the following reasons.

First, accounts of research practice are not always theoretically 'innocent'. That is, they very often derive from wider frameworks of ideas that carry explicit or implicit theoretical assumptions about the nature of social life in general, or the role of power, or the relation between institutions and social activity. In this sense, but for very different reasons, both MRT and GT have tended either to minimize the importance of these issues, or to construe them in such a way as to remove them from the orbit of routine discussions of research methods and strategy. The second reason, which may overlap with the first, has to do with the academic division of labour between 'theorists' and 'researchers' that I mentioned earlier.

This division of labour has meant more often than not that there has been a lack of dialogue between adherents, born out of 'protectiveness' towards their specialism. In turn, this has meant that discussions regarding the nature of social life, the relation between structure and agency and so on have been defined as exclusively 'theoretical' issues and problems which do not enter into research calculations. The approach outlined here has attempted to address these themes and issues in a way which registers both their empirical and theoretical aspects. In this sense, this approach treats what otherwise might seem to be irredeemably theoretical issues as integral aspects of research methods and strategy.

Research strategy, according to this view, must be sensitive to the temporal and social organizational characteristics of those things that are used as basic units of analysis. In this respect, questions about the social constitution of basic units of analysis (and how they articulate with each other) must be broached as essential components of the research process. That this is an intrinsic feature of my approach allows it to avoid treating data as 'pristine' confirmers or disconfirmers of a hypothesis, concept or theory. That is to say, what Gouldner (1971) has called 'domain assumptions' are brought up-front and seen to play an explicit and argued for role in the research. The public nature and accessibility of these assumptions allows them to act as points of departure for discussions concerning the evaluation of the research findings as a whole. This seems to be preferable to a situation where such assumptions are surreptitiously or unintentionally imported as part of an assumed 'neutrality' of research findings.

Clearly the strategies outlined in this book are of most relevance to those forms of social research which attempt to combine the analysis of social activity with the institutional forms that provide their backdrop. These strategies attempt to capture something of the interleaved nature of the ties that bind these two elements of social life together. Thus those forms of research that 'bracket' out one or the other of these elements for methodological purposes (see Giddens 1984) will be rather more peripheral to its concerns. However, as Giddens makes clear, in principle all social research should be rounded out with a concentration on both elements since they are equally important in the constitution of social life. These strategies attempt to address the interweaving of activity and institutions by stressing the importance of power, history and the layered nature of social life in the formulation of research strategy and the methods used to collect and classify data.

The connection between substantive theory and general theory

In so far as the realist approach concerns itself with the links between institutions and activities, then it is also concerned with the general theoretical issue of the macro–micro problem. Having insisted that the elements involved in this approach are both empirical and theoretical in nature, I would also want to argue the same for the macro–micro problem. In this respect the macro–micro problem must be freed from its association with purely theoretical debates and issues. It must be delivered into the arena of empirical research – although this must be done without sacrificing its theoretical import. The realist approach concentrates on the connection between theory developed from research and various aspects of the macro–micro problem. Therefore it forges a link between substantive theory (that is, theory pertinent to a particular substantive or research area) and general theory, which is relevant to many substantive areas.

It is necessary to establish such links in order that sociological knowledge advances on a broad front, with all aspects of empirical and theoretical endeavour harnessed together. Returning to the cooperative dialogue theme, this means that the academic specialization between 'theorists' and 'empirical researchers' must not be allowed to preempt the free flow and cross-fertilization of ideas between these domains of knowledge. Even though there are notable exceptions, there still persists rather more than a grain of truth in the idea that, on the one hand, researchers gather empirical data in relative isolation from general theoretical issues and, on the other, that theorists develop their ideas in the comfort of their armchairs.

The approach outlined here is intended to contribute to the erosion of this view. My underlying theme, therefore, has been to call for a closer tie between general theory and research. In this respect, general theory must concern itself with empirical evidence rather more than it has done hitherto (although I am not suggesting that the link between theory and evidence, in itself, is a straightforward matter). Conversely, very often empirical research would be strengthened by the incorporation of general theoretical issues and themes. Of course, this must be in the nature of a genuine integration and must not merely consist of the decorative use of theoretical 'buzz' words in order to add to the superficial 'glitter' of a research report.

There are several barriers to such crossing of boundaries which are all associated in some way with the core issue of academic specialization. One of the most formidable is contained in the fairly widespread misunderstanding that somehow general theory is really 'metatheory' and, therefore, that its use to empirical research is negligible. It hardly needs to be said that it is the hard-nosed empirical researcher who is most often heard to voice this complaint (although various ethnomethodologists come close to this view in their insistence that many theoretical ideas are too remote from the everyday world). However, as I have tried to press home throughout this book, such a view is erroneous in the extreme and, as a result, simply functions as a justification for ignoring the implications of general theory for research.

The mistake inherent in such a view is the assumption that all general theory is a kind of abstract story-telling which bears no significant relation to the 'real' empirical world. The view that general theory is too abstract and remote or that it is simply plain invention, misses the point entirely. The point is to understand what it is that such theory does attempt to represent. Subsidiary questions are: How does it do it? What sort of language and concepts does it use? This more constructive response would reveal two things. First, that there are different types of general theory which operate at different levels of abstraction. Secondly, that much general theory must be regarded as 'representing' the empirical world, although in a rather different sense from that implied in the grounded theory approach.

This is why I insisted in chapters 3 and 4 that research perspectives such as GT must not be allowed to monopolize the truth about the empirical world by definitional fiat. That is, the implicit claim that theories which are not grounded in the way defined in the GT approach (or any other which claims to be 'empirically grounded' as opposed to being 'theoretically adrift') are therefore to be discounted on the basis that they are simply speculative. The claim that such theories have no secure anchorage in the empirical world is a form of intellectual casuistry which must be countered at every opportunity.

Only by accommodating to the fact that different types of theory and social analysis represent the empirical world in different, but not necessarily competing, ways can we hope to fashion a rapprochement between substantive (research) theory and more general theories. This is also a necessary requirement for properly coming to terms with the macro–micro problem. This is for two main reasons. First, because its resolution involves tacking between aspects of social life (subjective and objective) which require different kinds of conceptual or theoretical depictions. Secondly, theories which fall on one side or the other of the macro–micro divide have often been construed as being incompatible. This is because, it is argued, they are competing explanations for the same phenomena (hence the arguments about whether social life is reducible to either macro or micro phenomena). While in some cases there are genuine incompatibilities, and yet other cases may be problematic in this regard, very often such theories reflect real differences both in levels of explanation and in the characteristics of social life to which they refer. It is in these cases that reconciliation is overdue.

The approach outlined here attempts to do this. It does so by treating general theories as potentially open, revisable and partial discourses rather than ones which are perfected, closed and hermetically sealed. This is made easier if the theory in question presents itself in a fairly open manner in the first place. The obverse is the case where 'schools of theory' or theoretical frameworks are used to defend rather dogmatic views, or to attack others which dare to take a different standpoint. Of course, it is not just a question of accessibility. It also has to do with the questions of explanatory adequacy and supporting (empirical) evidence. In this sense I have used some of the themes present in Giddens's structuration theory to feed into the main discussion of the development of theory from research. Structuration theory is useful in this respect because it can be drawn on in a partial way as a source of 'sensitizing devices' (Giddens 1990) which may be of relevance to empirical research.

However, noting the importance of dialogue and interchange between research theory and more general social theories should not deflect attention from the central objective of this realist approach. Above all, it represents a practical intervention in the world of social research. This approach is as much to do with strategies designed to sample, collect, order and classify empirical data as it is to do with analytical interpretation and the construction of theory. It is to these issues that the concluding section will turn. However, in this respect, these strategies have a direct line of descent from the empirical research traditions of MRT and GT. The connection with GT is particularly strong in so far as it re-emphasizes the importance of theory generation from ongoing empirical research. However, these strategies endeavour to widen the scope of 'empirically grounded' theory by widening its terms of reference and pointing to the importance of general theory as a complementary resource for theory construction.

New strategies: a practical guide

In this final section let me recap on some of the key features of the strategies I have outlined. This summary is an attempt to specify the distinctive features of what I have often referred to as a realist approach. I shall concentrate my attention on chapters 5 to 9, since it is in these chapters that the core of the 'new' strategies lies. However, it is important not to disconnect the focus of these chapters from the arguments set out in chapters 2, 3 and 4, since they provide an essential foundation. As I pointed out in chapter 1, this book may be read as a unified argument, as well as a resource which can be referred to for specific issues. For those readers engaged in the latter, I would refer them to the concluding sections of chapters 2, 3 and 4 for detailed summaries.

However, it is essential to bear in mind some of the broad themes of these chapters as I reiterate those in chapters 5 to 9. Chapter 2 emphasized that although the distinction between theory-testing and theory-generating research was useful for certain purposes, it should not be taken too far. Very often the concerns of the two types shade into each other in specific pieces of research, in other cases research has more descriptive or information-gathering aims. The field researcher should be aware of these intermediate forms and utilize aspects of them in their own research where relevant. To this end, chapter 2 concluded with some guidelines which describe specific ways in which theory-generating fieldwork may benefit from the use of aspects of theory-testing and 'intermediate' forms of research.

Chapters 3 and 4 were concerned with developing and amending the grounded theory approach with a view to expanding the range of theory-generating strategies available to it. In chapter 3, I pointed out that qualitative analysis and ethnography had been used and influenced by theoretical approaches other than interactionism and GT. Similarly, research using qualitative analysis and data is not all concerned with theory generation. Some qualitative approaches to research are anti-theoretical, while others are rather more concerned with information-gathering and problem-oriented aims. Yet others are concerned with clarifying or assessing the usefulness of particular concepts, or with applying theory and concepts from general theories. An essential part of my argument has been to stress that fieldwork which concentrates on developing 'new' or emergent theory may profitably draw on any of these other approaches (or even a combination of them) in order to further the goal of theory generation.

In this light, chapter 4 pressed ahead with the idea of extending the terms of reference of GT. This included the need to incorporate scientific realism into the humanistic framework of GT; the need to bring the structural features of social life (particularly power) to the forefront of field research; the need to expand the definition of GT, and for it to be open to the influence of general theory. As I said, these are all dealt with in detail in the concluding sections of the relevant chapters. The same, of course, is the case with chapters 5 to 9. The following discussion, therefore, simply serves to bring the general points together in order to have a clearer picture of what the new strategies add up to as a whole.

1   The research map and its uses

Chapter 5 outlined particular elements of society and social processes (self, situated activity, setting, context, history and power). The point of the map is to encourage the researcher to use it either to take an initial focus on a research topic, or to develop new directions for an ongoing project. The map is useful for fieldwork which has theory generation as a central objective because it encourages the researcher to be conscious of theoretical issues in the context of empirical research questions.

By the explicit focusing of research through the elements of the map, the researcher is forced to ask what is the relevance of this or that piece of empirical data for wider theoretical issues. For example, what do observations of interaction in a coffee bar or a workplace tell us about the relation between individual identity and social interaction? How is this social activity influenced by its social setting or context? How is power manifest in the observed data? What time-scales are relevant, and how do they help us understand the empirical data on the observed interaction? (For more detailed questions and research guidelines see the relevant sections of chapter 5.)

2   The notion of multistrategy research

The essence of the multistrategy approach is to use as many analytic or methodological 'cuts' into the data as are at one's disposal in order to achieve a dense empirical and theoretical coverage of the area. This also allows a flexibility of response which is needed to maximize the potential for theory generation. This flexibility must not be confused with an 'anything goes' attitude. In fact, the whole process is conditioned by the theoretical assumptions which underlie the research map. In short, these ensure that methods and strategies are used directly in the service of understanding the bonds that tie together the interpersonal world of everyday life with the more impersonal world of social institutions. They also ensure that this is done in a balanced manner which captures the mutual implication of macro and micro phenomena.

Flexibility of response is necessary for a number of reasons. First, the ongoing, developmental character of field research requires that particular methods and strategies are 'drawn in', utilized and so on in relation to the organic growth of the research project. In this sense, the researcher must remain responsive to the unanticipated nature of research problems and issues as they are 'thrown up' by the research itself. Secondly, flexibility of response ensures that the emergent categories and concepts of the research will not be prematurely 'fixed' and thus inhibit the further emergence of theoretical ideas.

3 Initiating and developing theory from fieldwork

(a) The typical problem for the researcher who wants to generate theory is how to get started. One way of approaching this is to use a background or sensitizing concept in order to give some provisional organization to the data, as well as to suggest further theoretical ideas. The background concept should be capable of handling both subjective and objective features of social life. Some reference to the unfolding nature of social activity across time and space would be an additional advantage. I examined the concept of 'career' in this respect (in chapter 7), although there are others that are suitable. Background or sensitizing concepts can be drawn either from empirical research or from more general bodies of theory. (For example, Foucault's notions of power, resistance and surveillance, as used by Bloor and McIntosh 1990, or Giddens's notion of the 'dialectic of control', as discussed in chapter 8.) However, the use of a background concept is not mandatory. The researcher should ask: Will a specific background concept help to stimulate my theoretical thinking about the area or problem in question? Will it help me to come up with further ideas, hypotheses, concepts, and so on? Will it help me organise the empirical data at my disposal?

(b) As Glaser and Strauss have shown, one powerful way of developing theoretical ideas from research is to engage in constant comparisons with other groups or situations which are similar to, or dissimilar from, that of the research focus. This encourages the researcher to ask questions concerning the subject of the research, for instance as to how, interaction in coffee bars, say, compares with interaction in families or on public transportation; or how professional–client relationships compare with those between customers and proprietors, or sportspersons and their agents.

(c) We can extend this further into the development of typologies or models which indicate the range of 'types' of groups, situations or relationships which exist for a given topic of research. These can refer to a diversity of forms of social phenomena, such as types of prison inmate, types of resistance strategies, types of religious or political organization, or types of labour market. The use of typologies allows comparative analysis to be more systematic, by indicating the range of comparable phenomena and by highlighting the differences and similarities that exist. I have emphasized the use of structural typologies in an effort to balance the existing emphasis on action typologies in this kind of fieldwork.

(d) Working with a typology also makes sampling more systematic and effective. This strategy builds on Glaser and Strauss's notion of theoretical sampling. By this, Glaser and Strauss mean that the researcher makes sampling an ongoing feature of the research. Groups and people are drawn into the research sample on the basis of their relevance to the emerging theory. In the same way that it makes comparative analysis more systematic, working with a typology makes theoretical sampling more ordered and elaborate. The inclusion of a structural typology has the advantage of adding a power dimension which is missing from many fieldwork analyses.

4   The dimensions of power, commitment and constraint

(a) The realist approach to fieldwork encourages the researcher to look for aspects of power in the data. The researcher should be aware of the different forms of power relationships and the resources on which they are based. Although these may empirically overlap, a good fieldwork analysis will always be clear about which elements of power are involved and how they interconnect. In particular, the researcher should be aware of types of power that are covert, and hence difficult to observe or detect in any straightforward sense. This elusiveness may be compounded by the lack of any obvious conflict or conflict of interest surrounding the the relationships. Some forms of power and domination lie very much 'behind the scenes' of the daily round of activities and interpersonal behaviour that are so often the focus of fieldwork studies. The researcher must understand how these forms of power operate and how they influence people's lives and behaviour.

(b) The researcher must also be aware of the way in which power can exert its influence over people's lives through subtle, and not so subtle, forms of constraint. This has to do with the resources available to groups and individuals (money, authority, property, knowledge, skills and so on). Resources enable people to do things – for example, the possession of knowledge and skills enables people to enter certain professions. However, lack of resources means that behaviour will be constrained. Typically, social settings and contexts provide examples of many forms of constraints and enablements in relation to daily activity. The intricacies that surround the intersection of constraints with social behaviour should be a focus for theory-generating fieldwork.

(c) The notion of commitment also reflects the dual nature of social activity (its objective and subjective aspects). It points to the nature of the bonds that tie people to certain kinds of social relations, settings and contexts. As with constraint, the researcher must be aware of the empirical variability of commitment. One of the central tasks of the approach I have outlined is to investigate the varying social circumstances and the corresponding social and psychological ties that enmesh people in these circumstances. In some sense, constraint and commitment are intertwined. The nature and degree of constraint are associated with particular forms and mechanisms of commitment. Again, a focus on commitment and the many issues that surround it is useful for the emergence of theoretical ideas, concepts and categories.

5 The historical dimension

History is the widest sense in which the passage of time is captured in research. The other elements of the research map represent different time frames and units of analysis and fit within the envelope of this larger sense. While it is unavoidable that the field researcher attends to the different senses of time in relation to self, situated activity, setting and context, this is not so with the historical dimension itself. It is not an absolute necessity to incorporate a historical dimension in field research which is essentially present centred, although without doubt the inclusion of a historical dimension will add depth to many analyses.

This depth derives from the fact that a historical dimension can give an indication of how the development of institutions over time have affected the lives of people. Particularly important, of course, is the manner in which power relations have emerged historically (gender, class, ethnic, professional, and so on). A historical dimension reveals that the way in which people live out their lives on a daily basis (that is, the routine interweaving of identities, interactions, settings and contexts) is intimately associated with the long-term evolution of institutions forms of power.

Final comment

In conclusion, let me elaborate a little on what I said in passing earlier in this chapter. I indicated that while my approach is defined somewhat in terms of an 'alternative' to MRT and GT (and their variants), I do not see it as an entirely separate direction in this regard. This is why the above summaries (and indeed the entire arguments on which they are based) should be viewed as 'guidelines' rather than 'rules of procedure'. To see them in this latter light would be to imbue them with a fixity and rigidity which I do not intend them to possess. In this sense, they should not be construed as a closed, dogmatic 'system'. Rather, they should be viewed as potentially revisable and negotiable in the light of further developments and influences. Of course, this is not to say that the approach is completely open to all and sundry influences. The interchange and dialogue I envisage must be governed by the theoretical presuppositions implicit in the strategies and underpinning the overall perspective that I have employed.

References

Abrams, P. 1982: *Historical Sociology*. Shepton Mallet: Open Books.

Acker, J. 1991: Hierarchies, jobs, bodies: a theory of gendered organisations. In J. Lorber and S. Farrell (eds), *The Social Construction of Gender,* London: Sage.

Alexander, J., Giesen, B., Münch, R. and Smelser, N. 1987: *The Macro–Micro Link.* Berkeley: University of California Press.

Archer, M. 1988: *Culture and Agency: The place of Culture in Social Theory.* Cambridge: Cambridge University Press.

Ashton, D. and Sung, J. 1989: The determinants of young adults' labour market status. Economic and Social Research Council, London.

Ashton, D., Maguire, M. and Spilsbury, M. 1990: *Restructuring the Labour Market: The Implications for Youth.* London: Macmillan.

Backett, K. 1990: Studying health in families: a qualitative approach. In S. Cunningham-Burley and N. McKeganey (eds), *Readings in Medical Sociology,* London: Routledge.

Ball, S. 1981: *Beachside Comprehensive: a Case Study of Secondary Schooling.* Cambridge: Cambridge University Press.

Barbour, R. 1985: Dealing with the transitional demands of professional socialization. *Sociological Review,* 33, 495–531.

Becker, H. 1952: The career of the Chicago public schoolteacher. *American Journal of Sociology,* 57, 470–7.

—— 1953: Becoming a marihuana user. *American Journal of Sociology,* 59, 235–42.

—— 1960: Notes on the concept of commitment. *American Journal of Sociology,* 66, 32–40.

—— 1963: *Outsiders.* Glencoe: Free Press.

—— 1970: *Sociological Work.* Chicago: Aldine.

Becker, H., Geer, B., Hughes, E. and Strauss, A. 1961: *Boys in White: Student Culture in Medical School.* Chicago: Chicago University Press.

Bell, C. 1968: *Middle Class Families.* London: Routledge.

Benson, D. 1974: Critical note: a revolution in sociology. *Sociology,* 8, 125–9.

Benson, D. and Hughes, J. 1983: *The Perspective of Ethnomethodology.* Harlow: Longman.

Benyon, H. 1973: *Working for Ford.* Harmondsworth: Penguin.

Bernstein, B. 1971: *Class Codes and Control,* vol. 1. London: Routledge.

—— 1973: *Class Codes and Control,* vol. 2. London: Routledge.

Bhaskar, R. 1979: *The Possibility of Naturalism.* Brighton: Harvester.

Blau, P. and Duncan, O. 1967: *The American Occupational Structure.* New York: Wiley.

Blauner, R. 1964: *Alienation and Freedom: The Factory Worker and his Industry.* Chicago: University of Chicago Press.

Bloor, M. and McIntosh, J. 1990: Surveillance and concealment: a comparison of techniques of client resistance in therapeutic communities and health visiting. In S. Cunningham-Burley and N. McKeganey (eds), *Readings in Medical Sociology*, London: Routledge.

Blumer, H. 1956: Sociological analysis and the variable. *American Sociological Review,* 21, 683–90.

—— 1966: Sociological implications of the thought of G. H. Mead. *American Journal of Sociology,* 71, 535–44.

—— 1969: *Symbolic Interactionism.* Englewood Cliffs, NJ: Prentice-Hall.

Bott, E. 1957: *Family and Social Network.* London: Tavistock.

Brewer, J. 1990: Talking about danger: the RUC and the paramilitary threat. *Sociology,* 24, 657–74.

Bruyn, S. 1966: *The Human Perspective in Sociology.* Englewood Cliffs, NJ: Prentice-Hall.

Bryman, A. 1988: *Quantity and Quality in Social Research.* London: Unwin.

Burawoy, M. 1979: *Manufacturing Consent.* Chicago: Chicago University Press.

Burgess, R. 1982: The practice of sociological research: some issues in school ethnography. In R. Burgess (ed.), *Exploring Society*, British Sociological Association, London, 115–35.

—— 1984: *In the Field.* London: Allen and Unwin.

Burns, T. and Stalker, G. 1961: *The Management of Innovation.* London: Tavistock.

Cain, M. 1973: *Society and the Policeman's Role.* London: Routledge.

Cavendish, R. 1982: *Women on the Line.* London: Routledge.

Charles, N. and Kerr M. 1986: Food for feminist thought. *Sociological Review,* 34, 537–72.

Clegg, S. 1989: *Frameworks of Power.* London: Sage.

Clegg, S. and Dunkerly, D. 1980: *Organisation, Class and Control.* London: Routledge.

Cockburn, C. 1983: *Brothers: Male Dominance and Technological Change.* London: Pluto.

Collin, A. and Young R. 1986: New directions for theories of career. *Human Relations,* 39, 837–53.

Collins, R. 1981: On the micro-foundations of macro-sociology. *American Journal of Sociology,* 86, 984–1014.

Dahrendorf, R. 1967: *Class and Class Conflict in Industrial Society.* London: Routledge.

Davis, F. 1959: The cabdriver and his fare: facets of a fleeting relationship. *American Journal of Sociology,* 65, 158–65.

—— 1963: *Passage Through Crisis*, Indianapolis: Bobbs-Merrill.

Delamont, S. 1976: *Interaction in the Classroom*, London: Methuen.

Delamont, S. and Hamilton, D. 1982: Classroom research: a critique and a new approach. In M. Stubbs and D. Hamilton (eds), *Explorations in Classroom Observation*, London: Wiley, 3–20.

Denzin, N. 1970: *The Research Act.* Chicago: Aldine.

Douglas, J. 1976: *Investigative Social Research.* Beverley Hills: Sage.

Douglas, J. Rasmussen, P. and Flanagan, C. 1977: *The Nude Beach.* Beverley Hills: Sage.

Durkheim, E. 1952: *Suicide: A Study in Sociology.* London: Routledge.

—— 1982: *The Rules of Sociological Method.* New York: Free Press.

Edwards, R. 1979: *Contested Terrain.* London: Heinemann.

Elias, N. 1978: *The Civilising Process,* vol. 1: *The History of Manners.* Oxford: Blackwell.

Etzioni, A. 1961: *A Comparative Analysis of Complex Organisations.* New York: Free Press.

Faulkner, R. 1973: Career concerns and mobility motivations of orchestra musicians. *Sociological Quarterly*, 14, 334–49.

Finnegan, R. 1989: *The Hidden Musicians: Music-making in an English Town.* Cambridge: Cambridge University Press.

Foucault, M. 1977: *Discipline and Punish: The Birth of the Prison.* Harmondsworth: Penguin.

Freidson, E. 1982: Occupational autonomy and labour market shelters. In P. Stewart & M. Cantor (eds), *Varieties of Work*, London: Sage.

Garabedian, P. 1963: Social roles and processes of socialization in the prison community. *Social Problems*, 11, 139–52.

Geer, B. 1968: Occupational commitment and the teaching profession. In H. Becker, B. Geer, D. Riesman and R. Weiss (eds), *Institutions and the Person,* Chicago: Aldine.

Giallombardo, R. 1966: Social roles in a prison for women. *Social Problems*, 13, 268–88.

Giddens, A. 1982: Power, the Dialectic of Control and Class Structuration. In A. Giddens and G. McKenzie (eds), *Social Class and the Division of labour*, Cambridge: Cambridge University Press.

—— 1984: *The Constitution of Society.* Cambridge: Polity.

—— 1987: *Social Theory and Modern Sociology.* Stanford: Stanford University Press.

—— 1990: Structuration theory and sociological analysis. In J. Clark, C. Modgil and Sohan Modgil (eds), *Consensus and Controversy: Anthony Giddens,* Basingstoke: Falmer.

Glaser, B. 1964: *Organizational Scientists: Their Professional Careers.* Indianapolis: Bobbs-Merrill.

—— 1968: *Organizational Careers: A Sourcebook for Theory.* Chicago: Aldine.

Glaser, B. and Strauss A. 1965: *Awareness of Dying.* Chicago: Aldine.

—— 1967: *The Discovery of Grounded Theory.* Chicago: Aldine.

—— 1971: *Status Passage.* London: Routledge.

Goffman, E. 1961: *Encounters.* New York: Bobbs-Merrill.

—— 1967: *Interaction Ritual.* New York: Doubleday Anchor.

—— 1968: *Asylums.* Harmondsworth: Penguin.

—— 1983: The interaction order. *American Sociological Review*, 48.

Gold, R. 1952: Janitors versus tenants: a status–income dilemma. *American Journal of Sociology*, 57, 486–93.

—— 1958: Roles in sociological field observation. *Social Forces*, 36, 217–23.

—— 1964: In the basement: the apartment building janitor. In P. Berger (ed.), *The Human Shape of Work.* South Bend, Ind.: Gateway.

Goldthorpe, J. 1980: *Social Mobility and Class Structure in Modern Britain.* Oxford: Clarendon.

Gouldner, A. 1954: *Patterns of Industrial Bureaucracy.* Glencoe: Free Press.

—— 1957: Cosmopolitans and locals: towards an analysis of latent social roles. *Administrative Science Quarterly*, 2, 281–306.

—— 1971: *The Coming Crisis in Western Sociology.* London: Heinemann.

Gross, N., Mason, W. and McEachern *Explorations in Role Analysis: Studies of the School Superintendency Role.* New York: Wiley.

Grusky, O. 1963: Managerial succession and organizational effectiveness. *American Journal of Sociology*, 69, 21–31.

Hammersley, M. 1985: From ethnography to theory: a programme and paradigm in the sociology of education. *Sociology*, 19, 244–59.

—— 1990: What's wrong with ethnography? The myth of theoretical description. *Sociology*, 24, 597–615.

Hargreaves, D. 1967: *Social Relations in a Secondary School.* London: Routledge.
—— 1972: *Interpersonal Relations in Education.* London: Routledge.
Harré, R. 1979: *Social Being.* Oxford: Blackwell.
—— 1981: Philosophical aspects of the micro–macro problem. In K. Knorr-Cetina and A. Cicourel (eds), *Advances in Social Theory and Methodology,* London: Routledge, 139–60.
Harré, R. and Secord, P. 1972: *The Explanation of Social Behaviour.* Oxford: Blackwell.
Harwood, R. 1971: *Sir Donald Wolfitt.* London: Secker and Warburg.
Hearn, H. and Stoll, P. 1975: Continuance commitment in low-status occupations: the cocktail waitress. *Sociological Quarterly,* 16, 105–14.
Hochschild, A. 1983: *The Managed Heart.* Berkeley: University of California Press.
Hughes, E. 1937: Institutional office and the person. *American Journal of Sociology,* 43, 404–13.
Humphreys, L. 1970: Tearoom Trade. London: Duckworth.
Kalleberg, A. 1983: Work and stratification: structural perspectives. *Work and Occupations,* 10, 251–9.
Kanter, R. 1989: Careers and the wealth of nations: a macro-perspective on the structure and implications of career forms. In M. Arthur, D. Hall and B. Lawrence (eds), *Handbook of Career Theory,* Cambridge: Cambridge University Press.
Keat, R. and Urry J. 1975: *Social Theory as Science.* London: Routledge.
Knorr-Cetina, K. 1981: The micro-sociological challenge of macro-sociology: towards a reconstruction of social theory and methodology. In K. Knorr-Cetina and A. Cicourel (eds), *Advances in Social Theory and Methodology,* London: Routledge, 1–47.
Knorr-Cetina, K. and Cicourel, A. (eds) 1981: *Advances in Social Theory and Methodology.* London: Routledge.
Krekel, R. 1980: Unequal opportunity structure and labour market segmentation. *Sociology,* 14, 525–49.
Kuhn, T. 1970: *The Structure of Scientific Revolutions.* Chicago: University of Chicago Press.
Lacey, C. 1966: Some sociological concomitants of academic streaming in a grammar school. *British Journal of Sociology,* 17.3, 245–62.
—— 1970: *Hightown Grammar: The School as a Social System.* Manchester: Manchester University Press.
—— 1976: Problems of sociological fieldwork: a review of the methodology of 'Hightown Grammar. In M. Shipman (ed.), *The Organization and Impact of Social Research,* London: Routledge.
Layder, D. 1976: Occupational careers in contemporary Britain: with special reference to the acting profession. Unpublished Ph.D. thesis, London School of Economics.
—— 1981: *Structure, Interaction and Social Theory.* London: Routledge.
—— 1982: Grounded theory: a constructive critique. *Journal for the theory of Social Behaviour,* 12, 103–23.
—— 1984: Sources and levels of commitment in actors' careers. *Work and Occupations,* 11, 147–62.
—— 1985: Power, structure and agency. *Journal for the Theory of Social Behaviour,* 15, 131–49.
—— 1987: Key issues in structuration theory: some critical remarks. *Current Perspectives in Social Theory,* 8, 25–46.
—— 1989: The macro–micro distinction, social relations and methodological bracketing. *Current Perspectives in Social Theory,* 9, 123–41.
—— 1990: *The Realist Image in Social Science.* London: Macmillan.

Lemert, E. 1962: Paranoia and the dynamics of exclusion. *Sociometry*, 25, 2–20.

Lofland, J. 1966: *Doomsday Cult: A Study of Conversion, Proselytization and Maintenance of Faith.* Englewood Cliffs, NJ: Prentice Hall.

—— 1971: *Analysing Social Settings.* Belmont, Calif.: Wadsworth.

Lofland, L. 1966: *In the Presence of Strangers: A Study of Behavior in Public Settings.* Working Paper 19, Centre for Research on Social Organization, University of Michigan.

Luckenbill, D. 1979: Power: a conceptual framework. *Symbolic Interaction*, 2, 97–114.

McHugh, P. 1969: Structured uncertainty and its resolution: the case of the professional actor. In S. Plog and R. Egerton (eds), *Changing Perspectives, in Mental Illness,* (New York: Rinehart and Winston.

McKeganey, N. 1990: Drug abuse in the community: needle-sharing and the risks of HIV infection. In S. Cunningham-Burley and N. McKeganey (eds), *Readings in Medical Sociology,* London: Routledge, 113–37.

McKeganey, N., Barnard, M. and Bloor, M. 1990: A comparison of HIV-related risk behaviour and risk reduction between female street working prostitutes and male rent boys in Glasgow. *Sociology of Health and Illness*, 12, 274–92.

Mead, G. H. 1967: *Mind, Self and Society.* Chicago: University of Chicago Press.

Merton, R. 1957: The role-set: problems in sociological theory. *British Journal of Sociology*, June.

—— 1967a: Research and sociological theory. In P. Rose (ed.), *The Study of Society,* New York: Random House.

—— 1967b: *On Theoretical Sociology.* New York: Free Press.

—— 1968: *Social Theory and Social Structure.* New York: Free Press.

Miles, N. and Huberman, A. 1984: *Qualitative Data Analysis.* Beverley Hills: Sage.

Nicholson, N. and West, M. 1989: Transitions, work histories, and careers. In M. Arthur, D. Hall and B. Lawrence (eds), *Handbook of Career Theory*, Cambridge: Cambridge University Press.

Nijsmans, M. 1991: Professional culture and organizational morality: an ethnographic account of a therapeutic organisation. *British Journal of Sociology*, 42, 1–19.

Nisbett, R. and Ross, L. 1980: *Human Inference: Strategies and Shortcomings of Social Judgement.* Englewood Cliffs, NJ: Prentice-Hall.

Outhwaite, W. 1988: *New Philosophies of Social Science: Realism, Hermeneutics and Critical Theory.* London: Macmillan.

Pahl, J. and Pahl, R. 1971: *Managers and their wives.* London: Allen Lane.

Parsons, T. 1951: *The Social System.* Glencoe: Free Press.

—— 1966: *Societies: Evolutionary and Comparative Perspectives.* Englewood Cliffs, NJ: Prentice-Hall.

Pawson, R. 1989: *A Measure for Measures.* London: Routledge.

Pinder, C. and Moore, L. (eds) 1980: *Middle-Range Theory and the Study of Organizations.* Boston: Martin Niuhoff.

Platt, J. 1981: Evidence and proof in documentary research. *Sociological Review*, 29, 31–66.

Pollert, A. 1981: *Girls, Wives, Factory Lives.* London: Macmillan.

Polsky, N. 1967: *Hustlers, Beats and Others.* Chicago: Aldine.

Preiss, J. and Ehrlich, H. 1966: *An Examination of Role Theory: the Case of the State Police.* Lincoln: University of Nebraska Press.

Rapoport, R. and Rapoport, R. 1971: *Dual-Career Families.* Harmondsworth: Penguin.

Rock, P. 1979: *The Making of Symbolic Interactionism.* London: Macmillan.

Rose, G. 1982: *Deciphering Social Research.* London: Macmillan.

Roth, J. 1963: *Timetables: Structuring the Passage of Time in Hospital Treatment and other Careers*. Indianapolis: Bobbs-Merrill.

Roy, D. 1973: Banana time: job satisfaction and informal interaction. In G. Salaman and K. Thompson (eds), *People and Organisations*, London: Longman.

Schatzman, L. and Strauss, A. 1973: *Field Research* Englewood Cliffs, NJ: Prentice Hall.

Scheff, T. 1966: *Being Mentally Ill*. Chicago: Aldine.

Scott, J. 1990: *A Matter of Record*. Cambridge: Polity.

Silverman, D. 1985: *Qualitative Methodology and Sociology*. Aldershot: Gower.

Sofer, C. 1970: *Men in Mid-Career*. Cambridge: Cambridge University Press.

Stacey, M. 1969: *Methods of Social Research*. Oxford: Pergamon.

Stanko, E. 1988: Keeping women in and out of line: sexual harassment and occupational segregation. In S. Walby (ed.), *Gender and Segregation at Work*, Milton Keynes: Open University Press.

Stebbins, R. 1970a: Career: the subjective approach. *Sociological Quarterly*, 11, 32–49.

—— 1970b: *Commitment to Deviance: The Nonprofessional Criminal in the Community*. Westport, Conn.: Greenwood Press.

Stinchcombe, A. 1959: Craft and bureaucratic administration of production. *Administrative Science Quarterly*, 4, 168–87.

Storr, A. 1989: *Churchill's Black Dog and other Phenomena of the Human Mind*. Glasgow: Collins.

Strauss, A. 1987: *Qualitative Analysis for Social Scientists*. Cambridge: Cambridge University Press.

Strauss, A., Fagerhaugh, S., Suczek, B. and Wiener, C. 1985: *The Social Organization of Medical Work*. Chicago: University of Chicago Press.

Stryker, S. 1981: *Symbolic Interactionism: A Social Structural Version*. Englewood Cliffs, NJ: Prentice-Hall.

Thomas, R. 1989: Blue-collar careers: meaning and choice in a world of constraints. In M. Arthur, D. Hall and B. Lawrence (eds), *Handbook of Career Theory*, Cambridge: Cambridge University Press.

Turnbull, C. 1973: *The Mountain People*. London: Cape.

Turner, R. 1962: Role-taking: process versus conformity. In A. Rose (ed.), *Human Behaviour and Social Processes*, Boston: Houghton Mifflin.

—— 1981: Unanswered questions in the convergence between structuralist and interactionist role theories. In H. Helle and S. Eisenstadt (eds), *Micro-Sociological Theory: Perspectives on Sociological Theory*, vol. 2, Beverley Hills: Sage.

Unruh, D. 1979: Characteristics and types of participation in social worlds. *Symbolic Interaction*, 2, 115–26.

Walby, S. (ed.) 1988: *Gender Segregation at Work*. Milton Keynes: Open University Press.

Weber, M. 1930: *The Protestant Ethic and the Spirit of Capitalism*. New York: Scribner's.

—— 1964: *The Theory of Economic and Social Organization*. New York: Free Press.

Whyte, W. 1943: *Street Corner Society*. Chicago: University of Chicago Press.

Willensky, H. 1961: Orderly careers and social participation: the impact of work history on social integration in the Middle Mass. *American Sociologial Review*, 26, 521–39.

Willis, P. 1977: *Learning to Labour*. Fainborough: Saxon House.

Wright, E. 1980: Class and occupation. *Theory and Society*, 9, 177–214.

Young, J. 1971: *The Drugtakers: The Social Meanings of Drug Life*. London: Paladin.

Index